Cheryl, my
Jewish friend—
I love you
Rachel

To Cheryl—
who is to-ply blessed—
Rabbi Yoel Kahn
11-8-89
20 Cheshvan 5750

TWICE BLESSED

TWICE
BLESSED

....

On Being Lesbian, Gay, *and* Jewish

EDITED BY

CHRISTIE BALKA AND ANDY ROSE

BEACON PRESS

Boston

Beacon Press
25 Beacon Street
Boston, Massachusetts 02108-2800

Beacon Press books
are published under the auspices of
the Unitarian Universalist Association of Congregations.

96 95 94 93 92 91 90 89   1 2 3 4 5 6 7 8

Test design by Molly Renda

Library of Congress Cataloging-in-Publication Data

Twice blessed : on being lesbian, gay, and Jewish / edited by Christie
Balka and Andy Rose.
p. cm.
Includes bibliographical references.
ISBN 0-8070-7908-1
1. Homosexuality—Religious aspects—Judaism. 2. Jewish gays—
United States. 3. Judaism—Doctrines. I. Balka, Christie.
II. Rose, Andy.
BM729.H65T85 1989
296'.08'664—dc20   89-42598

For Rebecca and Bruce

CONTENTS

....

ACKNOWLEDGMENTS

....

WE ARE BOTH GRATEFUL TO MANY PEOPLE WHO HAVE HELPED US bring this book to fruition.

To begin with, we thank Esther Cohen for initially suggesting the topic for this anthology while she worked at Adama Press. We thank the approximately thirty lesbian and gay Jews who met with us to help conceptualize the book, and Frances Goldin, who has shared her enthusiasm along with helpful suggestions about the manuscript. We also thank the twenty-five women and men who contributed to this anthology. All of them are taking personal and professional risks by writing here: they honor us with their integrity and their courage.

We wish to thank members of our respective communities of Philadelphia and San Francisco for the day-to-day celebrations and struggles that have helped clarify our vision for this book, and for frequent reminders of light at the end of the tunnel during the later stages of editing.

Finally, we acknowledge the many lesbian and gay Jews we know, and the many more we've never met, each of whom has a unique story that deserves to be heard. Our greatest frustration in editing this book was not finding a way to include the entire chorus of these voices.

Individually, we each have others to thank. Christie thanks "Sue Melia for her word processing skill, and Ursula Bowring, Lori Ginzberg, Faye Ginsburg, and Kate Kazin for helpful comments on the manuscript. In addition, I thank Rebecca, with whom I have shared life in the fullest sense while working on this anthology."

Andy offers the following acknowledgment: "My love and thanks go first to my life partner, Bruce, who has been patient and supportive in the midst of these extraordinary times, facing the challenges and tragedies that AIDS has brought into our lives. We face what must be faced, and life goes on. I am blessed with a partner who is able to go on with strength, tenacity, and a uniquely indomitable spark of life. My thanks go also to the rest of my family, along with so many wise and wonderful friends, who are all as eager as I am to see this book in print. Finally, I thank the far-flung members of the Lost Tribe, a group which gave me my first glimpse of being able to integrate my Jewishness, my gayness, and my political commitments."

INTRODUCTION

....

> The most persistent of all traditions relating to the observance of
> the day was the kindling of the Sabbath light on Friday eve-
> ning. . . . To conceal it from prying eyes, it was customary locally
> to kindle the light in a cellar, or to place it inside a pitcher; this
> similarity coming to be regarded as an essential observance.
> —CECIL ROTH, A History of the Marranos

IN FIFTEENTH-CENTURY SPAIN, THE INQUISITION DEMANDED THAT
all Jews convert or flee the country. However, some Jews took a different path, outwardly converting to Christianity while privately observing Jewish practices in their homes. Known as *conversos*,[1] these Jews
were thought to be anomalous in Jewish history. But in fact, homosexual Jews have experienced a fate similar to *conversos*. Frequently
during our five-thousand-year existence, we have been compelled to
hide our homosexual identities in order to survive as Jews.

While the essays in this anthology reflect a range of viewpoints and
life experiences, each is informed by lesbian or gay invisibility—the
experience of being as imperceptible in Jewish history, tradition, and
community life as were the *conversos* in their day. This invisibility
takes many forms, from that experienced by Adina Abramowitz, a
lesbian who grew up attending Yeshiva, to that experienced by Agnes
Herman, the mother of a gay man. Indeed, lesbian and gay invisibility is, in part, what moved Abramowitz, Herman, and twenty-five
others to share aspects of their lives, their struggles with history and
tradition, and their visions of contemporary Jewish life in this volume. As Jewish community activists and professionals, our own experiences of lesbian and gay invisibility—and our conviction that it
should be challenged—motivated us to edit this anthology.

Andy writes: "Growing up in Arizona in the 1950s and 1960s, I
learned that, as a Jew, if I didn't talk about my difference, people

1

would assume I was part of the majority, without my own culture, history, and beliefs. Fortunately, I developed an early appreciation for my Jewishness. I felt proud of my difference and excited, as the 1960s unfolded, to have a distinct cultural identity, especially one that valued justice so highly.

"As I grew up, I knew little or nothing about homosexuality. In the Hebrew schools and Jewish summer camps I attended, and the Jewish Community Centers in which my mother worked, homosexuality was referred to only in jokes or in disgust. There were no discussions about homosexuality. Nor were there curricula or role models of gay Jews—still largely as true today as it was twenty or thirty years ago.

"In my mid-twenties I began to find others who were looking for ways to integrate their Jewish identities and progressive political commitments. Then I discovered there were groups of lesbian and gay Jews reweaving the various threads of our identities. The possibility of integration—of being whole—was a revelation to me. It led me on a circuitous path to editing this book."

Christie writes: "Seeking refuge from the enforced heterosexuality of college life, I traveled to Israel at the age of eighteen. Kibbutz life was paradoxical: wearing my 'kibbutz uniform' (baggy pants, flannel shirt, and desert boots) to work in the fields was liberating in one sense. But facing the admonitions of older women, near-strangers who would accost me in the dining room, warning that I'd never find a marriage partner unless I plucked my eyebrows and wore makeup, was more oppressive than anything I'd ever experienced at home! It probably never occurred to those women that I lay awake at night thinking about making love to the woman asleep in the room next to mine.

"Four years later in Chicago, I met a woman with whom I became involved in my first significant lesbian relationship. Our courtship lasted over the summer, and we made love for the first time shortly before Rosh Hashanah. I remember walking into services at an egalitarian minyan that fall, my face flushed, feeling that the ground had shifted (and perhaps was still shifting) underneath me. I had marched in my first lesbian and gay pride parade that summer, publicly affirming my love for a woman. I remember looking around at familiar faces in the minyan, *davenning* a familiar service, and thinking that Judaism contained no roadmaps for my experience that year.

"Some years after that, I went to work in the Jewish community. As a lesbian Jewish communal professional, I received moderate support from heterosexual colleagues and some board members. Facing the prospect of nearly 100% job discrimination against open lesbians and gay men in the Jewish community, I did not feel comfortable coming out to everyone with whom I had professional contact. (This in itself presented difficulties, since I was expected to attend quasi-social events with a spouse.) One day at a board meeting, I reported on a new project involving women's organizations. After the report, one board member expressed reservations about the project, saying that it might result in our working with lesbian groups. I was astounded by this leap from *women* to *lesbian!* I thought surely my colleagues would respond to such an obvious example of lesbian-baiting. Silence filled the room. No words came from my colleagues or other board members, many of whom were veteran civil rights activists. It was as if I were the only one in the room who had heard the offending remark. After what seemed like a long time, the chair moved to the next item on the agenda. These are just a few of the instances of invisibility—all part of day-to-day life—that moved me to edit this anthology."

Lesbian and gay Jewish experience is not monolithic, as readers of this anthology will see. (This is also reflected in our decision to respect the contributors' individual preferences with regard to the transliteration of Hebrew and Yiddish terms.) Rather, it is influenced by the vicissitudes of religious identity, gender, age, class, geography, physical ability, and other factors. Nonetheless, lesbian and gay Jews share a distinct sensibility.

Many of us experience ourselves as "doubly other."[2] Positive representations of our sexual identities; our intimate relationships, friendships, communal networks; our language, art, and humor are absent from the majority culture. We are marginal in both Jewish and American culture, and some claim this provides us with special perspectives on both. For example, in an essay in this volume, Evelyn Torton Beck asserts that being "doubly other" enables Jewish lesbian-feminists to function as "a new prophetic minority" within Judaism.

We pay a price for our difference. We are subjected to *homophobia*, fear of lesbians and gay men, and *heterosexism*, institutionalized discrimination against lesbians and gay men. We face housing and employment discrimination, verbal harassment, physical violence,[3] and sometimes, rejection by family and friends. Twenty-five states still maintain sodomy laws, making sex in the privacy of our bedrooms a crime. Domestic partnership laws, which would enable partners of the same sex to enjoy the full legal privileges of marriage (e.g., spousal insurance benefits, the right to file joint tax returns, hospital visitation rights, and so on) exist in only a few cities.

Like Jews who assimilate, we learn to "pass"[4] as heterosexual—dressing the part, omitting a lover's gender from conversation, or refraining from public displays of affection. Passing hurts not only ourselves but also the Jewish communities in which we live, which don't reap the benefits of our authentic participation.

When the burden of passing becomes too great, lesbian and gay Jews find the courage to *come out.* Indeed, this is such a central part of our experience that coming-out stories have assumed the role of sacred text in lesbian and gay culture.[5] For Jews, and for lesbians and gay men, visibility is our key to finding each other, to building community, and to challenging myths and stereotypes about our people.

Once we come out, many lesbians and gay men develop a heightened awareness about the social construction of sexuality. Our sexual relations challenge Jewish tradition, which, as Judith Plaskow notes in an essay in this volume, assumes that sexual desire must be channeled primarily into procreation. While most modern Jews simply ignore these restrictions, lesbian and gay Jews bring fresh perspectives about the social construction of sexual desire, sexual ethics, and sexual variation to Jewish thinking about sexuality. These perspectives, which are just beginning to be explored in print, have the potential to transform Jewish sexual and family relations in some fundamental ways.

For many of us, sexual orientation functions as a lens through which we empathize with the oppression of others, and as a source of resistance to that oppression. Many well-known Jewish lesbian and gay activists have been inspired by Jewish history.[6] Like them, we understand *both* sexual orientation and Jewish identity as sources of resistance to oppression.

Both Jewish and lesbian and gay history teach that identity is not static: it is incumbent upon us to reshape it according to conditions in which we live at any given time. At Passover we are commanded to struggle in every generation for our freedom. As lesbians and gay men, we know that sexual identity is no more of a given, no more of a received identity, than is being Jewish. Both are subject to change from one generation to the next. Moreover, both can change within a lifetime, as we learn from those who come out later in life and those who identify as bisexual.

The visions of identity and community in this volume reflect the convergence of three movements that evolved in North America in late 1960s: Jewish renewal, feminism, and lesbian and gay liberation.[7] Inspired by the black liberation movement to reexamine race and ethnicity, an entire generation began to place a new value on ethnic pride and cultural pluralism. Like other ethnic groups, second- and third-generation American Jews began to reexamine the culture that many of our parents and grandparents eagerly sought to leave behind. This movement was fueled by Israel's 1967 Six Day War, which reaffirmed Jewish identity in many. Continuing in the two-century-old experimental tradition of American Judaism, mostly college-age Jews began to develop new forms of religious, cultural, and political expression which achieved a synthesis of Jewish tradition and the lessons of the post-Holocaust age.[8] Twenty years later, the results of these experiments are evident in new forms of Jewish art, prayer, community, and political activism that have inspired many contributors to this anthology.

Building on turn-of-the-century movements for women's equality, the second wave of feminism provided many contributors with a thorough understanding of how our personal experience is part of a larger system of male dominance. Feminists sought truths about every aspect of our culture—from history and political theory to art, literature, and science—by examining women's lived experience. Feminism defined gender as a social category inseparable from a larger context. Grounded in this understanding, the feminist movement has succeeded in changing some of the oppressive conditions under which we live. In addition, feminism provided fertile ground for a lesbian feminist movement to emerge in the late 1960s.[9]

The gay liberation movement shared with feminism an understanding that our personal and sexual identities are socially constructed and inseparable from a larger political context. While same-sex relationships have existed in all cultures, throughout all time, lesbians and gay men were first labeled "homosexual" by the Western medical establishment in the late nineteenth century. Some date the beginning of a distinct homosexual identity to this development, while others date it a century earlier. By the early twentieth century, the first "homophile rights" groups had appeared in the United States. These largely underground groups, which existed through the early 1960s, offered their members personal support as well as the hope of social acceptance and legal protection.[10] Prominent among these groups were the Daughters of Bilitis and the Mattachine Society, which enjoyed greatest popularity in the 1950s.[11]

But the modern gay liberation movement wasn't born until 1969, when patrons of the Stonewall Inn, a New York gay bar, spontaneously fought back against a police raid. This event transformed homosexuals' private fear into public rage. Like African Americans, who earlier in the decade had insisted on reclaiming the name "black" rather than being named by others, we rejected the label "homosexual" and took on the names "gay" and "lesbian." We devoted energy to coming out, reclaiming our past, creating a culture that joyously affirms our sexuality, and fighting for basic recognition and rights.

During these early years, the gay liberation movement, dominated by men, and the lesbian-feminist movement, worked separately though sometimes in a parallel fashion.[12] (There were, of course, situations in which we also worked together, particularly in minority communities where lesbians and gay men often face double invisibility. See, for example, Aliza Maggid's essay on the World Congress of Gay and Lesbian Jewish Organizations in this volume.) In the 1980s, improved trust, increased political sophistication, and the imperative to respond to outside threats—particularly from the political right and from AIDS—have brought our communities closer together. Although parts of the gay male community persist in their blindness to sexism, the sharp distinctions between the lesbian and gay male communities that existed in the 1970s have relaxed in the 1980s. (Our use of the term "lesbian and gay movement" in this anthology includes those parts of both communities that work together across gender lines, as well as the lesbian-feminist movement, and parts of both communities that remain essentially separate from one another.)

In the two decades since these movements first appeared, many of us have learned that claiming one part of our identity is an active choice that often leads to claiming other parts. It is a sign of the vitality of these movements that each has begun to incorporate teachings of the others. Lesbian and gay community Passover Seders, adult education courses in Jewish feminism, and the feminist process used by many havurot are but a few examples. In recent years an important body of theory exploring the intersections between Jewish identity, gender, sexual orientation, and other forms of identity has emerged. This theory can be found in works like *Nice Jewish Girls: A Lesbian Anthology*, edited by Evelyn Torton Beck; *The Tribe of Dina: A Jewish Women's Anthology*, edited by Melanie Kaye/Kantrowitz and Irena Klepfisz, and *Yours in Struggle: Three Feminist Perspectives on Racism and Anti-Semitism*, by Elly Bulkin, Minnie Bruce Pratt, and Barbara Smith. In addition, poetry, fiction, and liturgical material reflecting a lesbian or gay Jewish sensibility exists in great variety.[13]

Until the present generation, homophobia and heterosexism in the Jewish community led many lesbian and gay Jews to exile ourselves from the Jewish community, convinced that we were unwanted or did not belong. (This is particularly ironic given the deep-seated concern in the Jewish community over the impact of assimilation on the long-term survival and continuity of our people.)

Others of us have remained in the Jewish community, but have stayed in the closet. Like the fear that gripped the secret Jews of Spain, fear of discovery has often consumed the lives of those who felt compelled to choose this option.

The essays collected in this anthology point to a third alternative: one based neither on the exile of lesbian and gay Jews from the Jewish community nor on concealing our lesbian and gay identities. They speak to the blessing of affirming both our Jewish and our lesbian and gay identities, and to living our lives based on the wisdom of two cultures.

These essays also suggest prospects for bringing lesbian and gay experience to bear on Jewish history and tradition, family, and community life. These prospects will require fundamental change in our communities. They will require not only a willingness to include lesbian and gay Jews in our *minyanim*, but also a commitment to incorporate the experience of lesbian and gay Jews into our liturgy. They will require not only an openness to celebrating lesbian and gay life-cycle events in our synagogues to the extent that they mirror heterosexual life-cycle events, but also to the extent that they differ from, and at times challenge, heterosexual norms. They will require not simply a willingness to include lesbian and gay members in our communal organizations, but also a full commitment to mobilize the Jewish community in support of lesbian and gay rights.

Lesbian and gay Jews do not wish to live as the secret Jews of Spain.

We have begun to affirm our identities publicly. On the eve of the October 1987 National March for Lesbian and Gay Rights, the nation's largest civil rights march,[14] we witnessed a striking example of this. Nearly six hundred lesbian and gay Jews and our friends streamed into a Washington, D.C., auditorium designed for half our number, creating near-pandemonium as we greeted old friends, lovers, and strangers who seemed like family. The lights dimmed and we grew silent, settling into chairs, floors, windowsills, and laps. We lit the braided *havdallah* candle, we smelled the spices, we extinguished the candle in the wine. And we recited a blessing:

> Let us distinguish
> parts within the whole
>   and bless their differences.
> Like Sabbath and the six days of creation,
> may our lives be made holy
>   through relation.[15]

Christie Balka
Andy Rose
Passover 5749/1989

PART 1

··

Naming Ourselves

INTRODUCTION
....

Naming, in both Jewish and lesbian and gay culture, is an act of great importance. For Jews, naming signifies entrance into the covenant of our people. When a Jewish child is born, when one converts to Judaism, and at times of special significance, a Jew takes on a Hebrew name.

In lesbian and gay culture naming holds similar power. Naming our sexual orientation—coming out—breaks down our isolation. It enables us to take our place in a long tradition, and to join in community with others. Coming out is a continuous process that takes many forms, from private revelations to public celebrations of lesbian and gay pride.

In this section, five individuals describe growing up, coming out, and integrating their identities not only as lesbians and gay men, but also as disabled, working-class, and Sephardic Jews. Each has struggled against the mostly Christian, heterosexual assumptions of the majority culture to become visible against all odds. For some, Judaism has provided valuable insights about the importance of visibility and pride during this process, while for others it has presented an additional layer of conflict.

Lesbian and gay Jews exist in infinite variety. These essays are meant to be suggestive, not exhaustive, of our variety. But the point is clear: homosexuality among Jews, like homosexuality in general, cuts across all lines of age, class, physical ability, religion, and ethnic background. This diversity is a source of our strength.

Confessions of a "Feygele-Boichik"

....

Burt E. Schuman

WHEN FIRST APPROACHED ABOUT WRITING AN ESSAY ON MY EXPERI-
ences growing up Jewish and gay, I was filled with a mixture of terror
and embarrassment. I feared being perceived as a *schlemiel* who spent
the balance of his forty years as a marginal Jew and an ambivalent
gay. I dreaded appearing indifferent to the needs of my community
and cowardly in dealing with my parents. A paragon of courageous
activism I wasn't. Then it dawned on me that perhaps my story wasn't
so atypical, that other lesbian and gay Jews would identify with it.
I had to remind myself that not everyone can be a hero at twenty. The
question is how we respond to oppression *now*.

Though my feelings about being both Jewish and gay are very intense, the two have not always seemed related. My paths to Jewishness and gayness have in my mind's eye always resembled those of
U.S. 1 and Interstate 95 in New England—at times converging, at
times diverging and at times running parallel. They are curved and
convoluted, filled with sharp turns and sudden detours.

It is difficult to be sure which sensations came first—the sight of
shabbos candles on my grandmother's kitchen table or my brother's
bare chest, the sight of my great uncle wearing tefillin or my fantasies
of lying half-naked beside my second-grade deskmate, my first look at
a Torah scroll or my first view of "Spin and Marty" on television.
Some memories I've nurtured, others I've repressed; but it is through
these memories that I am coming to terms with my Jewish and gay
selves.

I was born in East Flatbush, Brooklyn, to an upwardly mobile, first-
generation Galician-Jewish family. My father came to the United States

12

when he was three; my mother was born in East Harlem. Both shared their generation's profound ambivalence toward Jewish religion and culture. For my father, Orthodox Judaism had proved severe and repressive, a reminder of his willful, autocratic father, who had forced him to quit school at the age of sixteen to work in the family bakery. For my mother, who was reared in a far more nurturing and tolerant environment, Orthodox Judaism appeared to be a barrier to first-class citizenship and the delights of the secular world.

By contrast, my maternal grandparents were deeply rooted in both Orthodox Judaism and Yiddish culture. They embodied the values of proud, self-educated Eastern European Jewish immigrants. To me these generational attitudes came to symbolize the positive and negative poles of Jewish identity—an all-encompassing and unashamed sense of religious and cultural identity at one end, and at the other, a confused and tortured assimilation into the middle-American mainstream. Often I have felt like an electrolyte flowing between the two.

When I was three my parents moved from East Flatbush to a garden apartment in Kew Gardens Hills, Queens. My earliest memories are of the objects and symbols of American mass culture: tricycles, beanies, football practice, 3D glasses, and "Howdy Doody," "Rootie Kazootie," and "Kukla, Fran, and Ollie" on TV. We were trained to cheer Adlai Stevenson and to boo Joe McCarthy, to root for Jackie Robinson and the rest of the Brooklyn Dodgers and to be as American as Horn and Hardart.

The only memories I have of Jewishness before the age of five were the moments when my parents would "talk Jewish" behind closed bedroom doors or when my mother would lapse into "Jewish" when chatting on the telephone.

I was five years old when I first entered a synagogue, on the occasion of my brother's bar mitzvah. I remember the long drive to Brooklyn, the endless hours sitting on hard wooden benches, squirming while my brother chanted from a raised podium and a gaggle of old men babbled incomprehensibly. If this was prayer, it certainly did not resemble anything Roy Rogers or Dale Evans did in their home. It was certainly very different from the prayers Miss Marinen made us recite before milk and cookies in first grade. It all seemed so strange, so foreign, so *un-American*.

It was only after the age of seven that my interest in Judaism began to take root, due in large measure to the growing bond I shared with my grandparents and great uncle. *Erev Shabbos* in their home was a truly magical event. The entire apartment seemed scrubbed and polished to a brilliant lustre. A feeling of joy pervaded their home, which was filled with the aromas of gefilte fish, chicken soup, potato pudding, *tsimmes*, boiled chicken, and chopped meat.

My grandfather and great uncle would return from synagogue looking radiant. The extended family gathered around the table in the living room–dining room—a festive table adorned with shabbos candles, the finest linen, gleaming silver, elegant crystal, and fine china. Everywhere, the echoes of conversation and conviviality would ripple through the air, along with wafts of Jewish-American and Yiddish humor. While we grew and changed, matured, went to college, and started careers, our lives somehow remained anchored around that table. There we were nurtured, loved unconditionally, and told we were special.

I began nagging my parents into letting me spend weekends at my grandparents' house. It was a particular treat for me to accompany my grandfather and great uncle—a talmudic scholar—to their shul on *shabbos* mornings. The atmosphere there was suggestive of a *shtibl* in a Galician *shtetl*. Men would rock back and forth with huge *taleysim* over their heads, spontaneously pouring forth with bits of *davening* in rapid-fire Galician or Lithuanian-accented Hebrew.

Passover was also a time of magic. My grandfather would conduct the seder dressed in a *kitl* and an elaborate headdress. We reclined on pillows, listened to a long recitation on the liberation from Egypt, ate sumptuous foods (including my grandmother's fried matzoh) and chanted some of the most beautiful melodies in the Jewish liturgy. Our one act of familial heresy occurred during the opening of the door for Elijah the Prophet; my great aunt would rush into the living room with a kerchief draped over her head, drink the fifth cup of wine, and run out the door. All this was done with a feeling of joy and fellowship.

There are other memories—*shabbos* strolls in the warm sun, lazy afternoons in the front yard with Yiddish papers spread across my grandfather's chest, Sunday breakfasts of Wheatena with the radio turned to WEVD's Yiddish broadcasts, and Sunday afternoons when my grandmother would be interrupted from her baking by the arrival of bearded old men with collection boxes and calendars.[1]

The contrast between my parents' and my grandparents' life-styles became more pronounced after we moved, in 1957, from our apartment in Kew Gardens Hills to a suburban, 1940s colonial in Hollis Hills, Queens. It was also the year that my brother went off to Brandeis University and I became an only child. The house, surrounded by a spacious lawn, tall trees, and a rock garden, looked as if it had sprung full-blown from the set of "Leave It to Beaver" or "Father Knows Best." Though the surrounding community was heavily Jewish, our block was not; many of the original owners were still living there.

In the fall, I was enrolled in the Hollis Hills Jewish Center and became a regular member of its junior congregation. My Hebrew school teacher was a youngish, progressive, secular Zionist whose warm personality and imaginative pedagogy (lots of games and folk songs) instilled a love of the Hebrew language and made me an eager learner. Despite the differences in style, this *yiddishkeit* was highly compatible with that of my grandparents.

At the same time, I became more keenly aware of my parents' ambivalence about their Jewish identity. Though they were supportive of my interest in Hebrew and Judaism, they set firm limits about *their* involvement. Friday night *kiddush* became an institution in our home, Hanukkah was regularly observed and ham and bacon disappeared from our table. However, they were adamant about not having "religion imposed on them," on not being forced to keep kosher or to give up travel, sports, and shopping on the sabbath.

Increasingly, I found their attitudes toward non-Jews rather puzzling. On the one hand, non-Jews were "the gentiles," whose traditional manners, Sunday dinners, and Christmases seemed so desirably "American." On the other hand, they were "the *goyim*," whose perceived blandness and provincialism was symbolized by the "Reader's Digest" or "Queen for a Day." (Italian-Americans were the exception to this rule and were considered "soul mates" by my parents.) These contradictory attitudes were painfully in evidence when my father's gentile business associates would come to dinner or when my father expressed fears about displaying an electric menorah in the window or mowing the lawn on Saturday.

Before adolescence, my gay feelings lay largely on the periphery of my consciousness, with the exception of an occasional crush or a fascination with bare male chests. As I grew older, however, I became keenly aware of being "different," though I was not aware of what that difference was. For many years I was able to compensate for those feelings by immersing myself in organized Judaism and, through religious and academic achievement, attracting attention and praise.

As I reached adolescence, however, I could not escape the feelings that kept rising to the surface. My fantasies and daydreams became more focused and more frightening. I dreamed constantly of meeting a male "pal" who would protect and comfort me. I took particular, furtive delight in the seminaked wrestling matches I had with one of my friends and in the thrilling sensation of bare skin on bare skin. Yet I was so terrified of these feelings that I turned a blind eye to some of the rituals of adolescence that were happening around me—stories of all-male strip poker sessions, games of "cookie," hints of fellatio by two boys who went home with me each day on the school bus, and the antics of a friend who would rush into my house, pronounce me "the epitome of feminine beauty and grace," and pounce on top of me.

The stronger these feelings became, the less protected I felt in my cocoon of *yiddishkeit*. Moreover, it seemed that many of my support systems were beginning to fall apart. By the time I entered high school, my grandmother began to complain about my not having a girlfriend, saying "I want to dance at your wedding." Teenage activities at the synagogue were centered around dances and socials; bare breasts replaced *Bereshit* as the main topic of male conversation. I felt awkward in the presence of formerly close friends who talked constantly about girls and paraded around with their girlfriends as if they were prize trophies. Cousins, and even members of my congregation, tried constantly to match me up with "a cute girl." Everywhere, the heterosexual noose was tightening; my one means to escape was to withdraw—physically and emotionally.

On rare occasions, I was able to use the growing civil rights movement as a diversion from my pain. By throwing myself into sit-ins, panel discussions, and voter registration projects, I could avoid dwelling on my loneliness and my sexual feelings. If I could find an oppressed people to champion, I did not have to deal with my *own* oppression. By assuming the posture of "leader," I could maintain a safe distance from my peers.

It was my involvement with the civil rights movement that precipitated a twelve-year break with organized Judaism. While trying to enlist the support of my congregation for a pro-integration boycott of the New York City public schools, I encountered a patronizing rabbi, vicious comments about "schvartzes" from leaders of the men's club, and a storm of hostility and outrage from congregants who feared that school integration would destroy their children's futures. The experience only added to the rage and alienation I already felt.

In 1965 I entered Queens College. My first two years of college were a sexual hell, made worse by the fact that I was living at home. Gay life, if it existed at all on campus, was well-hidden. If anyone was sending signals in my direction, I was oblivious. A good deal of my energy was spent trying to prove I was "normal" by going out on an endless series of first dates. While I had secret crushes on some of my best friends, I did not act on my gay feelings during my freshman and sophomore years.

I had planned an even greater escape from myself during my junior year in France. There, I was to become cosmopolitan and a bon vivant: I had not anticipated having my first sexual encounter with a man— least of all a German!

We met during a student orientation session in Nancy. For the rest of the student body, this coincided with the tail end of the summer session for students who had failed their exams in the spring; many were foreign medical students. My first love was friendly with a group of Norwegian medical students who were living in our dormitory complex. Slowly, almost imperceptibly, we found ourselves seated next to each other at mealtimes, going to cafes together, and taking long walks back to the dormitories from the student restaurant. When our orientation session had ended and several of us moved on to Reims to begin our formal studies, I found myself thinking about him almost obsessively.

I wrote to him as a trial balloon. To my amazement, he wrote back and expressed interest in cultivating a friendship. Soon, we were writing to one another regularly, and our letters grew more and more affectionate. Often, they contained long digressions on the nature of friendship and love, and mutual assurances that there was no *malentendu*. On two brief visits to Nancy, we found ourselves chatting away in bistros for hours, reluctant to part.

On my third visit the inevitable happened. I could find no accommodation for the night; he suggested I spend it in his room, which conveniently had one double bed. He had no difficulty convincing me to stay another night.

Despite our intimacies, I had never revealed the fact that I was Jewish. That evening, while we were having dinner with some of my American classmates, I did something rather strange. I began to throw Yiddish phrases into the conversation and a few of my classmates followed suit. This left my friend disconcerted and confused.

The next morning, which was a Saturday, we were awakened by chimes from a nearby clock tower. Sleepily, I muttered, "I guess people are going to church." He answered, "Why church? This is Saturday . . . Does this have anything to do with your using Yiddish?"

This led to a long and loving dialogue about his Germanness and my Jewishness, about the Holocaust and survival in postwar Germany. Though the romance soon faded—except for an occasional tryst when he was in the United States—we have remained close friends for twenty years.

After returning from Europe I spent a great deal of time running away from what I had discovered about myself. I was a gay Jew, a *feygele-boichik*, and no degree of playacting could alter the truth. I could not play at being French, for the blatant anti-Semitism I had been exposed to in Reims made me realize how alienated I would be from that society. I could not play at being a macho Don Juan, for it was hard to sustain a compelling sexual interest in women. I could not play at being a platonic chum with the male friends I wanted to ravish, because sooner or later my possessiveness and jealousy drove them away.

Slowly, timidly, I began to come to terms with my gayness, and later with my Jewishness. Moving to my first apartment and beginning my teaching career made it easier. But even my separation from the nest could not help peel away the layers of fear, suspicion, and paranoia that had formed around my psyche. I remember circling around the block no less than five times before entering my first Greenwich Village bar. I remember heading for the subway with my coat collar turned up and my hat pulled down over my ears, afraid that my principal or one of my father's friends would see me. When I answered advertisements in the *East Village Other*, I insisted on meeting my dates in "neutral" territory and dreaded their looking or dressing too "nelly." Gradually, I began to relax and enjoy my newly found life-style. I relished the thrill of the search, the moment when my love interest would agree to come home with me, and the excitement of the first sexual contact. To my amazement, I discovered that sexuality was an integral part of my life.

My exploration of gay life yielded other dividends. During a mutual confession, I discovered that my best friend from teenage work camp was also a "club member." A hushed admission to my London-based brother that I was "a screaming, raving queen" was answered by the quip, "So am I." At that moment, we experienced simultaneously a sense of giddy exultation and profound sadness—joy that we had no more reason to hide, and sorrow over the years wasted spinning webs of deceit. Today, my brother and I enjoy a caring, trusting, and completely candid relationship. We even, on occasion, visit bars and discos together when I'm in London or he's in New York.

My return to *yiddishkeit* and complete acceptance of my Jewishness was as long and arduous a journey as the discovery of my gayness. The same denial, the same ferocity of self-deception came into play with painfully negative results.

Finally, one Sunday, I found myself in the Jewish Museum surrounded by ritual silver and enormous blow-ups of Roman Vishniac's photographs of the vanished shtetls of Poland and Hungary. Confronted so baldly with the images of my immediate past, I was smitten by an overwhelming, incapacitating sense of loss.

The journey continued through a study of the Yiddish language, Yiddish music, and a flirtation with Jewish socialism. But secular *yiddishkeit* was not enough. I needed a spiritual home—but where?

While waiting in line for—of all things—tickets for the Grand Kabuki, I found myself conversing with a man who waxed enthusiastically about Congregation Beth Simchat Torah, New York's lesbian and gay synagogue. The very mention of such a place evoked bizarre and surreal images for me: drag queens in pink diaphanous *taleysim* screaming, "Kiss my *tsitsit!*"; muscular, butch women in leather dragging their fem lovers to the bima for *aliyot*.

To my surprise, I found an updated version of my grandfather's *shul*. Everywhere, there were manifestations of great faith and intense *yiddishkeit*, from men and women shaking back and forth with huge *taleysim* over their heads to passionate singing and rite of passage ceremonies. The members of this congregation treated me like family, and the congregation became an important resting place, a way station on my Jewish journey.

Gradually I felt the need for a religious home that was theologically less traditional and politically more progressive. That home is Stephen Wise Free Synagogue, where I live happily as an openly gay man in a pluralistic Jewish family. This family has raised its voice loudly and unequivocally for lesbian and gay rights—demonstrated by its conference on lesbian and gay Jews in 1986, and by its passionate support of a resolution on the inclusion of lesbian and gay Jews in the Jewish community at the last Union of American Hebrew Congregations biennial convention.

Acceptance into a Jewish spiritual home has enabled me to love myself more both as a gay man and as a Jew. I've become an active member of our lay-led *chevra tefila,* serve on the Ritual Committee, and even lead study sessions. My work with the choir has progressed to the point where my cantor asks me to substitute for her on occasion. None of this could have occurred if I were still in the closet: I simply would have been too alienated.

Recently, I submitted my new-found sense of identity to the ultimate challenge: accepting the directorship of a Jewish agency whose constituency ranges from Orthodox to Reform Jews. This has been quite a change from working for a human rights agency, where being openly gay was "politically correct." Here, however, I tread carefully. I do not, at this time, choose to "inflict" my issues on the agency. I have my own vehicles for expressing my activism. However, the death from AIDS of a previous openly gay director has muted any open expressions of heterosexism within our community. Whatever they may have felt about the issue from the standpoint of *halacha,* our Orthodox rabbis never rejected this man. They were extraordinarily loving and supportive throughout his illness and eulogized him at his funeral. This expression of Judaism at its best, of *gmilut chassadim,* means far more to me than ideological correctness.

For now, I am at peace. I feel like a mensch.

Growing Up in Yeshiva

....

Adina Abramowitz

I GREW UP IN A WARM, VIBRANT MODERN ORTHODOX COMMUNITY in Washington, D.C. Though my parents were Conservative Jews, we joined an Orthodox synagogue when my family moved to Washington, and I attended an Orthodox Hebrew Day School—a modern yeshiva—from nursery school through ninth grade. My yeshiva training gave me a tremendous knowledge of Jewish texts, traditions, and practice. From yeshiva I also learned that all my social needs could *and should* be met inside the Jewish community. My early experiences in yeshiva continue, to this day, to inform my Jewish identity. Despite whatever conflicts I have had between being a lesbian and being a Jew, it has never been an option for me to leave Judaism. My beliefs and practices today are quite different from what I was taught as a child, but I still draw upon the knowledge and the love of Torah that I got during my yeshiva years.

Whenever I go to lesbian and gay pride events, especially if they are in Washington, I look for people who graduated from my yeshiva. Surely I can't be the only lesbian or gay graduate of the Hebrew Academy of Washington!

My parents came from fairly assimilated backgrounds. I ended up at a yeshiva, in part, because they wanted me to have the Jewish education they didn't have. There was always a tension between what I was learning at school and what my family observed at home. During my first few years in school, I resolved this conflict by making demands that we be more observant at home, to which my parents willingly agreed. But beginning with fourth grade, I tended to be less observant at school. At ten I stopped participating in daily morning *davening*. I became an intellectual rebel, challenging the rabbis on laws that seemed prejudiced or hypocritical. I was smart and serious, and the principal and rabbis couldn't ignore my knowledge of text. The peak of my rebellion occurred in eighth grade when I made fun of the *davening*, and the principal called me into his office and grilled me on my beliefs about God. When I got back to my classroom the girls had written "Free Adina" all over the blackboard.

Despite my rebelling, my days in yeshiva were happy, and I received a fine Jewish education. Maimonides' Levels of Tzedaka taught me about empowerment, and the Prophets (my favorite Hebrew subject) taught me about social justice. As a result of studying Jewish history and living in Washington during the sixties and seventies, I always knew that I would be a political activist. At twelve and thirteen I watched various protests and wondered which cause I would champion later on.

In sixth grade, the boys and girls were separated for Hebrew studies so the boys could be initiated into the practice of learning Talmud. During the next four years, the sixteen girls in my class became very close. Bar mitzvah parties, dances, and other heterosexual rites of passage crept up on us. The boys didn't always invite me, and when I went I felt nervous and awkward. I felt betrayed by these boys, who, up until the previous year, had been my buddies because I was a "tomboy." The girls told me I would have to stop playing sports with the boys if I ever wanted to have a boyfriend. The rules were changing fast, and I didn't understand why.

Yeshiva taught me that girls were safe and boys were not. Why else were girls allowed to spend time together unsupervised, yet co-ed dance parties were thought to be evil and would probably "make us into drug addicts"?

After yeshiva, I attended the local public school. The two years I spent there were very difficult, as I was largely unprepared for the social scene. During the seven-minute breaks between periods boys would seek out their girlfriends and neck—we used to call it "the seven-minute fuck." The drugs in high school shocked me. I saw students shoot up in public before classes started. Taking care of your body is a very positive Jewish value that I had learned in yeshiva and that was reenforced by my parents. Seeing students use drugs countered everything I had learned.

Compared to yeshiva, high school was not very academically challenging. What was I supposed to hang my ego on, if not intellectual accomplishment? In public school I was suddenly considered to be very religious. That was disconcerting after nine years of being from "the liberal family." In public school, my religious observance became an anthropological curiosity.

I didn't make many new friends in high school, and I certainly didn't have any boyfriends. My buddies were the other kids from yeshiva who chose to go to public school. Most of us went to *midrasha*— a Jewish studies program that met every Sunday morning and two evenings a week. I was much less interested in boys than my girlfriends, and would occasionally wonder if I was a lesbian, but I would quickly push that thought away.

When it came time to choose a college, I knew I wanted to continue my dual-track education. My first choice was to go to Barnard College and attend the Jewish Theological Seminary (JTS) part-time. Even though I visited Barnard as a senior in high school, somehow I didn't notice the strong lesbian presence on campus or the fact that all the Jews I met were Orthodox. When I arrived at Barnard as a freshman, I was again totally unprepared for the social scene. My fantasies about going away to school were always about the intellectual stimulation. On the first day of orientation, I met many of the women (all of a sudden we were women!) who became my friends throughout college, including the woman who later became my first lover. All of us were Jews, and most of us were Orthodox.

During my first year at Barnard, I struggled to fit into the Orthodox community, which was the only active Jewish presence on campus. I took classes at both Barnard and JTS. The seminary was an eye-opening experience for me: it offered an acceptable Jewish worldview that reconciled many of my inner beliefs with what I had been taught in yeshiva. Instead of believing in the Torah being given by God to Moses, I studied "critical theory," which postulated that the texts were written over a long period by various people and groups and that the compilation of these texts were the holy documents of our tradition. Instead of a fixed view of *halakha*, there was an understanding that the law had changed over time to fit the culture and environment where Jews lived. Yet the social implications of attending JTS were a disaster. One *frume* Barnard woman, upon hearing that I was attending classes there, said "But that's an *apikoros* [heretical] place."

At the end of my first year at Barnard my study partner, best friend, and constant companion admitted that she had "sexual feelings" for me. She was one of the other women taking classes at both Barnard and JTS, and she came from an observant family in Boston. Together we began to struggle over the various "women in Judaism" issues. I was drawn to her but was also very scared. After much anguish, we decided to "give in" and experiment with being lovers. What followed was a year and a half of a loving, guilt-ridden, closeted relationship. Every two or three weeks we would break up because there was no way to reconcile our relationship with our Jewish beliefs, and we would never be accepted by the Jewish community anyway. Shortly thereafter, we would get back together and start the process all over again. Meanwhile we continued to try to fit into the Orthodox social scene. Although we were known as a duo, we were not out to anyone but our roommates and a few select friends.

During this relationship I went into therapy for the first time with a counselor from Barnard's mental health office. As a fairly traditional therapist, she believed that lesbianism was a phase that many women at women's colleges were "susceptible to." She also didn't really believe that modern people could be religious. To her the conflict between my sexuality and my religious beliefs was a myth—the former was a phase and the latter a neurosis.

Although I knew a number of self-accepting lesbians during my first two years in college, I didn't allow myself to get close to them. None of these women were Jewish-identified, and some of them thought it was strange that I was. I felt judged by them because they rejected all organized religion as patriarchal and seemed to regard spirituality as a frill we couldn't afford during this period of struggle for more "basic" women's rights. In order to include them in my inner social circle, I would have had to overcome two lessons that I learned well at yeshiva: that my own sexuality was unacceptable, and that all my social needs should be filled inside the Jewish community.

When I was at home during the summers I attended the Conservative shul in which I had grown up. I was lonely, conflicted, and confused. I would look at the adults whom I had known since I was a kid and wonder, "Can I trust any of them with my problems?" I didn't come out to anyone. I realize now that I had never heard the words "gay" or "lesbian" spoken in that shul. No wonder I felt isolated.

During my junior year in college I lived in Israel and studied at Hebrew University. My lover from Barnard was also there, but we had promised ourselves that we would not export our relationship to Israel. This year would give me a chance to decide if I was seriously interested in making aliyah.

In Israel, I quickly became friends with a group of Americans who were Reconstructionist, and *chavurah* Jews. They believed that modern thought and contemporary culture could and should be integrated into Jewish life. This opened up the possibility that there could also be a place for feminism and perhaps even gay and lesbian Jews inside the Jewish community. We formed a minyan that met every other week. Here, for the first time, I saw women participating equally with men in all aspects of the Shabbat service, and I was very moved. Here was a Judaism that dealt with the world of emotions as well as intellect. Over the course of the year I rejected Orthodoxy as a worldview. I realized that I believe the "truth" derives from many sources, while my Orthodox friends believe it originates from only one source.

That year, my social life was divided between my new friends who were in the minyan and a group of Orthodox friends from Barnard who were studying in men's and women's yeshivot. I spent most of my *Shabbatot* with one of these two groups. As the year progressed, I felt increasingly alienated from the Orthodox group. Almost all of the Orthodox group practiced *negiyah*—not touching a member of the opposite sex. A great deal of physical affection took place between members of the same sex. The assumption that this was nonsexual made me very uncomfortable, because it denied what I was feeling more and more often toward women. The thought that I was a lesbian sometimes seemed inevitable, though it did not seem possible.

Shortly before Passover, on a walk that began two hours before Shabbat, a woman from the *chavurah* community came out to me. She was a rabbinical student who had been lovers for most of that year with another student. We were both so excited to connect with another Jewish lesbian that we got absurdly lost and barely made it back to the house before Shabbat.

The world turned upside down for me in that moment of honesty. During the seder, and the next few weeks, all I could think about was how my isolation was over. When I realized a few weeks later that I was in love with a woman, I had someone to talk to. "I didn't come all the way to Israel to get involved with a woman," I said to my newfound lesbian friend. I was in anguish again. I felt as if I had failed, that I was weak and couldn't resist temptation. Despite the fact that I had two Jewish lesbians to share my struggles with in Israel, I still did not feel that this was a viable life-style. My cocoon had grown from just me to three people—hardly a minyan!

When I came back from Israel for my senior year I decided I wanted a relationship that would succeed or fail on the basis of emotional compatibility, not sexual orientation. I met and went out for a year with a man who was a graduate student at JTS. Heterosexual privilege was quite a shock to me. For the first time in my life, my partner and I could hold hands on the street. In my relationships with women I had almost never shared affection or even simple touching in public. (Perhaps this was the lesbian form of *negiyah!*) His friends accepted me, and they accepted us as a couple with no questions. That was quite a switch from the scary, cautious process of coming out to a few selected friends when I was with women. I felt judged by my lesbian friends but welcomed by many Jewish friends. I heard via the grapevine that my old therapist was pleased I was "cured." Despite this newfound heterosexual privilege, I was so used to being in the closet that most of the people who attended our minyan never realized that he and I were together.

That relationship did end because of emotional incompatibility. Without making a conscious decision to do so, I went back to being with women. I felt like I had come home, which was totally unexpected. For a brief period I attended a Left-leaning church in Greenwich Village that had a gay minister. On Shabbat I would go to the minyan and be in the closet, and on Sunday I would go to church and explore what it felt like to be accepted as a lesbian in a religious setting. I was surprised at how meaningful the services were to me—the emotional experience was not that different from the minyan. In 1979, I marched in my first Gay Pride parade with a group from that church.

In my second year after graduating from college, in December 1980, I attended the founding conference of New Jewish Agenda and signed up for the lesbian and gay affinity group. That may have been my first conscious act of self-acceptance and pride. I was twenty-two years old and had been carrying around the conflict between my Jewish and lesbian identity for five years. Just being in a room with over thirty people who put the words "gay" and "lesbian" together with "Jewish" was immensely healing. I don't remember anything we talked about. I do remember the sense of affirmation I felt in that setting.

As I was becoming more secure in my lesbian identity, I ended what was to be my last relationship with a woman who was ambivalent about her sexual identity. No relationship at all was better than a relationship that didn't affirm my lesbian identity. After all of the years of debate, I decided on New Year's Eve, 1980, to try calling myself a lesbian for one month. Almost immediately I felt enormous relief. Although my struggles with my sexual orientation were by no means over, I have not questioned my lesbian identity since that moment.

During my coming out process, I longed to find a Jewish partner. Since that didn't seem possible, I decided to be open to a relationship with a Christian woman who was also an activist. I felt we understood each other spiritually, and this might be enough to make it work. Up until that point, I believed that sharing a Jewish home was so important that only another observant Jewish woman could be my partner. Although we broke up for other reasons, that relationship taught me an important lesson. Having an observant Jewish partner no longer seemed like a prerequisite for a relationship.

Having given up on finding a Jewish partner, I then met a woman who was not only Jewish and observant, but had also gone to yeshiva! During our relationship, we shared Jewish holidays, became famous for the Shabbat dinners we made for our friends, and had a great time laughing over the Yiddish-English-Hebrew mailings she still gets from her Brooklyn yeshiva. We were accepted in our community as a couple, and our *simches* were shared by our friends. I had finally found and helped to create a Jewish community that nurtured all of me.

Since my mid-twenties, I have been out to my family and my Jewish community. Although coming out to them was wrenching and painful for me, I have been met mostly with acceptance. My family in particular has grown to appreciate my choices and has learned to support me in ways I never would have thought possible.

There have been a few times when the two strands of my identity were able more fully to merge. I was privileged to tell my personal story at a retreat held by the Reconstructionist Rabbinical College when the college was in the process of deciding whether to admit openly gay and lesbian students. At the retreat, I was able to be open and vulnerable, yet at the same time strong and unafraid. The students were moved, and I felt that sharing my story opened up more than a few minds and hearts.

The following summer I helped plan, and then officiated at a commitment ceremony for a lesbian couple who are both close friends of mine. (One member of the couple was the woman who had come out to me in Israel.) We rewrote most of the traditional Jewish wedding ceremony, adding our own values about relationships and changing the "God language." We also added writings by Adrienne Rich, lyrics by songwriter Margie Adam, and new rituals. At the ceremony, the women spoke to each other and I spoke to both of them individually and as a couple. When it was over, there wasn't a dry eye in the group. Many of the lesbian couples had a look of deep longing for the affirmation these two women received for their life choice. My feet didn't touch the ground for two weeks. I was euphoric.

Another experience that moved me deeply was a *Havdalah* service which I helped plan the night before the 1987 March on Washington for Lesbian and Gay Rights. We invited a number of performing artists who are gay and lesbian and Jewish to give a concert, and we asked Rabbi Yoel Kahn of San Francisco's Congregation Sha'ar Zahav and singer/songwriter Ronnie Gilbert to do the Havdalah service. Approximately six hundred people crowded into the room, with more in the hallway, to hear Ronnie Gilbert sing the *berachot* from *Havdalah*, and to hear Ruth Pelham, Elliot Pilshaw, and Alix Dobkin perform. The audience was ecstatic from the very beginning. Old friends who hadn't seen each other in years were reunited. Yoel Kahn said, "Everyone I want to come to my wedding is here tonight." My parents were in the audience. On that night a lesbian and gay Jewish community was visibly present, and we expressed our pride and love for each other.

I know that most gay men and lesbians have trouble coming out. Yet I feel that the Jewish community put me in a double bind that kept the conflict over my sexuality brewing for many years longer than necessary. The Jewish community kept gays and lesbians totally invisible, yet all my social needs were supposed to be filled by this community. When I was in Israel, I confided in the Hillel rabbi about my dilemma. He said no Jewish community should reject me as long as "I didn't go around proselytizing." I asked him if that meant I should stay in the closet. He said yes. He had no answer to the obvious question of how I was supposed to meet a Jewish woman to be my partner.

My struggle to integrate my Jewish and lesbian identities was really two separate, yet interwoven, struggles. First, I had to figure out a way to be Jewish that included the celebration of difference, that recognized and honored women's experience (including our emotional selves), that respected tradition without coming from a purely halakhic framework, and that attempted to integrate *tikkun olam*—repairing the world—into ritual practice. Second, I had to figure out how to accept myself as a lesbian, to love myself, to come out to the important people in my life from a place of strength, and to find other lesbians with whom to share triumphs and disasters. In my conflicts over my Jewish identity, there were many resources available to help me, and these struggles often seemed more productive. There was a whole community to talk with about feminist language about God, or about how Jews should respond to United States policy in Central America. My struggles over my sexual identity were much more private and painful. Much of this work went on in the privacy of a therapist's office, by myself, or in long talks with the few lesbians in my life.

One aspect of coming out in the Jewish community was made easier by my yeshiva years. Every Jewish community I've been involved with respects learning and having a "Jewish background." When I first came out to folks at the Germantown minyan (where I *davened* regularly for three years), they already had a high regard for me because of my regular *d'vrei torah*. That made it harder for people to reject me, as they already valued my contribution to the community. Yet I wonder what it must be like for others who don't share my background.

Recently, I have become involved in creating a new synagogue based on the concept that prayer, study, and social action are all necessary components of a complete Jewish life. It is called Mishkan Shalom (Sanctuary of Peace) and the statement of principles openly announces that gay and lesbian Jews are valued members of the community. I am now involved with a woman I met in the synagogue. When my lover told our rabbi that we were together, his reaction was very warm: "*Mazel tov*, you're the first *shidekh* in the shul." When I told my mother about this new relationship, she said excitedly, "And you met her at the shul . . ."; to which I added, "Yeah Mom, it's a dream come true—meeting a woman at shul."

Different like Moses

Alan D. Zamochnick

I ALWAYS ENJOY THE SEDER AT PESACH. TO ME IT REPRESENTS THE continuous celebration of liberation from our own *Mitzrayim,* our narrow places of oppression and despair. As a child, not quite able to understand what the seder meant, I vividly remember my mother taking me aside and, with a child's book about Passover, patiently explaining the story of the Exodus and of Moses. To this day, the part of the story I remember most is that Moses was a person with a disability, like me. My mother described the story of the burning coals with which Pharaoh had tested Moses' intelligence and determined his fate. Pharaoh had placed a plate of burning coals on one side and a plate of sparkling coins and jewelry on the other. If the infant Moses was intelligent he would be attracted to the sparkling jewelry and coins and would be killed, as a threat to Pharaoh's heirs. On the other hand, if he were attracted to the hot black coals, he would be perceived as not very intelligent and would be allowed to live. Legend has it that Moses started to reach for the jewelry and coins. At the last moment, however, an angel pushed the baby's hands into the hot steamy coals. The coals burned his hand and he put it in his mouth to lick the burns, injuring his tongue. From then on, Moses, our teacher and leader, had difficulty speaking.

Growing up with cerebral palsy and a severe hearing impairment was not easy. I attended a public day school for orthopedically disabled children. Often at school, teachers who had no understanding of deafness would criticize me for not paying attention, telling me to listen harder. Classmates would shy away from me because they had difficulty understanding me, and I would shy away from them when things became too difficult for me to hear or to attempt to guess what was going on.

Despite my limited social experience and communication skills, I was an eager learner. When I could understand what was being discussed, I was bright and extremely observant; so much so, that when my family first suspected I had hearing problems, it took the doctors quite a few years and several kinds of tests before they positively identified my deafness. Having cerebral palsy made things more complicated, as many people believed that if you had cerebral palsy, you were also mentally retarded. My parents knew that I was too observant to be either retarded or unwilling to listen and suspected the problem to be something else: possibly a hearing impairment.

I came from a family that valued books and learning, but like most middle-class American families in the 1950s and 1960s, we were also hooked on television. There were times when my brother and I needed help with our schoolwork, and we would turn to our father, the mathematics expert of the family: he could make the most complicated math problem seem simple. But he worked long hours. The trick was to catch him as soon as he came home late at night, before he could relax. Once he relaxed it was too late—he'd eat and then before we knew it, he'd fall asleep at the dining room table with the TV set blaring.

I remember one time in particular, when I was in junior high school, I succeeded in hijacking him for help with algebra. He had just turned on the TV, and it was blaring a detective story. My father was explaining the algebra problem to me, and I was trying to understand what he was saying by looking at him and attempting to hear him over the TV. He kept telling me to look at the paper he was showing me, not at him. But when I looked at the paper, I could not follow my father's lips. It was an exhausting experience. Only one-third of English phonetic sounds can be clearly read on the lips by a person fluent in the language. For a person in my situation—depending on both lipreading and hearing the words simultaneously—it was an impossible task. Somehow I managed to guess a quarter of what he was explaining and tried to figure out the loose ends.

Both my hearing impairment and my cerebral palsy interfered with my social life. Interpersonal communications were difficult at best, even with a hearing aid. Books were my world. Because of my limited social experiences, I had difficulty understanding fiction and preferred reading books on history and geography, and about foreign countries. I longed to be with other children but could not make a real connection and felt distant from my peers.

During the 1960s, as the African, West Indian, and South Pacific island nations were becoming independent, I followed their progress with a hawk's eye. As I gained better control of my physical movements, I would go downtown myself, buy several different newspapers, and compose a composite "chapter" in a scrapbook for each new nation the day it became independent. I saw these former European colonies as mirror images of myself and my desire to escape my early adolescent isolation. This hobby helped me develop a more independent self-image.

At the same time, I began to take an interest in my Jewish heritage. One Hanukkah, I attempted to follow my brother as he sang traditional prayers. I sang the way I thought I heard them and practically created my own language. That was not new: I had also ruined the *Star Spangled Banner* and other songs we were taught in school assemblies. Those renditions were legendary. What was new was that I became aware of my brother's preparations for becoming bar mitzvah.

Without knowing quite what it was about, I launched a campaign to go to Hebrew School myself. We did not live in a Jewish neighborhood and the synagogue was about half a mile away. At first my father doubted that I could succeed, partly because of my physical disabilities and partly because some of my public school teachers had told him I was not very bright, not realizing that my hearing impairment might be preventing me from responding appropriately or causing me to appear shy. With my mother's support, I managed to persuade him to let me try. In a sense, I experienced "mainstreaming" in Hebrew School before this was considered an acceptable practice in educating children with disabilities. It was both challenging and frustrating I didn't fully learn Hebrew until adulthood, but I enjoyed learning about the history and religious traditions of our people, about our people's attachment to *Eretz Yisrael*, and about the many famous people who were Jewish. On my own, I also read about the Nazi Holocaust and the Jewish resistance.

Also at this time, I accidentally bumped into the word "homosexual" in some reading material. I may have come across the word in a textbook. I was immediately intrigued, not knowing why. By this time, I had developed a fascination for hairy male chests. Not sure what it all meant, but sensing it was wrong, I did not discuss it with my mother. Girls were beautiful, but this was something else and for some reason, it was more emotionally charged. That was my first recognition that I might be even more different than I had previously imagined. As was my habit, I tried to read everything I could find on the word, only to be frustrated by restrictive shelves in libraries and bookstore clerks telling me I was not supposed to be asking for such materials. "You're too young!" some people would say. One person even advised me to wait until I was in medical school. Faced with such barriers by people who normally took the extra effort to understand me, I basically dropped the subject, still occasionally pursuing it in encyclopedias once I was finished looking up other subjects.

Interestingly, my mother was the one who brought up the issue of sex one evening. She drew basic pictures of male and female anatomy and explained them to me. She also explained the reproductive functions of the sex organs. Finally, she spoke about "sexual hygiene," indicating that I should not let anyone, woman or man, touch my penis. For some reason, that last statement triggered an adolescent temper tantrum. I told Mother that I understood why a woman should not touch my penis, but why not a man? I remember yelling that statement very rapidly, and either she did not understand me or she let the question go without an answer. She did not, however, bring up sex again, and when I raised the issue later, we discussed it in terms of "hygiene" and dating girls, based primarily on my observations of my brother's dates.

In high school, my social activities were extremely limited. I was fighting a school system that had rigid ideas about the futures of people with severe disabilities. The idea was that people with cerebral palsy, and those with communicative disabilities, had no future except in a sheltered workshop environment. But I could never stick to that mold. My high school homeroom teacher recognized this and encouraged me to learn additional things on my own. Along with my mother, she encouraged me to have a healthy disrespect for "the system" by showing the authorities what I could do when given the opportunity to break down the barriers of ignorance. By showing me how to disagree constructively with the authorities, she encouraged me to think about prejudices against persons with disabilities and minorities. This greatly influenced my political interests and participation in the social movements of the late sixties and the seventies.

My teacher could not, however, help me with social skills. Several years before, I had attended a summer camp for children and adolescents with disabilities. While there I met some campers from the local school for deaf children. I was fascinated by their use of sign language and attempted to learn some signs from them. I was surprised how difficult it was for me at first to form the letters of the manual alphabet. And yet, it fascinated me. That summer I came home spelling words by hand. When my mother saw me spelling out a word, she was very annoyed. A speech teacher had told her never to let me learn sign language because I would lose the motivation to use speech. This was ironic, considering that I later attended Gallaudet College (now Gallaudet University), the world's only liberal arts college for deaf students. Learning sign language actually helped me improve my speech skills since it provided the visual clues to sounds I misunderstood or did not hear.

At Gallaudet I was able to gain many of the social skills I had previously lacked. I even had opportunities to date women. Bit by bit, I also began to notice that it was difficult finding women who were interested in dating. It was never mentioned openly, but it didn't take long to discover that some of the women would refuse to date me because I had cerebral palsy. But there was another factor at work. I could go only so far with dating and no further. Every time I felt serious about a woman, I found I could not get myself to go beyond a certain emotional point. It seemed I kept hitting an internal brick wall. At first I thought it was simply because I was not ready for such a relationship. At the same time, however, I noticed again that I was attracted to hairy male chests and male genitals. I knew by then that these were homosexual feelings, and I was afraid of them. I also was aware that students on campus who were suspected of being "fairies" were severely harassed. On the other hand, I really did enjoy the company of women. Not quite knowing what to do, I submerged my sexual feelings, allowing them to emerge only in private or while viewing photos of nude men in "girlie" magazines. I did not quite know what my sexual orientation was. In abnormal psychology class I learned about the homosexual stereotype and the resulting social stigmatization. I could not identify with it, but the erotic images of the hairy nude male kept floating back into my mind's eye.

Once, on a trip home from visiting a college friend in Connecticut, I decided to spend time in New York. Curiosity got the best of me and I decided to visit a male movie theater. I stumbled in the dark to find a seat. I watched the movie for an hour and got very bored, for I could not follow the dialogue. There was also very little physical action, which was ironic for such a movie. Besides, the men in the film had smooth chests. I walked out before anything really happened. And yet, images from that film kept returning to my mind.

I also slowly became aware of the movement for gay rights. While a senior in high school, I had witnessed a homophile rights demonstration in front of Independence Hall in Philadelphia on the Fourth of July with fascination and awe.[1] I did not dare join the demonstration. It just was not my time.

At Gallaudet I was a respected opinion columnist at the student newspaper, writing on national and international affairs, openly voicing my opposition to the United States' involvement in Vietnam and my hopes for peace in the Middle East. And I wrote about the rights of minorities in America. In my last article before graduating from Gallaudet, I wrote about deaf people as a minority group that should stand up for its rights. Nowhere in these columns did I mention the rights of gay people. It was too sensitive an issue for me. I knew only vaguely about the Stonewall Riot in New York, where gay and lesbian people finally rebelled against police harassment in 1969.

After graduation from Gallaudet in 1970, I went to graduate school at New York University. I had always felt drawn to urban life and wanted to live in the biggest of big cities. I was attracted to New York, in part, because of its large and varied Jewish community. Also, I would have the opportunity to visit the all-male movie theaters when I felt I needed sexual relief without having to explain to my parents where I was going and then feeling guilty about lying to them.

New York marked a new chapter in my life. For the first time, I was living and interacting with my hearing peers on an equal footing. The program I enrolled in, Communication in Education, was the closest I was able to get to the teaching field. Because I was enrolled through the Deafness Research and Training Center, I was able to qualify for sign language interpreter services and take courses in Deafness Studies.

New York was also where I came to know my sexual orientation. Though I was not ready to come out to myself, I would go to the male movie theaters for sexual relief and occasional encounters. While I did not form relationships with people I met in these movie theaters, I was able for the first time to explore my sexual needs and tensions. Ironically, this was a time of great activism by the first wave of the gay liberation movement, yet I was not part of it. I did not know how to express my sexuality openly in an environment that was inhospitable to gays. Since I was closeted, I did not know anyone else who was gay in the dorm where I lived. I had heard and read about gay people being mugged, beaten, and killed. The one organization I probably would have felt most comfortable joining, New York's gay Jewish group, had not yet been founded.

Meanwhile, I had other battles to face. I wanted to be a teacher or counselor of multidisabled hearing impaired and deaf youths and adults. While my advisers at NYU were more forward-looking than those in many graduate-level programs, they still had nagging questions as to whether I had the physical ability to make myself understood by deaf people.

Still, I was engaged with the world and able fully to enjoy all that New York had to offer. And then something happened. In my second year as a graduate student, I was busy working in two agencies with multidisabled deaf and communicatively impaired adults in summer programs, when I suddenly had a severe cerebral muscle spasm in my neck. I was paralyzed for a few hours and simply could not move because of the intense pain. At that point, I became addicted to Valium.

Outwardly, the drug appeared to work in relieving painful muscle spasms as my neck muscles kept pulling in opposite directions. After a few days I was able to return to work and eventually complete my studies and receive my degree as planned. Inwardly, however, the drug was causing me to become emotionally depressed. Looking back, the most frightening thing was that I did not even know this until several factors combined to escalate my depression. All the while I was taking the drug under medical supervision.

For seven years this drug clouded my perceptions and damaged my self-image. For a variety of reasons, including my disabilities and my reluctance to live in areas with limited public transportation, I was unable to obtain a permanent full-time job. I was back at home with my parents and working part-time teaching communications skills to severely disabled adults in a sheltered employment program. Because I was depressed, I was getting more respiratory infections than usual, which caused me to stay home from work more often. In addition, my sexual experiences were limited to encounters I had at all-male movie theaters. I had few real opportunities for sexual outlets and I became emotionally frustrated. On several occasions I experienced fits of violent self-hatred.

After several of these episodes, I decided on my own that it was time for me to kick the Valium habit. I decided something had to be done, and fast. At first I tried to go cold turkey, but that made matters worse. Following my mother's suggestion, I slowly decreased the amount of Valium I took. This took almost a year, but it worked.

After I successfully withdrew from Valium, I noticed my old urge to get involved return. I joined a number of disability rights advocacy groups and reconnected with the world. However, there was still something missing in my life.

At some point I picked up a flyer that mentioned Beth Ahavah, Philadelphia's lesbian and gay synagogue. I remember staring at the name with interest, yet I was not quite sure about going. At first I put off attending a service, not certain how I would be accepted and a little scared about going. Finally, during Passover in 1979, I decided to go to a Shabbat evening service. I was late in arriving and found the congregation in the midst of the *Amidah* service. Trying to enter quietly, I tripped over a narrow step at the entrance and almost fell into the congregation, literally. Everyone looked up, and I was so embarrassed! One guy handed me a siddur and the others resumed *davening.* At the close of the service the wine cups were passed around for the *kiddush.* I wanted wine but noticed that the plastic cups were so tiny I could not hold one without spilling it. Finally the man leading the service that evening, Jerry Silverman, asked me if I wanted some wine. I said yes, but mentioned that I could not hold the cup. He brought a cup of wine to where I was and held it for me to drink it. That was the beginning of a wonderful friendship that continues to this day.

In coming to Beth Ahavah, I was finally able to come to terms with my being gay. Here were real, loving people, with real names—and Jewish at that! By accepting me for who I was, members of Beth Ahavah helped me make a major transition in my life. A short time after coming out to myself, I came out to my parents. Within a year I had a new job and was working on becoming independent.

Coming out to myself was difficult. I had been fighting all these years to show people I was like everyone else. I asked people to give me the opportunity to show them I really was like everyone else. In accepting the idea that I was gay I realized that I was not like everyone else: I was different in terms of my emotional needs and physical desires. I had never attempted to hide my disabilities or my Jewishness, but sexuality was another matter. I actually relied on my understanding of Judaism to accept myself. Attending services at Beth Ahavah, I was slowly able to accept and embrace my sexuality as part of my whole being.

Judaism contains some interesting contradictions in its attitude toward people with disabilities. In addition to Moses, we have several other biblical role models with disabilities, including Isaac, who was blind and may have suffered severe mental trauma; Leah "of small eyes"; and Jacob, who wrestled all night and acquired not only a new name, Israel ("God-wrestler"), but also a mobility impairment. Miriam had leprosy; Elijah is reported to have had a disability in one hand; and Job seems to have had a clear case of manic depression. These and other examples indicate that people with disabilities were in positions of leadership among the Jewish people in biblical times.

At the same time, Talmudic laws and interpretation make it difficult for people with disabilities to become fully accepted and integrated into Jewish life. These laws, especially those that apply to deaf people, mirror a lack of acceptance in the larger societies in which Jews have lived. The Talmud speaks of the *cheresh*, those who can neither hear nor speak and were considered not fully responsible. They were prohibited from marrying, from making contracts, and from buying and selling property, and they were exempted from participating in Jewish religious life. The deaf persons who could not speak were placed in the same category as the lunatic (*shoteh*) and the minor (*katan*).[2]

Regardless of their original intent, these laws hinder the integration of Jews with disabilities into religious life to this day. Many of the obstacles center around work. For example, Judaism views carrying a wheelchair up a flight of stairs and sign language interpretation as work, which is prohibited on Shabbat and festival days. This effectively prevents many observant Jews from sharing their religious life in a Jewish context with Jews with disabilities. Non-Jewish sign language interpreters, for example, may not be familiar with Jewish liturgy and may not know the appropriate signs to express certain Jewish religious concepts. They would use religious signs expressed in mainstream deaf culture, which often convey Christian religious concepts in English-speaking societies.

Moses is the biblical figure I can most identify with by virtue of his disability. Not only is it a challenge for him to be understood by others, but his brother Aaron is at his side interpreting for him when he speaks. This is a powerful image in my life since I find I communicate most effectively and understand best when using a sign language interpreter. Moses is a leader who shows that leaders also are human and have human needs.

The concept of *tikkun olam*—to mend, rejuvenate, make the world a better place for all people—is at the core of my Jewish identity, the core of my political and social activism, and motivates me to become a loving, understanding individual. Almost everything I identify with as being Jewish radiates from this ideal.

In 1988, nine years after I joined Beth Ahavah, I was drafted to be synagogue president. Like Moses, I was reluctant to pursue a leadership role. Over the years I had found I could be most influential as a voice behind the scenes. My election as president made me realize how much I was accepted by my peers.

Despite this and other experiences that have made me realize that I am accepted, I have also had moments of deep loneliness. I have always wanted to be in a loving, enduring relationship with another man and I have not yet had this opportunity. Yet I have many friends, I am working for a federal civil rights agency on disability rights and rights of persons with AIDS, and I am independent. I have expanded my own *Mitzrayim*, my own "narrow places."

You Didn't Talk about These Things: Growing Up Jewish, Lesbian, and Working Class

······························

Felice Yeskel

LUCKILY, I HAVE NEVER BEEN PLAGUED WITH CONFUSION ABOUT MY Jewish identity. I learned Jewish pride at home.

I have never been unsure that I am a lesbian. I did have a hard time accepting this part of myself and trusting that others would accept me, but the fact that I love women was always a given. Unfortunately, I did not learn lesbian pride at home. I learned fear, shame, and secrecy. I learned lesbian pride from other lesbians: through reading books like *Rubyfruit Jungle;*[1] on the streets of Berkeley, California; at women's music festivals; at political demonstrations; and in bed.

To this day, when I call myself working class, I wonder if this is accurate. Pride in being working class is, for me, another thing altogether. I had a context for developing as a Jew at home and a context for coming out as a lesbian in a supportive lesbian community. But there was nowhere to go to develop working-class pride, and what I learned both at home and in various social change movements was shame, not pride.

There are many ways to be Jewish, lesbian, and working class. Each of us has a story to tell, and mine is no more or less typical, illuminating, or relevant than any other. It is influenced by the fact that I am white (I have blue eyes, fair skin, and I "don't look Jewish"), Ashkenazi, thirty-five years old, and currently able-bodied. I grew up in New York City, where I was labeled "intellectually gifted" by the school system, and I have thought of myself as a radical for many years.

My father was an immigrant from Poland; he came to the United

States when he was nine. He grew up in "the projects" in Newark, New Jersey. He died four years ago, after a series of nonmalignant brain tumors which began when I was five and seriously disabled him. My mom was born in New York City of Russian-Jewish parents. She lived in Manhattan her whole life, until six years ago when my parents moved to Florida. My father came from a poor-to-working-class background, while my mother's background was lower middle class. I'm their only child.

One of my primary experiences of growing up is that of being different, or at least of feeling different. While the "reason" that I felt different changed from year to year, my experience of alienation remained the same. Being a Jew, a lesbian, and not being middle class were three of the biggest reasons.

It is unclear to me which difference I noticed first. Perhaps it was being a tomboy, the only girl on the playground playing skellies[2] and ring-a-levio[3] with the boys. My mother's reaction, more than the difference itself, was significant: she was horrified by my ripped jeans and dislike of jump rope and dolls. She hoped that I wouldn't stand out, and she used to ask, "Why can't you be like the other girls?" on a daily basis. My sense that I was not like other girls grew into the knowledge that I was a lesbian.

Perhaps my alienation had something to do with my experience at Hunter College Elementary School, a public school for "intellectually gifted" children on Park Avenue. My mother's desire for upward mobility and her tendency to push me conspired to get me, via months of standardized tests, into Hunter. At age five I found myself uptown, and not at the local elementary school with my friends from the playground.

At Hunter I felt shame when I had to tell kids what my father did. He was a bagman, and I thought he was the only one in the world. *Well, have you ever heard of a bagman?* When I asked him what I should put on forms in the space for father's occupation, he said "peddler." I wasn't sure which was worse: being a bagman or a peddler. Why couldn't he do something "normal"? Most of the kids from Hunter lived uptown. Their parents had gone to college and were professionals. Some even had doormen. Again, I found myself in the position of being different and not having a name for my difference. Then, like now, you didn't talk about these things (but you did change your behavior because of them).

I did not invite anybody from school home to my apartment, although I did go to their homes to play. I did not tell stories of cutting school and going to work with my father in his big red truck, coming home covered with flour from the bags he collected. I did not tell of the Sunday morning ritual I shared with my father: we would go down to the Lower East Side, a few blocks from where we lived, to buy breakfast—bialies, herring, carp, and whitefish. My father would speak Yiddish with the men who sold things from pushcarts, and they gave me free tastes of things to eat.

I also did not tell my school friends about my father's parents, who lived in a tenement in Newark, New Jersey. My grandmother wore rubber bands on her wrist so she could reuse them. My grandfather wore a yarmulke all the time. They were more comfortable speaking Yiddish than English. They seemed very foreign and Old World to me, fascinating and repulsive at the same time.

My life with my family seemed so different from my life at school. Even though a third of the kids at school were Jewish, I didn't think they had any idea about my life at home. They seemed more American, more "normal." Their lives looked like the lives I saw on TV.

At school I was led to believe in a more expansive reality. My classmates and I were told, "You are the best, the brightest, the most verbal. Anything is possible for you." This was the myth of the American dream: if you apply yourself and work hard you can do anything you want.

While my mother seemed to believe this message about me, this was not how she acted about herself. Her version of "anything is possible" was diluted by constant reminders of anti-Semitism. It seemed like she believed something like: "You can make it, no thanks to the prejudiced *goyim* who want to keep Jews from really making it." At home I had constant reminders of being Jewish (and being oppressed), while at school we were all just American. The attitude that "we're better than them" that I got from my mother about being Jewish was similar to the attitude about working class and poor people that I learned at school.

As a result, I didn't feel at home anywhere: my worlds were cut off from each other. I felt different from the kids in my neighborhood because I felt smarter and therefore better than them. But I felt like something was wrong with me, although I couldn't put my finger on what it was. I didn't feel as good as the kids at school, who didn't have to pass because they were already "there." During those years I wanted to be "normal" more than anything else.

Contributing to my confusion, there was a low-intensity class-war going on between my parents, and I was the arena in which it was played out. My mother gave me the message that my brain would get me anywhere and that I must get somewhere, while my father wanted me to do whatever would make me happy. Every week the three of us went out to dinner. I often felt embarrassed and ashamed, like "Who are we kidding?" Anybody who bothered to look at us could tell that we didn't belong and we weren't what we were pretending to be. It felt very uptight, sometimes like torture. My mother was on guard about everything my father and I did or said, lest something "wrong" slip out. She promised that if I learned to eat and act properly she would take me to the Top of the Sixes—a fancy restaurant. While appearance was crucial to my mother, my father didn't care about it at all. His attitude was, if the food tasted good, what difference did it make where you ate it?

My father was accepting of our circumstances and accepting of me just the way I was. My mother wanted more for us. As a result she was critical of my father and me all the time. Her criticisms had to do with how we looked and what people would think. My mother prepared me to pass in the world I have lived in since I started Hunter. My father could offer me no help in that world, but offered unconditional love and a safe haven in which to rest.

As an only child, all of my parents' hopes and dreams centered on me. My mother wanted me to have an easier and better life than she had. To her that meant living a comfortable upper-middle-class life in suburbia with a professional man, raising children, and perhaps even having meaningful work. Because I was "bright" I could make it: my brain was my ticket out.

But when I was eleven, I realized I was a lesbian. I found "the L word" in a dictionary, and I knew it was me. Again I had the sense of difference, of another shameful secret to keep. Just as my father had been the only bagman in the world, I was now the only lesbian in the world.

Realizing I was a lesbian made me feel as if I was throwing a huge wrench into the parental plan. I thought about killing myself just about every day. How could I destroy my parents' happiness? My struggle to come out as a lesbian and accept my identity was a long, lonely, and painful struggle. As a child, I felt personally responsible for the survival of the Jewish people. If the Jewish family was the primary agent of Jewish survival, where did I, as a lesbian, fit in?

In addition to guilt, I feel like an anomaly in my family. I have no other unmarried relatives who are my age. Adult status is bestowed on those who have a family of their own (read: husband and kids)— all others are eternally children. At thirty-five, I find myself still a child in the eyes of my family, with no clearly defined adult role.

"You can only trust your family: everyone else will screw you in the end." This was another message I received from my parents, aunts, uncles, and grandparents. We have a close family, which means that everyone feels they have the right to comment on everything you do: relationships ("so, *nu?*"), kids ("when?"), clothes ("when are you going to get some?"), work ("when are you going to get a 'real' job?"), life-style choices ("when are you going to start living like a *mentsh?*"). This is quite a different cultural context to come out in than that faced by my upper-middle-class WASP friends, whose parents would die before asking anything that personal!

And then there were the comments about my love life. From the age of thirteen I heard comments like: "So, what boy are you interested in?" "So, why don't you go to the temple dances?" "So, when are you going to get married and make me a grandmother?" There was a definite heterosexual agenda, and lots of pressure to stick to it.

But unlike many other lesbians, I never worried about being disowned. The thought was incomprehensible to me. I worried about hurting my family and letting them down, but not about losing them. Our worlds had sharply divided in many ways years earlier, but we had come to accept that. When my grandfather would ask me about my life, and I would tell him, omitting my lesbianism (echoes of my mother's words, "You'll give him a heart attack; he's too old—don't upset him," ringing in my ears), he'd shake his head and say, "You're meshuggeneh but if you're happy, it's o.k. with me." Though we may not have understood each other, we knew we would always be close and love each other.

Like many of my generation, I became politicized through the anti-war movement when I was in high school. My personal politics, however, were much more involved in the struggle to wear pants to school and keep my non-conscious butch integrity. This integrity was hard to pull off as a teenager, and I have vivid memories of my mother calling me a transvestite for wanting to shop in the army-navy store.

As I grew into an adult, I received a scholarship-financed education at a private college. (My roommate had a convertible sports car and a kidney-shaped swimming pool in her suburban backyard.) In college, I encountered the Women's Liberation Movement. Finally I found validation for my own reality. I struggled, along with others of my generation, to live a life-style that was consistent with my values. Dropping out of a Ph.D. program in counseling psychology, I emigrated (a time-honored Jewish tradition) to Berkeley, California, which allowed me to come out at last! Through three bra-less years of separatism I developed intense pride in my lesbian self. Coming out to my family was the release from fear and guilt that I needed, and I haven't been in the closet since.

My struggle to find work and define a life-style that I can live with integrity is ongoing. Over the years, I have lived alone, with my current lover, in group houses, and in an intentional community of 125 people. I have worked in a variety of jobs: as a camp counselor, therapist, trainer, researcher, educator, grass roots organizer, and administrator. In each position my goal has been to work for social change and to earn a living. Over the past five years I have worked at the University of Massachusetts as an advocate for gay, lesbian, and bisexual concerns. Equally significant as my work for money has been my grass roots activism on a broad range of issues.

It wasn't clear to me when I came out as a lesbian and dropped out of graduate school, and it still isn't clear today which disappointment is worse to my family: being a lesbian or choosing not to travel the route of middle-class professionalism. I *feel* more guilty letting my family down in the class arena, as if they invested in me and made a bad investment. Financially, I'm not in a position to take care of my widowed mother in her old age, and while she doesn't expect me to play that role, I wish I could.

While I feel wonderful about the social change work I've committed my life to, I feel inner conflict about the potential comfort and security I'm giving up. This conflict is exacerbated when I'm surrounded by downwardly mobile lesbians from upper-middle-class backgrounds who behave self-righteously about their choices. My worries about security are played out in the unconscious choices I make about money. The fact that I compulsively save money means that I've bailed out lots of upper-middle-class friends when the phone company has threatened to disconnect their service for lack of payment.

My saving habits can be deceptive. If I often have more money than my friends whose families own big suburban houses and summer homes, how could I possibly be working class? The only reason the thought ever entered my mind was because a Jewish working-class friend of mine said, "Felice, I think you're working class." When she said it I felt like I'd been insulted, so powerfully had I internalized the classism of society and my training. The only other working-class people I had met were not Jewish, and their experience seemed very different from mine. But meeting another working-class Jew and realizing that we had something in common that transcended our Jewish connection made me start to think about it.

Class issues, like issues about sexuality, are taboo. Here in the United States, we live in a "classless society": we believe we are all middle class. Maybe there are a few unfortunate poor people (we read about them in the newspapers) and some very lucky rich ones (we see them on TV), but the people we know and see are middle class. Those of us who are different feel pressure to pass as middle class or keep our culture to ourselves.

Those of us who picked the passing option may feel different but we don't know why; we often think we're middle class too. As gay, lesbian, and bisexual Jews, we learn to survive in a Christian, heterosexual society that renders us invisible. We understand the pressure to assimilate quite well. Many of us deal with this by forming communities that affirm and support us living in a multicultural world. But the myth of class mobility, especially for Jews (and the reality for some of us), makes working-class community more difficult to find.

Because class is a function of both culture and resources, Jewish working-class culture often masquerades as middle class. Often I have found myself the only Jew in a working-class context. Usually, I am surrounded by working-class Catholics, whose concerns are different from mine. And, I've been told hundreds of times (mostly by upper-middle-class people), "You can't be working class, you have a college education." Jewish culture stresses education, so I knew I was going to college one way or another, whether my family had the money or not. Often people are surprised to hear a Jew say she's working class. Stereotypes die hard, and everyone knows "Jews have money." Too often this assumption is made by Jews about other Jews.

Writing this down feels like disloyalty to my family. I am nervous about sharing all these things I was taught to hide. But my experience as a Jewish working-class lesbian has taught me that silence about difference creates ignorance, fear, and isolation. I have a dream of being welcome as a working-class Jewish lesbian in the Jewish and lesbian communities. I have a dream of finding a working-class community that is inclusive of my experience. Silence gets in the way of this dream. It feels scary to break the silence, but I know that taking this risk will help others take similar risks. Soon these worlds we thought were so homogenous will reveal their true cultural diversity. So please consider telling your story too.

Hiding Is Unhealthy for the Soul

....

Rachel Wahba

SOMETIMES IT HAPPENS BEFORE YOU EVEN KNOW IT. YOU FIND YOURself passing through life quietly, politely not "flaunting" those differences about yourself that the other person may not easily understand, integrate, or like. To pass through, quietly whenever possible, without making noise, is more often thought of as "appropriate" rather than as "giving up." But I think it comes close to being just that. I know that when I don't expect to be understood, I am quiet. And if being seen feels dangerous, sometimes I hide.

When I wear my *Shaddai*,[1] my star of David, I am visible as a Jew. And the gold band on my finger indicates that I am "married." Both symbols concretely represent primary identities that are very important to me. Most people recognize my star of David for what it is: a Jewish identity symbol. With my ring, the assumption is that I am married to a man.

My *Shaddai* kept me from feeling truly "stateless" growing up as a Jewish child without a country. It affirmed my identity and my sense of belonging and continuity, reflecting my ties to my people who, throughout the centuries in the Middle East, North Africa, and Europe, were made to wear the star of David as a symbol of shame. As a young teenager, pictures of Jews in Nazi Europe wearing the yellow star made me feel proud and angry, not ashamed. Forced to or freely, I can wear my *Shaddai* in strength.

My identity as a lesbian would not be an issue if we were not, in a sense, "stateless," if this choice were considered a natural, viable, and legitimate way of life. For me, unlike being a stateless Jewish child raised with a positive Jewish identity and schooled in anti-Semitism on all fronts, my lesbian identity came later in life, as I stumbled on the possibility in a feminist studies class in the mid-1970s. It was a previously unimaginable option: it was a new expression of my self and a new avenue for growth out of unequal relationships and the traps of internalized sexism. It gave me a sense of coming together and being part of a community, something I had not yet experienced in the United States.

My *Shaddai* was made for my mother by her father, and when I was born she gave it to me. Most days I wear it out. Some days I wear it inside comfortably, naturally; other days I know I am hiding. On those days I feel vulnerable somehow. My *Shaddai* looks too big and too obvious, maybe too "blatant" in a world that wants the Jew to assimilate. Someone might come up to me and yell, "Hey! You! You Jew!" like that hateful man did to my brother one morning as he rode the bus to work. El never rode public transportation to his job again. I try to stay away from angry places, and I drive my car everywhere. I hear my mother's words, spoken from her experience as a Jew in Baghdad: "You never know [what danger awaits you]. Be careful [have eyes in the back of your head] because you never know."

She was sixteen, my mother, during the Rashid Ali Rebellion.[2] It broke out suddenly, and I imagine them—my granny, my mother, her sister, her brother, and her aging blind grandmother—hiding from the frenzied mobs who were randomly killing Jews and looting Jewish homes for endless hours. My mother, Khatoon/Katie, slept with her shoes on for weeks, ready to run from rooftop to rooftop at a moment's notice. She told me that the British (who still had military bases in Iraq) waited two days before they stopped the murdering, plundering mobs: it was a good way to let the rioters blow off steam, and the Jews were considered dispensable. My mother remembers seeing the Tigris filled with furniture: Jewish homes and lives floating down the river.

She was a scared but proud Jewish girl. Her mother was less scared, having been raised in the relative safety of Singapore, then a British colony, before returning to Iraq. My grandfather knew he had to get the family out of Baghdad because granny would not keep quiet about the anti-Jewish outrages. Her English (and her arrogance) saved her— the Arabs saw her as British, not as a Jew.

If you were a Jew in Iraq, you "never knew" what would happen to you. I remember hearing so many stories (because I had "big ears," they said) as my family and their friends sat and talked after dinner, in Japan, about their lives in Iraq, Egypt, Syria, Lebanon, Afghanistan, Burma, India, Germany, Poland, Russia, and China. I grew up among Jews who could no longer live in their native lands. And I grew up without a native land.

I didn't have to face the rape threats and taunts about future pogroms that my mother, as a Jewish girl, faced as she walked the narrow alley streets of Baghdad. In postwar Japan, it was being a brown-skinned foreigner that had its difficult moments. My brother and I never knew when some schoolboy would yell, "*kurombo!*" (slang for "darky") or "*gaijin!*" (pejorative term for foreigner), alerting everyone on the street, where the finger-pointing and giggling filled us with shame.

On the street in Japan, "Jew" was not the issue. It was, however, an issue in the Catholic missionary schools I attended. From my parents I learned about Moslem anti-Semitism and from Stella Maris, my school, I learned about Christian anti-Semitism. I heard over and over again how the Jews killed Christ, and that I should repent and put on a crucifix instead of continuing to wear my *Shaddai*. Why was I so stubborn? Sister Joan, whom I so adored and wanted to please, would coax me with, "But Rachel, Jesus was a Jew, just like you."

At Stella Maris I learned how the nuns there justified the Holocaust: "Such terrible events will continue to happen to Jews until they accept Christ." I remember my first oral book report in the seventh grade about Eichmann and what happened in Germany under Hitler. My German classmate, Helga, got very defensive, proclaiming that "Hitler wasn't so bad." Her father had told her that Hitler "built good roads for Germany." For the rest of the hour, the class discussed whether or not Hitler was all bad, and concluded that if at the last minute he had repented, he would, being a baptized Catholic, end up in Heaven after doing time in Purgatory, while Jews (unbaptized) would never be allowed in Heaven. I continued to wear my *Shaddai*. Some days it was much harder than others.

My father, Maurice/Moshe/Moussa, and his father Eliahu, and his father, and so on down the line were all Egyptian. On his mother Rachelle/Rahel's side, they were originally from Spain, Palestine, and Algeria. Life in Egypt was less oppressive for Jews than in my mother's Iraq, where her family dates back as far as they can trace it, perhaps since the Babylonian Exile (approximately 2,600 years ago). Egypt was more cosmopolitan and less insulated than Iraq, with more Western influence. But my father has stories, too, about why he had to leave Egypt. The underlying second- and third-class citizenship of Jews in Moslem lands always existed. Some times were better than others, but a Jew could never feel fully safe. There was never a sense of ease, or security, or recourse when things were bad. Under Islam, security for Jews was always up to the whim of the current regime. There were special laws created for Jews and often a special tax for all *Dimmis* (unbelievers, including Christians and Jews), with yet another tax only for Jews. Over the centuries (at different times) Jews had to wear cowbells around their necks, were forbidden to live in houses taller than those of their Moslem neighbors, were barred from higher education, and were subject to *Chtaka*, a ritual of hitting any Jewish passerby on the head while reciting a sacramental phrase. And of course there was always the fear of pogroms at any time, especially during the holy days, theirs and ours.

With the rise of Hitler in the West, my father witnessed the excitement in Egypt. Books proliferated, with *Mein Kampf* translated into Arabic and displayed everywhere. My father said to himself, it is finished, time to leave forever. Meanwhile in Iraq, the Grand Mufti was making plans to welcome Hitler and finish off the Jews in Arab lands.

My parents fled from their native lands and met in Bombay, India. They married and had me and then my brother. My father made his way to Japan, drawn by its safe harbor and business possibilities. After a long delay because of our stateless status, the rest of us joined him there and began to wait for our chance to immigrate to the United States.[3] It was a long wait: over twenty years.

It was 1964 when I arrived in Los Angeles as a college student. I was so happy and excited to finally be here and to realize my childhood dream, which was to be an American Jew! I was disappointed to discover, though, that I was out of synch with many of my peers who had become, or were fast becoming, highly assimilated "Jewish Americans." Also, most of the Jews I met had never known, or entertained the idea of, an "Arab Jew." They wondered how that could be. Had my family migrated from Russia or Europe to the Middle East at some point? Was I part Moslem, part Jew?

At first I didn't understand why my background was so hard to comprehend. After all, the Ashkenazim knew they were originally Polish Jews, or German Jews, or Russian or Hungarian or Rumanian.

And predating earlier migrations to Europe, I wondered where they thought their people originated from anyway. In the small but very cosmopolitan Jewish community in Japan, I grew up understanding that we are one people, dispersed. Our differences, Western/Ashkenazi and Eastern/Sephardic, had more to do with regional acculturation in language, music, food, customs, rhythms, and superstitions. Our alikeness, going much deeper than our differences, lay in the similarity of our values, shared sacred texts, ritual cycles of the week and year, and our sense of history and continuity.

I realized that while I had read many books by prolific Ashkenazi authors, it was not the same the other way around. Twenty years ago there was little written about "Eastern Jewry" in comparison to writings on Western Jewry.[4] Primarily shopkeepers and merchants, Jews in Arab countries did not want to make noise and call attention to themselves. Without our share of writers and publishers to tell our stories, it is not surprising that often Ashkenazim (and the world at large) don't know about us.

One of my most exciting discoveries, however, were the books of Albert Memmi,[5] a Tunisian Jew who is now, like many North African Jews, a French citizen. Memmi, a professor of sociology at the Sorbonne, wrote books on Jews in Arab lands that provided information and validation I had been missing. I bought all the copies I could find and ordered more from the publisher, so that I could convey a better sense of the history and experience of Arab Jews to my friends.

To most American Ashkenazi Jews, Sephardic means "from Spain," and you speak Ladino. And if not Ladino, then why not Yiddish? Jews who know me well, particularly those who grew up speaking or hearing Yiddish in the home, will look at me every so often and remark, "You really don't speak Yiddish?" Yiddish for Ashkenazis is so often synonymous with "Jewish." They sense my strong Jewish identity and know that I am an immigrant, so it's confusing to them that Yiddish is not in my bones.

Jews in most Arab countries spoke Judeo-Arabic, a dialect, rather than a developed language like Yiddish or Ladino. It is Arabic interspersed with Hebrew words and excludes Koranic language, which differentiates it from the more classical Islamic Arabic. My mother told me that in Iraq, once you opened your mouth they could tell you were a Jew: different.

The Sephardim were not "Jewish Arabs"; they were Arab Jews

(they could not assimilate into Arab culture unless they actually converted to Islam). My family, and the people in the Jewish community
in Japan, were Jews first. We lived with American Jews and European
Jews. We shared a strong and undiluted bond as Jews. Somehow,
along the way, we had either actively resisted or were simply not
allowed to assimilate.

And so when I am defined, as I have been at times, as a "Jewish
lesbian," I feel misunderstood. Suddenly my identity is switched.
"Jew," the defining noun, becomes a descriptive adjective. But
the continuity cannot be broken so easily. I am a Jew, and I have
become a lesbian, and so I am a lesbian Jew. It goes so deep and so
far back, generations upon generations. Then the other identities follow: Sephardic, woman, lesbian, daughter, sister, mother, friend,
lover, "wife."

The parallels between being a Jew and a lesbian are obvious. We
struggle against prejudice and for civil rights, and we struggle for
the right to be visible without fear. We strive to preserve self-respect
and maintain self-esteem in the face of bigotry and ignorance. As lesbians, gays and Jews, we face issues of assimilating, "passing," or
coming out.

As a lesbian, every time I go outside my San Francisco gay enclave,
I am automatically put in the position of either "coming out" or "being
in the closet." I don't "look gay" according to the prevailing stereo-
typic images; I wear a wedding band; and I have a daughter who lives
with me. People assume I am straight and (heterosexually) married.
How I feel and respond to these assumptions changes with each
situation—from natural, self-confident ease to painful inner conflict.
There is usually no context for coming out, which makes communicating difficult at times. I could get a response I'm not ready for.
I might go into long explanations I am not asked for, or that aren't
necessary. I fear that someone who doesn't know me will put me in
some category that has little to do with the totality of who I am.
It sometimes takes a lot of familiarizing in order to be seen or feel
understood.

A recent experience brought this home for me. At a post-conference
cocktail party, I was talking with someone I very much like and ad-
mire, first briefly about the conference and then quickly gravitating to
a Jewish topic. As different as our histories are, we experience a special bond based on our strong identities as Jews. But when she asked

me whether I had remarried, I jumped into the closet, saying "no."
I knew she had meant "married to a man." And when she later asked,
"You're still close to your in-laws?" I again wanted to come out (of the
closet I had leapt into), but the best I could do was to say, "Oh, that's a
whole other story for another time." Since we meet only briefly at
these annual conferences, "another time" doesn't come easily.

Particularly with people I feel an affinity with, I want to be able to
stay with wherever the conversation goes. It is distressing to exclude
and censor out important aspects of my life, the things other people
talk about freely, specifically in regard to my mate. But how do I mention my spouse when we don't yet have a commonly understood term
to describe a lesbian or gay mate? "Significant other," "lover" (more
fitting for an affair or a new romance), "mate," and "partner" all
sound strained or sterile. I like the poetic sound of "soul-mate" or
"love of my life" better than all the above, but how does one interject
these words into a heterosexually assumed conversation about "hus-
bands" and "wives"? Just to say her name, which is clearly not representative of the opposite sex, is awkward. My lesbian lover/partner/
soul-mate/"wife" is not merely my "friend." Mis-naming the relationship immediately propels me into the closet, and I am there until I get
myself out.

I worry (at my most insecure moments) whether people will react
negatively to who I am and what I am saying. Am I being too loud,
overexposing myself, "flaunting my life-style," embarrassing someone, or generally making others uncomfortable? And how is this different from wearing my *Shaddai* and having someone ask me, "Why
do you have to wear such a big one?"

My mother would probably want to know why I am writing this
essay—about the lesbian part—why do I have to be so public about
it? (She would like the Jewish part—we're not in Iraq anymore.) The
lesbian part is still "a very different experience from what I know,
from my upbringing and background," she says. And of course, I
understand that. She is my mother and my love for her is unconditional, as hers is for me. We are fortunate to live in the same city, so
that my lesbian life-style becomes more familiar and less alien to her
each day.

When I first came out, my mother thought our relationship was
severed. My father was horrified. They screamed and they cried.
They hoped I would reunite with my husband or marry another man.
It felt very "abnormal" to them. Now our family is back to normal,

because the familiarity and the ordinariness of it makes it so. And for my daughter, living with her mom and Judy is what is normal; it's life as usual.

My parents and my in-laws have become family, as I had thought they would. When Judy's parents come to visit, they stay with my parents. Their geographical backgrounds are totally different: my parents are "wandering Jews," immigrants from Arab countries, while Judy's parents are New York Jews whose families came from Russia and Poland. They all share similar values, understand anti-Semitism, care deeply about Israel, talk endlessly about things Jewish, and argue passionately about political issues.

A year ago, an incident took place while Judy's parents were visiting, prompting me to write to the four of them. After nine years, I wanted to say it out loud: that Judy and I were as "married" as any married couple, and that they were "in-laws" to each other. Everyone was behaving as if this were so, but the words remained unspoken, omitted, avoided. I felt then, as I feel now, that it is important to speak the words, and so I share parts of what I wrote.

We live in a world that is frightened of differences. So when we as lesbians are considered different, there is a great pressure to be quiet, to be happy with tolerance and to hide. As I write this letter, I realize this is a "coming-out" to you as a married couple. No, not legally, because we don't have that basic human right (yet) . . .

You, our family, give us more acceptance than most if not all of our friends get from their families. We are "privileged gays" in that respect. How unique it is to have the parents of a lesbian couple actually relate to each other, let alone visit with and stay in each others' homes! Our friends envy us. You have been so wonderful to us as a couple in so many ways, and we have been blessed as individuals and as a couple to have parents like you, parents we can be proud of. We do not take that for granted.

You, our mothers and our fathers, have been forced to deal with us because we choose to be openly gay. We did not bring each other to you as "roommates" or pose as your single daughters. This was not in your plans or your upbringing, and maybe you resent being made to deal with choices your children have unilaterally made.

Judy and I have a relationship that continues to grow and

deepen. Like you, we have found soul-mates in each other. We have worked hard in our relationship and on ourselves, and have learned a lot over the years, individually and together. So when, by omission, you don't speak to what is in fact a nine-year marriage, it invalidates what we have. Like all marriages, with its ups and downs, critical points, and pain and joy, ours needs the same respect and acknowledgment that every relationship needs. And as we get older, it becomes less acceptable to pretend, to accept invalidation, even in ways that may seem insignificant.

Recently, when we were all together, you toasted your "special friendship" with each other, and I said, "you're not just friends, you're in-laws." The mood became uncomfortable, and you insisted that it was being friends that was important. So we dropped it. Only I haven't. I keep wondering how you would have reacted if we were a heterosexual couple.

Sister Joan, my favorite nun and an early mentor of mine, told me year after year that she was "praying for my soul." She liked me, but could not fully accept me, because I was a Jew. I learned in that school to be a very proud Jew who had to be strong despite the difference, a Jew who felt very connected to her people and to God, and felt absolutely no reason to be Christianized.

As you all know, hiding is very unhealthy for the soul. We don't hide as Jews when we wear our Magen Davids, form an anti-defamation league, support Israel, fail to assimilate and remain proud to be Jews. We never stop "coming out" as Jews every time we speak up and refuse to disappear. As Jews we all know how important it is to have a voice, and to be openly visible. And when you are gay in a heterosexual society, it's the same: you never stop "coming out."

Coming out has to be better for the soul than passing through life in various shades of invisibility. It can be uncomfortable and even frightening at times. But not to do so leaves us disconnected, somehow. So I take a space, as I have here, and open it, shedding light on differences and similarities. And I think it is true that when differences are understood, the similarities are always greater.

PART 2

....

Reclaiming Our History

INTRODUCTION

....

As lesbian and gay Jews, history is central to our lives. But recorded history is neither objective nor immutable. In this section, authors analyze, reinterpret, and reclaim Jewish texts and history, challenging the heterosexist assumptions that Jews have made about our past.

The biblical passage of Leviticus 18:22, which labels homosexuality an abomination, is fundamental to Jewish discussions of homosexuality. Rebecca T. Alpert analyzes this text and notes the absence of lesbian and gay perspectives from contemporary interpretations of it. She addresses the importance of confronting the verse directly and emotionally, and she asks how we might use this text in our struggle for lesbian and gay liberation.

Using traditional tools of interpretation, Faith Rogow examines the absence of lesbian and gay experience from Jewish historical understanding. Rogow discusses the traditional biases and the methodological challenges inherent in historical research on lesbian and gay themes. She notes the importance of understanding the striking historical parallels between Jewish and gay experience and offers her own reinterpretations of particular texts, urging Jewish historians to do the same and arguing that Jewish self-understanding will be marred if the voices of lesbian and gay Jews remain absent from history.

In search of lesbian and gay role models, Jody Hirsh continues the *midrashic* process begun by Faith Rogow, examining both well-known and lesser-known figures in biblical and medieval Jewish literature. His interpretations will surely create possibilities for those who are willing to question their heterosexist assumptions about the text.

Finally, Jeffrey Shandler shares an oral history of Gerry Faier, a Jewish lesbian whose life spans the twentieth century. Her experience adds a new dimension to our understanding of twentieth-century American Jewish history. While the stories of previous generations of lesbian and gay Jews can now only be reconstructed from often elusive records, Gerry's is the first generation whose experience need not be lost to us.

These essays will be discomfiting to readers who believe that historical truth can only be found by divorcing oneself from lived experience. We include them here precisely to challenge that assumption, and to inspire further research on lesbian and gay themes in Jewish history.

In God's Image:
Coming to Terms with Leviticus

....

Rebecca T. Alpert

JOAN AND LESLIE HAVE BEEN LOVERS FOR THE PAST FIVE YEARS. THIS
year, they decided to go home for the Jewish holidays to Joan's family
in upstate New York. It was an important milestone. Joan's parents had
become more comfortable with their daughter's lesbian life-style and
lover; this would be a way of acknowledging the growth in the relationships among Leslie, Joan, her parents, and her younger brother.

Joan's family is deeply involved in their local Conservative synagogue, and it was truly an act of courage for all of them to go to Kol
Nidre services together. Joan was excited—proud of her family and
eager to reenter the Jewish life she had left behind. Leslie was scared,
but interested in learning more about involvement in the Jewish community. Although Leslie's parents are Jewish, she was raised without
religious training.

Yom Kippur evening turned out to be a good experience. The congregants were friendly and welcoming to Joan and her "friend." Religiously, too, the women were moved by the powerful experience of
communal prayer. They decided that night to spend the entire next
day in shul, continuing their fasting and waiting for the stirring blast
of the *shofar* to bring an end to the day.

All went well until the afternoon service. The rabbi explained that
for the Torah portion, they would be reading from the book of Leviticus, chapter 18, a description of forbidden sexual practices. Why
read that on the holiest day of the year? No explanation was offered.
As the Torah was read, Joan and Leslie followed along in the transla-

tion until they read the words: "Do not lie with a male as one lies with a woman; it is an abomination." [1]

Joan and Leslie froze, recognizing the meaning for them as lesbians, even though the language refers only to men. They looked at one another, disappointment spreading across Joan's face while a tear formed in the corner of Leslie's eye, as if to say, "This place is really not for us, after all."

Three times a year, on Yom Kippur afternoon and then twice during the annual cycle of Torah readings, every year for the past 2,500 years, Jews around the world have listened to the public reading of the words of Leviticus declaring a sexual act between two men "an abomination." When the prohibition is read from Leviticus 20, during the third yearly reading, it is declared not only an abomination, but also a capital crime.

What could be more profoundly alienating than to know that the most sacred text of your people, read aloud on the holiest day of the year, calls that which is central to your life an abomination? What could be more terrifying than to know that what for you is a sacred loving act was considered by your ancestors to be punishable by death?

Coming to terms with Leviticus may be the greatest single struggle facing gay men and lesbians seeking to find a religious home within the Jewish community. Before we examine strategies for all of us to cope with this dilemma, we must understand the power and authority of this text: What is Leviticus, and why is it so important?

Leviticus is the third book of the Pentateuch, the five books of Moses. These books comprise the story of the birth of our people and the beginnings of the Jewish legal system. Traditionally, they are understood as revelation—God's words, written down by Moses, God's prophet, on Mt. Sinai. Thus, these words are considered not only a record of our past, but God's explanation of God's will for the people of Israel as well. Laws codified in these books are the ultimate source of authority and are the starting point for the later development of Jewish civilization. According to strict interpretation of Jewish law, no law stated in the Torah can ever be nullified or abrogated.

Beyond its implications for the Jewish legal system, the Torah has deep symbolic power. It is preserved on a handwritten parchment scroll. It is kept in the ark, a sacred space at the front or center of every synagogue, under a flame that burns perpetually. It is adorned with a special cover and ornaments. It is removed from the ark with great pageantry to be chanted aloud three times weekly. The public reading of Torah is the central event of the Sabbath morning service. To be called to the Torah to recite the blessing for reading from the scroll is a great honor. Blessing and reading from the Torah forms the central experience of the bar/bat mitzvah ceremony. (Imagine, if you will, the adolescent who thinks he or she might be gay having to read from Leviticus 18 or 20 at the rite of passage!)

Clearly, the words of the Torah cannot be dismissed lightly, nor would we wish them to be. The Torah contains concepts that are vital to us: that we should love our neighbors as ourselves and deal respectfully with the stranger, the poor, and the lonely in society. The Torah instructs us to all see ourselves as having been created in God's image, and therefore as the bearers of holiness in the world. It also contains wonderful and challenging stories of the world's beginnings and our people's journey from slavery to freedom.

Those of us who choose to remain identified with the Jewish tradition do so in part because of the foundation laid by Torah. We cannot simply excise what we do not like; it is our heritage and the primary text of our people. Yet a piercing question arises and reverberates through our lives: How do we live as Jews when the same text that tells us we were created in God's image also tells us that our sacred loving acts are punishable by death by decree of that same God?

This question may impel us to deny the power of Leviticus, but in truth we cannot. For all of us involved in any way in Jewish life, this text has authority. It has authority in that it is used by others to support the belief that homosexuality is wrong. (Of course, this is true not only for Jews. Leviticus is quoted by right-wing Christian religious groups to the same end.) And whether we ourselves consciously accept the authority of the text or not, we would be foolish to think that it does not affect us deeply, sometimes in subtle or insidious ways. For those of us who are lesbian or gay, it can undermine our pride in ourselves, feeding our own homophobia as well as that of others.

Let me suggest, then, three methods of coming to terms with Leviticus. We can, as did our ancestors, interpret the text to enable us to function with it on its own terms. We can, like biblical scholars, treat the text as a historical record and draw conclusions based on the way it functions in a given context. Or we can encounter the text directly with our emotions and our self-knowledge, allowing it to move us to anger, and then beyond anger, to action.

Each method comes to terms with the text's authority in a different way. Through interpreting the text we stay within the system and redirect it. Through historical reasoning we place limits on the text's authority by examining it with the lens of another system. Through encountering the text emotionally, we confront it and therefore use it as an instrument of transformation.

The Interpretive Method

Midrash—the process of making commentary to interpret the text—is a vital aspect of attempts throughout Jewish history to make the Bible come alive. Throughout the generations, interpreters have sought to make the text accessible to their contemporaries who may not understand its original meaning. The text may be ambiguous, unclear, or redundant. A word or custom may be unfamiliar and need explanation. One part of the text may contradict another part, and a resolution of the conflict is necessary. The same word or phrase may be repeated, seemingly without purpose, and commentators have sought to explain these repetitions by assigning different meanings to them. Finally, there are cases in which the grammar or syntax is unusual and lends itself to providing a new interpretation.

While interpretive methods are legitimate and widely practiced, it should be noted that many would claim that the text is not really in need of interpretation. It stands on its own as God's word.

With this understanding as our background, let us look at how Leviticus 18:22 and 20:13 have been interpreted by traditional Jewish commentators. We find that this prohibition is mentioned less often than others in the Torah. Some have assumed that this lack of discussion is due to the fact that homosexuality was not common among Jews. Suffice to say that we can only speculate about the extent of homosexual practice, but we can say with certainty that the subject was not considered problematic enough to require extensive public discussion. For whatever reason, to be sure, homosexuality was not a visible issue in the Jewish world until contemporary times.

Most of the interpretations of Leviticus 18:22 hinge on an unclear word—*to'evah*—which is generally translated as "abomination." In fact, the meaning of this word is obscure. Therefore, interpreters have taken the opportunity to translate it in ways that explain the prohibition. After all, the text never tells us why lying with a man is *to'evah*, but only that it is.

What might *to'evah* mean? According to the second-century commentator Bar Kapparah, it means *"to'eh ata ba*—you go astray because of it" (see Babylonian Talmud, Nedarim 51b). This play on words has been taken to mean that it is not intrinsically an evil to engage in homosexual acts, but rather that they have negative consequences. Bar Kapparah did not spell out those negative consequences—rather, it was left to later commentators to interpret his interpretation.

Certain medieval texts suggest that one is being led astray from the main function of sexual behavior, namely procreation. Some Rabbinic commentators assume that to go astray means to abandon your wife and to disrupt family life. This interpretation is reinforced by medieval commentator Saadiah Gaon's general pronouncement that the Bible's moral legislation is directed at preserving the structure of the family (*Emunot ve-Deot* 3:1). Finally, modern commentator R. Baruch haLevi Epstein, author of the commentary *Torah Temimah*, suggests that going astray means not following the anatomically appropriate manner of sexual union.[2]

The most well-known biblical commentator, Rashi, who lived in eleventh-century France, had but one comment on the subject. Wanting to make the text clearer to his readers, he explained rather graphically the meaning of the phrase, "as with a woman": "He enters as the painting stick is inserted in the tube."

In the contemporary era, traditional Jews have had to come to terms with the fact that gay men and lesbians have made ourselves a presence in the Jewish community. The most serious and thorough traditional response on the subject has been made by Norman Lamm.[3] Lamm affirms the text as it is simply understood—a strong prohibition against homosexuality. While he claims interpretation to be unnecessary to explain the text, in fact, he makes an interpretation of his own of the meaning of *to'evah*: "The very variety of interpretations of *to'evah* points to a far more fundamental meaning, namely, that an act characterized as an abomination is prima facie disgusting and cannot be further defined or explained."[4] While the term *to'evah* is not a problem for Lamm, the fact that this is considered a capital crime is at least distressing. But since capital punishment was one of the things the rabbis interpreted out of existence by making it impossible to convict someone of a capital crime, Lamm does oppose penalizing homosexual behavior.

It is not only Orthodox Jews who assert interpretations to substantiate their antihomosexual points of view. Note the following responsum by the well-known Reform rabbi, Solomon Freehof: "In Scripture (Leviticus 18:22) homosexuality is considered to be an 'abomination.' So too in Leviticus 20:13. If Scripture calls it an abomination, it means that it is more than a violation of a mere legal enactment, it reveals a deep-rooted ethical attitude."[5]

So far, we have examined traditional interpretations of the text. These interpretations either support the plain meaning of the text, explain difficult or unclear words in the verse, or use the text to create legal pronouncements on unrelated subjects.

Yet the interpretive method is also used to alter the meaning of other biblical verses, sometimes even contravening the original meaning. This fact creates an opportunity among contemporary commentators to alter or expand the meaning of our verse.

Contemporary commentators in the first instance see a contradiction between Leviticus 18:22 and the idea as stated in Genesis that we were all created in God's image. This contradiction must be resolved. We must assume that those of us who were created lesbian and gay are also in God's image, and that acts central to our identity cannot therefore be an abomination.[6]

In another interpretation, it is pointed out that the text refers only to certain sexual acts, not to same-sex love relationships. Therefore, the text is not relevant to a style of life and love and family of which it was ignorant.

It has often been pointed out that lesbians are not included in the Leviticus prohibition. This fact has led to a variety of interpretations: that women's sexual activities don't matter, that lesbian activity is acceptable, or that the absence of this rule makes the ruling against gay men invalid.

Perhaps the text is addressing the issue of sexual experimentation. According to this interpretation, straight men who are considering a "fling" and in the process hurting their current partner should refrain from doing so.

Another contemporary commentator, Arthur Waskow, has suggested that the text is only trying to tell us not to make love to a male as if he were a female—that is to say, gay love and straight love are indeed different.[7] One should not be confused with the other. (The acts do not evoke the same feelings or fulfill the same commandments.)

To some readers, this whole process of textual interpretation may seem irrational and unnecessary, and even amusing. Why go to the trouble to validate this text? Why play by these rules? There are many gay and lesbian Jews who feel compelled by the absolute authority and immutability of the Torah text. For them this is the only solution that will enable them to affirm both their gay and Jewish selves, and help them to feel whole. And for all of us, as noted earlier, the traditional interpretations affect us in subtle and destructive ways. It is for these reasons that more creative work needs to take place in the area of interpreting the text.

Biblical Criticism

A little more than one hundred years ago, Jewish and Christian thinkers began to study the Bible as a document created by human hands. The early biblical critics' questioning of divine authorship is viewed as commonplace today, but in their times their views were heretical.

Biblical scholars sought to place the Bible in its context in the Ancient Near East. They explained much of what was unclear in the biblical text by reference to practices in other cultures. They explained redundancies as the result of compilation of documents by multiple authors. They introduced the concept of evolution and attempted to date biblical materials. Biblical critics developed sensitivity to the nuances of the text, developing concerns about linguistic and literary patterns.

The viewpoint of biblical criticism enables us to look at our verse in its historical, linguistic, and cultural context and understand it in a new, more objective light. Of course, we must bear in mind that complete objectivity is unattainable. Even looking at the text from outside, we are bound by our own cultural norms and expectations. In truth, we are looking at our verse through another kind of lens. While we think the approach of biblical criticism is a valid way to look at the text, we do not think that we have found in this method a way of obtaining "the truth."

From this perspective we certainly see the simple meaning of the text—that in biblical times, homosexual acts were forbidden. Yet this method does not require that we affirm the truth of that reality for today. We can, as biblical critics, acknowledge the need for a reexamination of biblical norms. (After all, the Bible also countenanced other things we no longer accept as moral—slavery and a second-class status for women and people with disabilities, for example.)

Furthermore, we can explain why homosexual acts were considered *to'evah* from a different perspective, by examining parallel linguistic uses of the word. We discover that *to'evah* is actually a technical term used to refer to a forbidden idolatrous act. From this information, we may conclude that the references in Leviticus are specific to cultic practices of homosexuality, and not sexual relationships as we know them today. This explanation is supported by reference to the other legal condemnation of homosexuality in Deuteronomy, which directly interdicts homosexual practices related to cultic worship.

Second, we understand that much of the Bible is an effort to make the separations between acts considered holy and those considered profane, to create an ordered perception of the universe. Accordingly, the sexual prohibitions described fit into the larger category of laws about kosher foods, the separation of the sexes and their clothing, and the prohibitions against plowing with two types of animals and of mixing certain types of fabric. We can reexamine, today, which of these separations are still meaningful.

Looking at the text from the outside also enables us to explain the repetition of the law as being derived from two different sources, written at different times. So the death penalty may have been applied at one period in biblical history, but not at another time.

Through this approach, we are able to step back from the text and ask questions about how the text functioned. We can see from some of the suggestions above that the text functioned to keep order and define it and to separate the Israelite people from the practices of their neighbors. This gives us the opportunity to conclude that values may be disengaged from specific laws, and that there may be other means of perpetuating values if we indeed still share them today. Further, if we are not bound by the assumptions of divine authorship, we can assert that while the prohibition against homosexual acts functioned in its time, it is no longer appropriate to our ethical sensibilities today.

Encountering the Text

There is one last approach for coping with Leviticus. In this method, we confront the text directly. We do not look to the midrashist or the scholar to interpret the text for us. Rather we face the text in its immediacy—seeking its meaning in our lives, coming to terms with all that implies, and then going beyond it.

To face the simple meaning of Leviticus is to acknowledge the source of much of lesbian and gay oppression. The Bible does tell us that sexual acts between people of the same sex are *to'evah*—an abomination—and that they are punishable by death. And we know very well that this text has given generations the permission to find those of us who are lesbian or gay disgusting, to use Norman Lamm's word; to hate us; and even to do violence against us.

In our encounter with Leviticus, we experience the pain and terror and anger that this statement arouses in us. We imagine the untold damage done to generations of men, women, and children who experienced same-sex feelings and were forced to cloak or repress them. We reflect on those who acted on those feelings and were forced to feel shame and guilt and to fear for their lives. We remember how we felt when we first heard those words and knew their holy source. And we get angry—at the power these words have had over our lives, at the pain we have experienced in no small part because of these words.

Then, if we can, we grow beyond the rage. We begin to see these words as tools with which to educate people about the deep-rooted history of lesbian and gay oppression. We begin to use these very words to begin to break down the silence that surrounds us.

We proclaim the two consecutive weeks in the spring during which these words are read (*Parshat Ahare Mot* and *Parshat Kedoshim*) as Jewish Lesbian and Gay Awareness Weeks. During this time we urge that Torah study sessions be held in every synagogue to open the discussion of the role of gay and lesbian Jews in the community. Those of us who can take the risks of visibility must make ourselves available to tell our stories—of our alienation from the community, and of our desire to return. Each of us can tell the story of what this prohibition has meant in our lives—how we have struggled with it, and where we are on the road to resolution. And we expect to be listened to, with full attention and respect, as we do so.

In this way, we can transform Torah from a stumbling block to an entry path. We become more honest with ourselves and with our community about the barriers to our involvement, about our need for separate places to worship, and about our demand to be accepted as an integral part of Jewish life.

Whether we try interpreting, criticizing, or confronting, there are no easy answers for coming to terms with Leviticus. But we cannot desist from the challenge of finding creative solutions to deal with this dimension of our oppression. To be whole as Jewish lesbians and gay men we must acknowledge with what great difficulty those pieces of our lives fit together. But we must also demand—of ourselves and of our community—that those pieces be made to fit.

We marvel at the fact that words written thousands of years ago still have so much power to affect our lives. Words are powerful. Now it is up to us to make the words that will transform our lives and give new meaning to our existence as gay and lesbian Jews.

Speaking the Unspeakable:
Gays, Jews, and Historical Inquiry

....

Faith Rogow

> Whatever is unnamed, undepicted in images, whatever is omitted
> from biography, censored in collections of letters, whatever is
> misnamed as something else, made difficult-to-come-by, what-
> ever is buried in the memory by the collapse of meaning under an
> inadequate or lying language—this will become not merely un-
> spoken, but *unspeakable*.[1]—ADRIENNE RICH

AS JEWS, OUR TIES TO HISTORY ARE NOT CASUAL, AND RIGHTLY SO.
Our understanding of history shapes our view of economic, social,
and foreign policy. Moreover, our religious identity is based on our
understanding of our history. As noted historian Michael Meyer has
explained:

> For modern Jews, a conception of their past is no mere aca-
> demic matter. It is vital to their self-definition. Contemporary
> forms of Jewish identity are all rooted in some view of Jewish
> history which sustains them and serves as their legitimation. . . .
> Traditional Jewish faith rests neither on abstract speculations
> nor on a revelation given to a single prophet: it is people's collec-
> tive and continuing response to a Divine will manifest to it in the
> early stages of its historical existence and determining its fate
> down to the present time.[2]

As testimony to the importance of history in Jewish life, we have devoted significant communal resources to preserving our historical
record, and we often gauge our people's future by how well we have
passed down customs from one generation to the next. Given the cen-

trality of history to Jewish life, it is astonishing that so many Jewish scholars ignore the most basic techniques of historical research when studying gay Jews.[3] The attitude reflected in most scholarship from Jewish sources on gays ranges from ambivalent to openly hostile. This essay will explore the faulty historical assumptions on which these opinions are based. It will offer, as well, an investigation of the multifaceted intersections of gay and Jewish history.

Despite the difficulties of using sacred texts as historical sources, Jews rely on such texts to interpret the world, so historians must also depend on them to help decipher Jewish experience. In the best tradition of Jewish scholarship, we learn the most from our texts by asking them as many questions as our imagination allows. The better our questions, the better our answers. Those who attempt to silence questioners threaten that learning process. Thus, there is reason to be wary of those who restrict the interpretation of text to a heterosexist perspective. Such people often use texts, especially the Bible, as a weapon to discredit perceived enemies. Unfortunately, innumerable Jewish scholars have done just that, justifying homophobia by claiming that God declared homosexuality a sin, an affront to the Divine order of the world.[4] Historically, such a claim is difficult to sustain, raising more questions than it answers.

Perhaps the most common claim is that the existence of gay Jews is a new phenomenon, that in the past, gay Jews were a rarity.[5] Such arguments are based on a rabbinic response to R. Judah, who forbade two bachelors from sleeping together under the same blanket because they might be sexually tempted or besmirch their reputations (Mishnah, Kiddushin 4:14). The Sages, however, disagreed, maintaining that the ruling was not necessary because homosexuality was so uncommon in the Jewish community that the feared results were not likely to occur (Babylonian Talmud, Kiddushin 82a). This decision was subsequently codified by Maimonides in the *Mishneh Torah* and reaffirmed five hundred years later by R. Joel Sirkes.[6]

For the historian, accepting these sources at face value is problematic in several ways. First, to conclude from them that there were no gay Jews is curious in light of the fact that the issue was discussed in the text. In general, communities do not make laws to restrict behavior that does not occur. In addition, this conclusion ignores an intervening ruling by R. Joseph Caro that two men should not be alone together because of the prevalence of homosexuality. It also fails to account for the motives behind R. Judah's initial decision.[7] Finally, the position that gay Jews were a rarity ignores the findings of contemporary historians of the gay experience. Though gay history is a new field, evidence to date suggests that in all ages and all places there were lesbians and gay men.[8] If this was not true of the Jewish community, scholars need to explain why the Jewish community was such an aberration.

John Boswell is a contemporary historian whose work has focused on biblical text. In his classic study, *Christianity, Social Tolerance and Homosexuality*, he notes that comparatively few biblical passages actually deal with homosexuality. The lack of references might suggest that homosexuality was rare in ancient Israel, but it is equally possible that scant references are indicative not of a lack of numbers, but of a lack of concern. That is, the text does not spend a great deal of time on the subject because it was not considered abnormal or disturbing to our ancestors and therefore did not merit attention.

Of the existent passages, Boswell focuses on the story of Sodom (Genesis 19) as the most influential on modern attitudes. Briefly, Lot takes two angels into his household, only to have a crowd of Sodomite men demand that they be handed over so that the crowd might "know" (*neydah/yodah*) them. Lot refuses, calling the request "wicked" and offers his daughters as a substitute. The Sodomite men persist and ultimately God destroys the city. The traditional interpretation concludes that the crowd intended to have homosexual relations with the angels and that homosexuality was such a severe sin that it brought destruction on the city.

Boswell notes that the word "know" is very rarely used in a sexual sense: "In only ten of its 943 occurrences in the Old Testament does it have the sense of carnal knowledge."[9] He subsequently points out that "Sodom is used as a symbol of evil in dozens of places, but not in a single instance is the sin of the Sodomites specified as homosexuality." It is quite possible that the ancient Israelites understood the sin of the Sodomites to be something other than homosexuality altogether. Boswell provides several alternative explanations, including transgressions against prevailing norms of hospitality. He cites the parallel story in Judges 19, noting that Jewish sources "have overwhelmingly failed to interpret this as one of homosexuality," despite repetition of the identical phrase, "that we may *know* him."[10] Even if one rejected Boswell's interpretation, it is still not clear that homosexuality is the source of Sodom's "wickedness." Rather, as in Judges 19, the issue at hand is quite plausibly rape.

Boswell's arguments are further strengthened if one examines the passage directly preceding the Sodom story, in which we are told that Lot's visitors are angels sent by God to destroy the city. Rumor of such intent would certainly be enough to arouse an angry mob, and their demand to "know" the visitors might have been no more than a request for reassurance that Lot was not endangering the city by housing these visitors. It is also puzzling that Abraham would debate with God over the impending destruction of Sodom, if the residents were widely known as homosexuals and Abraham's tribe saw homosexuality as evil. In other passages (e.g., Deuteronomy 23:18) the term Sodomite is used in tandem with harlot, the former describing men and the latter describing women. The connotation is one of prostitution, not homosexuality. In other instances, the term "Sodomite" has been incorrectly given as the English translation for the word *kadesh*. Again, *kadeshim* were prostitutes, but there is nothing in the text itself that suggests they were homosexual prostitutes. In fact, if the traditional interpreters are correct and the Hebrews abhorred homosexuality, it seems strange that they would use a term based on the word "holy" (*kadosh*) to describe homosexuals.

The other biblical text routinely used to justify homophobia is Leviticus 18:22, which states that "a man should not lie with a man as with a woman. It is an abomination." Here again, Boswell notes that the terminology is not as obvious as interpreters have implied. He explains that the term *to'evah* (usually translated as "abomination") more often signifies something that is ritually unclean rather than something that is intrinsically evil. That is, homosexual relations are condemned not because the sexuality expressed is somehow evil, but because the ancient Hebrews considered such relations idolatrous. In fact, in several instances *to'evah* actually means "idol."[11] Whether something that was idolatrous in ancient times is necessarily idolatrous today is a separate issue that cannot be adequately covered in the scope of this essay. What should be clear, however, is that biblical passages cited to characterize homosexuality as evil and against God's natural order do not necessarily condemn homosexuality at all, but rather, may censure those who commit rape, idolatry, or reject important customs of hospitality. [Editors' note: For an extended discussion of this text, see the essay by Rebecca T. Alpert in this volume.]

To further understand these passages we can look to related texts. Certainly the most famous declaration of same-sex love is between David and Jonathan: "The soul of Jonathan was knit with the soul of David, and Jonathan loved him as his own soul. . . . Then Jonathan made a covenant with David, because he loved him as his own soul" (1 Samuel 18:1–3). David is no minor character—our Jewish messianic hopes rest on a return to his era—so it is reasonable to take him as an appropriate Jewish role model. Moreover, the text makes no negative comment on this love, leading the reader to assume it elicited no concern, at least by the text's redactors, if not always by David and Jonathan's contemporaries. Thus, if other texts are interpreted to be a condemnation of same-sex love, they need to be reconciled with this text.[12] Heterosexist interpretations have insisted that David and Jonathan loved each other platonically, and, therefore, this is not an instance of homosexuality. This explanation, however, is based on an incomplete definition of homosexuality that limits gay identity to the sexual act.

Beyond Traditional Interpretation: Gay *Midrash*

Jewish history also incorporates a method of textual exegesis known as *midrash,* a type of commentary in story form. Since Talmudic times, each generation of Jews has used this interpretive method to cull contemporary meaning from the sacred texts. Through the use of *midrash* we broaden our concept of history so that we may approach the text with fresh vision. One way to achieve such vision is to question the heterosexist assumptions on which our traditional stories are based. The tale of Dina (Genesis 34) offers one example. Having just moved to a new place, Dina "went out to see the daughters of the land." She is spotted by a local man, Shechem, who rapes her, tries to console her with "comforting" words, and eventually asks her family for her hand in marriage. Dina's brothers agree, all the while planning to attack Shechem's tribe as revenge because their sister had been "defiled." The story ends with the slaughter of all the men of Shechem's tribe.

One could imagine this as the story of a heterosexual man who expects all women to pay homage to his sexual prowess but is confronted by a woman who responds with indifference. Shechem sees Dina's interest in women and takes it upon himself to "convert" this

lesbian by raping her. We can imagine that Shechem's "comforting"
words to Dina were really a self-justification, claiming he loved her
enough to make her into a "real woman." While modern society has
often condoned such behavior by looking the other way, Genesis
gives us an example of communal outrage at such treatment of a lesbian. (Sexism, however, is still apparent in the story: at no point
is Dina ever consulted—she appears powerless in the face of both
Shechem and her brothers.)

Another text worthy of reconsideration[13] is the story of Rachel and
Akiba. In the traditional version of the tale, Rachel, daughter of a
wealthy family, recognizes the genius of poor, bedraggled Akiba. She
marries him against her family's wishes, losing her inheritance as a
result. Akiba leaves her to seek entrance to an academy, and though
he disappears for many years, her faith in him is eventually justified
because he returns as one of Israel's greatest scholars. Even then,
however, the obligations of leadership keep Akiba from staying with
Rachel.

Related exclusively from the heterosexual male point of view, the
tale portrays Rachel as a role model because, in the service of a great
male scholar, she is totally selfless. The account is puzzling because
we are told that the result of this great love is that the couple never
sees each other. According to the story, they do not even attempt
to see each other, despite prevailing norms that would have expected
Akiba to father children.

But perhaps Rachel and Akiba were not heterosexual, and though
living in very different worlds, both needed the heterosexual "cover"
of marriage to gain respect and credibility in a homophobic world.
They had agreed before the marriage that Akiba would go off to the
all-male world of scholars, and that Rachel would survive not as a
woman alone, but through the support of other women. They did not
need to see each other because they had no intentions of consummat-
ing the marriage. Instead of a story of heterosexual sacrifice, we have
an example of gays using the institutions of the dominant culture to
survive.

The Practice of Gay History

The brief examples above point to two main trends in the practice of
gay history. The first could be dubbed the "great gays" method, while
the second goes beyond this to examine how events differ when

viewed from a gay point of view. The "great gays" method attempts to gain legitimacy for a hated minority by pointing out that some of society's accepted heroes belonged to that minority, as in the case of David and Jonathan. It also provides evidence to counter the claims that gays did not exist by uncovering the accomplishments of individual gays.

The Jewish community has done a particularly comprehensive job of denying itself heroes simply by excluding gays from the historical record. One notable example is Dr. Magnus Hirschfeld, an accomplished scientist in Weimar Germany who is generally recognized as the father of sexology, the science of human fertility and sexuality. Despite his prolific work as a scholar and his considerable contributions to the biological sciences, Hirschfeld is absent from all Jewish encyclopedias and biographical collections of great Jews. His work, as well as that of the Institute for Sexual Research, which he founded and directed, were ultimately destroyed by Hitler. In a response that highlights the irony of denial, the German Jewish community failed to react to the burning of the Institute, attributing Hitler's act to anti-gay sentiment. Germany's gays tended to view the act as part of Hitler's campaign against the Jews, rather than taking it as a signal that they, too, might be endangered.

Uncovering gay Jews of the past is not likely to be an easy task. Because in so many places and times it has been dangerous to be publicly labeled a homosexual, gays leave few written records identifying themselves as such. Most accounts of gay experience come from antagonistic sources, some of which deliberately falsify records to suit their point of view.[14] In some cases gay records exist, but families who control them block access because they do not want a person's gayness revealed publicly. In other instances, academic institutions impede research by stigmatizing those who choose to study the gay experience, threatening researchers with denial of jobs or vital recommendations or implying that their work is somehow less than serious. Even when we can identify gay subjects, the historian must be careful not to endanger the subject's life or well-being through public exposure.

An additional difficulty associated with the "great gays" approach is defining who is gay. Just as Jewish historians have difficulty identifying who is a Jew (for example, is a Jew one who is born of a Jewish mother? one who is actively observant? one who has converted as a Reform Jew?), so, too, do historians of the gay experience disagree about who should be considered gay. If an individual centers his or

her life around persons of the same sex but does not have genital contact, is he or she gay? What about a person who lives publicly as a
heterosexual but privately seeks homosexual experiences?[15]

Historians even disagree about whether the definition of homosexuality has changed over time. One school of thought, exemplified
by Judy Grahn, asserts that homosexuality has changed over time,
but as is the case with Jews, we can trace a continuous gay culture
from ancient times to the present.[16] Other scholars insist that the entire gay experience is historically specific, noting that the lives of gay
individuals in cultures that accepted homosexuality were significantly
different than in societies that condemned gays, and the experiences
of gay men were not necessarily identical to those of lesbians.[17] Another school of thought, exemplified by Jeffrey Weeks, maintains that
homosexual behavior is essentially universal, although gay identity is
historically specific.[18] Boswell adds that in many cultures, homosexual
behavior was not a determinant of one's core identity. He notes that
the Bible has no word for "homosexual," and he concludes that the
ancients viewed homosexuality as a behavior rather than an identity.[19]

Just as definitions have differed through the ages, so has terminology. The words used to describe people who love others of the
same sex are relatively new. "Homosexual" was first used by the
Western medical community in 1869 and "gay" was coined many decades later. As historian Jonathan Katz has pointed out, every term
"gives material body to a particular historical concept" and provides a
clue "to the often fundamentally different ideas and judgments"
about those we call "gay."[20] Thus, it is somewhat inaccurate to use
terminology from one era to refer to events or people from a different
era. Labeling someone who lived a thousand years ago "gay" could
be confusing because it implies their experience was parallel to that
faced by gays today. On the other hand, using historically accurate
but unfamiliar terminology can be equally confusing. (In this essay, I
have used the terminology of the 1980s to provide the modern reader
with a frame of reference, recognizing that while such usage gives the
reader a better general idea of the subject, it partially obscures the
variations in gay experience throughout history.) More important
than choice of terminology is the recognition that, ultimately, labels
alone (particularly labels not freely chosen) cannot tell us how individuals "named, thought of, and evaluated themselves, or their acts,
feelings, and relations, or how they were perceived and responded to
by others."[21]

Some authors have mistakenly approached the "who is a gay" issue as an attempt to discover a cause for homosexuality.[22] At worst, such attempts are motivated by a hope that once a cause is found, a "cure" will soon follow. At best, they sidetrack us from the more significant historical inquiry into the manifestations and lessons of gay heritage. Frank Kameny, a Jew and an early leader of the Mattachine Society (the first U.S. gay rights organization), addressed this issue in the 1950s by comparing gays with other minorities:

> I do not see any great interest on the part of the B'nai B'rith Anti-Defamation League in the possibility of solving problems of anti-Semitism by converting Jews to Christians. . . . We are interested in obtaining rights for our respective minorities *as* Negroes, *as* Jews, and *as Homosexuals*. Why we are Negroes, Jews, or Homosexuals is totally irrelevant, and whether we can be changed to Whites, Christians, or heterosexuals is equally irrelevant.[23]

Jews need not solve all these historical issues in order to begin incorporating gays and lesbians into our history books. A simple beginning would entail claiming as our own those Jews who have been leaders in the gay rights movement. Further, Jews need not solve the theoretical issues in order to gain from the second stage of doing gay history, which goes beyond simple identification of "great gays" by looking for new ways our tradition speaks to us when we take off our heterosexist blinders. The story of Rachel and Akiba is but one example.

Commonalities and Consequences

The Jewish community stands to gain insight about the ways we have been oppressed by examining the oppression of gays. The frequency with which gay experience parallels Jewish experience is striking. Boswell writes, "Most societies . . . which freely tolerate religious diversity also accept sexual variation, and the fate of Jews and gay people has been almost identical throughout European history, from early Christian hostility to extermination in concentration camps . . . even the same methods of propaganda were used against Jews and Gay people—picturing them as animals bent on the destruction of the children of the majority."[24] These parallels have also been discernible in America, from popular culture to the rhetoric of right-wing hate groups. For example, the 1947 American film *Crossfire*, an adaptation of Richard Brook's novel *The Brick Foxhole*, easily substituted a Jew for the gay murder victim in the original. The film was acclaimed as a mature treatment of anti-Semitism, with no mention that the plot intended to explore homophobia. Not only have many societies associated Jews and gays, but gays themselves have noted the similarities, as in the 1951 "Missions and Purposes" of the Mattachine Society, which stated that one organizational goal was to develop "an ethical homosexual culture . . . paralleling the emerging cultures of our fellow minorities—the Negro, Mexican, and Jewish Peoples."

Jews have generally been slower to acknowledge similarities. As in *Crossfire*, too often the gay experience is obscured in relation to the Jewish experience.[25] Few *Yom HaShoah* (Holocaust Remembrance Day) observances include laments for the loss of gay life, though tens of thousands of gays, as well as six million Jews, were among Hitler's victims.[26]

The Jewish community's opposition to examining the experience of gay Jews stems, in part, from the accusation that gays pose a threat to the Jewish community. Echoing fears expressed by every denomination, Orthodox rabbi Abraham B. Hecht has stated that if homosexuality is not stopped, "the institution of marriage will go out of style and children will become strange creatures—unwanted and unloved."[27] Nathaniel Lehrman takes this position as well, claiming it is based on empirical evidence and "the lessons of history."[28] Yet, these claims to historicity are never backed up with historical examples because overwhelming historical evidence contradicts their conclusion. Many societies have accepted homosexuality fully and none has experienced the eradication of heterosexuality, marriage, or children.[29] In fact, no historical evidence exists to suggest that gays do not wish to bear and raise children. One need only look at the spate of recent publications on gay parenting and the cases brought before American courts in which gays are fighting to keep their children, to see the falsehood of this position.[30] [Editor's note: see essays in this volume by Martha Ackelsberg, Judith Plaskow, Evelyn Torton Beck, and Linda Holtzman for further discussion of this issue.]

A similar denial of historical fact is routinely presented by Jewish writers who oppose gay civil rights. Their argument is threefold. First, in what Ellen Umansky has aptly called the "domino theory of immorality," a variety of scholars have warned that the granting of civil rights to gays will result in certain and widespread moral depravity, a claim easily proven ahistorical by the evidence cited in the previous paragraph.[31] A second approach insists that gays do not really experience discrimination and therefore are not in need of legal protection.[32] The well-documented rise in physical attacks on gays in the 1980s and the Hardwick case (in which the Supreme Court found a gay man guilty of sodomy after being discovered with a lover in his bedroom) provide ample proof that this claim is mistaken.[33] Finally, these authors have chosen to ignore the parallel experience of gays and Jews. Those Jews who oppose gay civil rights have mistakenly defined gays as being so different from themselves, they erroneously conclude that what happens to gays has no effect on Jews. Moreover, their denial ignores the thousands of Jews who are also gay. Historically, American Jews have defended civil rights not only because moral standards dictated action, but also because Jews have seen the protection of minorities as being in our own best interest. If Jews now break this historical pattern and refuse to recognize the interests we share with gays, we inevitably perpetuate discrimination and we must ask why. Are we Jews afraid to confront gay history because it would force us to confront the oppressor as well as the oppressed in us? Will we continue to deny gay experience merely because it reminds us that we have not always lived up to our own moral standards?

Ironically, while Jews have failed to recognize gay voices as part of the diversity of Jewish history, gays have been increasingly present in Jewish literature. Though this is certainly a positive step, it does not signal impending widespread acceptance of gays by the Jewish community. The Jewish Publication Society's reissue of Jo Sinclair's novel *Wasteland* is a prime example of the community's ambivalence. One of *Wasteland's* stronger characters is a lesbian. Interestingly, the character is blond; that is, she does not "look Jewish." The portrayal allows the reader to see the character as physically different, as "other," and perhaps as somehow less than truly Jewish. Another book in the same JPS series, *Allegra Maud Goldman* by Edith Konecky, tells the story of an adolescent Jewish girl struggling toward adulthood and, along the way, discovering what it means to be a Jewish female in America. She finds herself attracted to women, and though the story ends before she sexually matures, her independent and adventurous nature leads the reader to assume she will eventually identify herself as a lesbian. The other Jewish characters, however, describe her attraction to women as abnormal, assuring the reader that the pro-

tagonist is unusual and will not receive approval from the mainstream
Jewish community. It is no coincidence that these portrayals of gay
Jews have been limited to fiction, which can easily be criticized as a
misrepresentation of reality. Nor is it coincidental that the Jewish
community, usually quick to take pride in its successful authors, has
generally ignored writers of gay works, even when those writers are
as accomplished as Tony Award–winning Harvey Fierstein (*Torch
Song Trilogy*).[34]

Unless Jews come to accept gays as part of our history, we are in
danger of creating the "unspeakable" which Adrienne Rich describes
in the quotation that prefaced this essay. Yet, the risk is not that the
gay voice will be buried, for the gay community will continue to explore its heritage with or without the support of the Jewish community. The danger is that an authentic Jewish voice will be silenced and
that an opportunity to better understand our tradition will be lost.

Just as we eagerly study other subgroups of Jews, we must begin to
look at the experience of Jews who center their lives in the gay community. Gays, knowing what it feels like to be excluded from society,
have long based their politics on the principle of inclusion, cooperat-
ing with other oppressed groups even when those groups have seemingly conflicting needs. Perhaps the lessons of gay coalition-building
can provide models for Jewish-Arab or Jewish-black dialogues. The
gay community has also exhibited an enormous amount of creativity
in developing new family structures and support networks. These
new models may very well be the key to Jewish survival in a world of
increasing mobility. Finally, gays remind American Jews of what it is
like to live with constant injustice. In the face of oppression, Jews are
commanded to pursue justice, but when our immediate surroundings
are comfortable, it is easy to forget that others suffer. Contact with the
gay community could reignite our communal anger and lead us back
to the activism that inspires us to be "a light to the nations."

When the Jewish community silences, omits, or distorts gay voices,
it denies us access to a piece of our history. Rather than leading to
a greater understanding of Jewish tradition, it guarantees that our
understanding will remain incomplete. When our prejudices cause us
to limit the questions we ask, our scholarship is sure to become stale
and dogmatic. As Rabbi Chanina ben Dosa said: "When conscience
takes precedence over learning, learning endures; but when learning
takes precedence over conscience, learning does not endure."[35]

In Search of Role Models

....

Jody Hirsh

FOR CENTURIES NOW, IT HAS BEEN ASSUMED THAT HOMOSEXUALITY was anathema to all upright Jews. Modern scholars such as Robert Gordis have told us that Judaism has maintained a "persistent feeling of revulsion toward homosexuality."[1] Such an assumption has colored our perception of Jewish history to such an extent that even obviously positive images of homosexuality in Jewish sources and Jewish tradition have been overlooked or even radically reinterpreted in order to invalidate any potentially positive attitudes. Now, as we reexamine our assumptions and our history, we find that positive gay and lesbian role models exist in all periods of Jewish history.[2] Centuries of denial and invalidation, however, have made such role models all but invisible to the modern Jew—even to gay Jews.

If gay role models have been invisible, the religious and academic worlds, in their refusal to acknowledge the gay experience in Jewish history, have reinforced that invisibility. Consider, for example, the following biblical statement describing the farewell of David and Jonathan, which may reveal much about their relationship. Jonathan, afraid for David's life, has arranged to warn him of the danger by a prearranged signal involving shooting arrows and calling out instructions to his young servant:

> And Jonathan gave his weapons unto his lad, and said unto him: "Go, carry them to the city." And as soon as the lad was gone, David arose out of a place toward the South, and fell on his face to the ground, and bowed down three times; and they kissed one another, and wept one with another until David exceeded.[3]

83

This "revised standard" translation based on the King James Bible informs us that David "exceeded," an obscure reference to say the least. The Hebrew is clearer. It reads, "until David *became large*" (*ad David higdil*). The reference, I think, is to physical arousal. Such a reading, however, has never been suggested by biblical scholars: the pioneering *Lexicon of Biblical Hebrew* by Brown, Driver, and Briggs, the standard reference work used by generations of English-speaking Old Testament students, tell us that *higdil* means to magnify, become great, or become large—except once in all the Hebrew literature, *higdil* means "to weep greatly"![4] While I have found no other place that *higdil* refers to male sexual arousal, such an interpretation seems far less a distortion than "to weep greatly." Furthermore, a physical relationship is certainly supported by David's famous lament over Jonathan:

> I am distressed for thee, my brother Jonathan:
> Very pleasant hast thou been unto me:
> Wonderful was thy love to me.
> Passing the love of women.[5]

The book of Ruth provides a model of a primary relationship between two women, Ruth and her mother-in-law Naomi. Although Jonathan and David were probably actual historical figures, Ruth and Naomi were apparently fictional ones figuring in this fifth-century B.C.E. equivalent of a historical novel set in the thirteenth century B.C.E. The story tells of a Judean woman, Naomi, who moves with her family from Judea to a foreign country, Moab, in order to escape a famine. When Naomi's husband and two sons die in Moab, Naomi decides to leave her two daughters-in-law and return to Judea. One daughter-in-law, however, insists upon remaining with her, and even marries a distant relative of Naomi's in order to provide some security for both women. Traditional interpretations of this tale insist that the essence concerns Ruth's realization that the Hebrew God is the only real God, and hence she tells Naomi that Naomi's God will, in fact, be her God.

Yet the essential point of the story is not Ruth's "conversion" to Judaism. Her adopting Naomi's God is in no way remarkable. Ancient polytheistic people believed that the gods' powers were geographical; hence, moving from Moab to Judea would have necessitated changing religions. What is remarkable, however, is the devotion between Ruth and Naomi. Why didn't Ruth return to Moab like Naomi's other daughter-in-law, Orpah? The key is in Ruth's commitment to Naomi.

Ruth follows Naomi's advice and even tricks Naomi's kinsman Boaz into thinking that he has participated in the sexual intrigues of the threshing season by sleeping with her. Women alone and unmarried, without the conventional family structure to protect and support them, were vulnerable to financial insecurity and physical danger. Ruth marries Boaz in order to protect and support her mother-in-law, a commitment which should have been rendered void by the death of Ruth's husband, Naomi's son. The primary devotion to Naomi, rather than exclusively a commitment to the Jewish people, couldn't be clearer:

> And Ruth said: "Entreat me not to leave thee, and to return from following after thee; for whither thou goest, I will go; and where thou lodgest, I will lodge: thy people shall be my people, and thy God my God; where thou diest, will I die, and there will I be buried; the Lord do so to me, and more also, if aught but death part thee and me."[6]

There is no implication that the relationship between Ruth and Naomi is a physical one. Nevertheless, Ruth's primary reason for marrying Boaz is for the benefit of Naomi. The entire story, in fact, hinges on the strength of the women's primary commitment to each other.

Of all the biblical tales, the story of Joseph is by far the most complex with regard to the gay subtext. The story chronicles the life of Joseph, the favorite son of Jacob, who is, at the beginning, an unpleasant, gossiping "daddy's boy" who carries tales of his brothers to his father. He infuriates his brothers further by interpreting dreams which imply that he will rule over them. After being sold as a slave, Joseph is taken to Egypt where he serves in the house of Potiphar, a high Egyptian official. After being falsely accused by Potiphar's wife, he is thrown into prison only to be remembered as an interpreter of dreams at a moment of crisis. He becomes the right-hand man to the Pharaoh, able to save his own family from famine and responsible for bringing the children of Israel to Egypt.

Joseph's story is one of suffering and growth. After years of enslavement, imprisonment, and suffering, Joseph changes: he shows great sensitivity and sympathy in seeing his brothers again. Rather than taking vengeance on them, he demonstrates his stature and humanity: "Then Joseph could not refrain himself before all them that stood by him; and he cried: 'cause every man to go out from me.' And there stood no man with him while Joseph made himself known unto his brethren. And he wept aloud; and the Egyptians heard, and the house of Pharaoh heard. And Joseph said unto his brethren: 'I am Joseph; doth my father yet live?'"[7]

Our first glimpses of Joseph establish him as a character akin to a shaman or oracle: he is an interpreter of dreams and foreteller of the future. His celebrated "coat of many colors" (*k'tonet passim*) is, in fact, an article of women's clothing. Such a coat is described one other time in the Bible explaining that "with such robes were the king's daughters that were virgins apparelled."[8] According to historian Arthur Evans, "The first shamans (or healer priests) in nature societies were women. The first male shamans imitated women by taking on their roles and wearing their clothing."[9] This explanation gives us considerable understanding of a major aspect of Joseph's role in the history of the Jewish people.

Joseph's adventures in the house of Potiphar in Egypt reinforce the image of Joseph as a gay man. Biblical commentators have long noted the importance of the selection and order of details in the normally sparse biblical narrative. The description of Joseph's advancement in Potiphar's house is indeed revealing:

> And Joseph was brought down to Egypt; and Potiphar, an officer of Pharaoh's, the captain of the guard, an Egyptian, bought him of the hand of Ishmaelites, that had brought him down thither. And the Lord was with Joseph, and he was a prosperous man; and he was in the house of his master the Egyptian. And his master saw that the Lord was with him, and that the Lord made all that he did to prosper in his hand. And Joseph found favour in his sight, and he ministered unto him. . . . And Joseph was of beautiful form, and fair to look upon.[10]

The physical appearance of Joseph is added clearly in order to explain Joseph's success: Potiphar advanced Joseph in his house in part because he was "fair to look upon." Even the early rabbis could not ignore the implication. In an attempt to explain the use of the word *saris* (eunuch)[11] in describing Potiphar, we are told: "This implies that he was castrated, teaching that he [Potiphar] purchased him for the purpose of sexual intercourse."[12] Of course the rabbis insist that the attraction was not mutual, that Joseph couldn't have been homosexual—an interpretation that is contradicted by the text. Potiphar's wife attempts to seduce Joseph:

> And it came to pass, as she [Potiphar's wife] spoke to Joseph day by day, that he hearkened not unto her, to lie by her, or to be with her. And it came to pass on a certain day, when he went into the house to do his work, and there was none of the men of the house there within, that she caught him by his garment, saying: "Lie with me." And he left his garment in her hand, and fled, and got him out.[13]

The traditional explanation of Joseph's behavior is that he is "pure" or "holy" and therefore resists her advances. He, in fact, does mention earlier that lying with her would be a sin against God. Such restraint at this point in the story, however, is unlikely. Joseph has several ordeals to survive before he grows to the stature of the man we see at the conclusion of the story. At this point, he is still the undisciplined teenager whom we have met at the beginning of the tale. He has an unmatched opportunity. Potiphar's wife has seen to it that no one is home. He flees from her partly from fear, but partly from disinclination, despite her beauty. Potiphar's wrath, as well, results partly from his possessiveness of Joseph. Potiphar's wife has accused Joseph of attempting to rape her. Potiphar is angry because it seems as if Joseph would consider someone else as a bed-partner.

Joseph's success story, even in prison, is dependent on the kindness of other men—the jailer, the butler, and the baker, also referred to as *sarisim* (eunuchs). He grows, becomes a hero, and is the *savior* of his family and of the Israelite people. The events that shape Joseph's life have an effect on more people than him alone. And not only is Joseph's "gayness" not condemned; it is part of God's plan for the deliverance of the Jewish people.

How can such positive views of homosexuality in biblical times be reconciled in light of the apparent prohibition of homosexuality of Leviticus 20? Much has been written in this book and in other sources about the possible meaning of this ambiguous injunction [Editor's note: See the essay by Rebecca T. Alpert in this volume.] Whether it refers to ritual prostitution only, or to the fact that "appropriate" men's sexual practice with men is different than that with women (as Arthur Waskow has suggested),[14] or simply that it represented a fear of "wasting seed" (i.e., without intending to procreate), there clearly are alternative interpretations. The existence of gay biblical role models alone shows that Leviticus can't be seen as a universal prohibition of homosexuality.

The data aren't totally positive, however, in that "gay" biblical figures aren't gay in the modern sense of being exclusively homosexual or developing an exclusively "gay" life-style. It is clear that however we interpret the "gayness" of biblical role models, the norm was to be married and have children regardless of whom one was really able to love, or even prefer. The first of the 613 biblical commandments is, after all, to be fruitful and multiply. David, Jonathan, Ruth, Naomi, and Joseph all had children. In all five cases, however, their relationships with loved ones of the same sex were pivotal relationships in their lives as well as in the significance for the Jewish people.

Nowhere is the invalidation of the gay Jewish experience clearer than in the modern representation of the world of medieval Jewry. It is a surprise even to the most well-informed modern Jews that the pivotal tenth-century philosopher, Sa'adya Gaon of Iraq, was known for his sexual adventures as well as for his influence in matters of Jewish law. According to medievalist Norman Roth, "In the controversy between Sa'adya Gaon and the exilarch David b. Zakkai, Khalaf Ibn Sarjada accused the Gaon of homosexual acts . . . and stated that the youth of Nehardea (in Iraq) had wearied themselves in *pursuing* him. . . . [The] accusations against Sa'adya were based on reliable testimony which the latter never attempted to refute, although he carefully refuted all the other charges against him."[15]

Few Jews realize that many famous poets and scholars of the Golden Age of Spanish Jewry are known as well for their homoerotic poetry. Poets of the stature of Judah Ha-Levi, Moses Ibn Ezra, Solomon Ibn Gabirol, and others wrote poetry that clearly could not be interpreted as other than homosexual. Most of this poetry is not frequently translated into English and is therefore inaccessible to the average Jewish reader. The few homoerotic poems translated are generally not recognizable as such in English. The following innocuous Judah Ha-Levi poem (twelfth century), for example, has been published often:

> Awake my friend, from your slumber.
> I, awake, am satiated by your image.

> If you see someone kiss your lips in a dream,
> I will make your dreams come true.[16]

In Hebrew, all nouns, adjectives, and *verbs* are masculine or feminine. All words in this poem referring to either the speaker or the beloved are masculine. Many scholars have attempted to deny the overt homosexuality of such lines by claiming that the poet intended his speaker to be female (but the verbs indicate that the speaker is male), or that the poet is addressing his son (but a kiss on the lips seems strange), or even that the poem is actually about the relationship between God and Israel (really!).

Other poems, such as the following one by Moses Ibn Ezra (twelfthcentury) are considerably less ambiguous:

THE TREACHEROUS FAWN

> My heart's desire and my eye's delight:
> The hart beside me and a cup in my right hand!
> Many denounce me for loving,
> But I pay no heed.
> Come to me, fawn, and I shall vanquish them.
> Time will consume them and death
> Will shepherd them away.
> Oh come to me, fawn, let me feast
> On the nectar of your lips
> Until I am satisfied.
>
> Why, why would they discourage me?
> If there be any sin or guilt in being ravished
> By your beauty—let the Lord be my judge!
> Do not let your heart be swayed by the words of my
>   tormentor.
> That obstinate man.
> Oh, come put me to the test!
>
> He was lured and we went to his mother's house.
> There he bent his back to my heavy yoke.
> Night and day I alone was with him.
> I took off his clothes and he took off mine.
> I sucked at his lips and he suckled me.
>
> But once his eyes had done away with my heart,
> His hand fastened the yoke of my sin,

And he looked for grievances against me.
He raged and shouted in fury:
"Enough! Leave me alone!
Do not drive me to crime,
Do not lead me astray!"

Oh, do not be unrelenting in your anger, fawn.
Show me the wonders of your love, My friend;
Kiss your friend and fulfill his desire.
If you wish to let me live—give me life;
But if you would kill—then kill me![17]

The references to others denouncing the poet, or to the lover's fear of being led astray, attest to some stigma attached to this relationship. However, the poet's attitude, complete with nearly direct quotation from the biblical Song of Songs, is not one of shame or embarrassment. Such relationships were not universally stigmatized by Jewish medieval society, at least among the intellectual elite. This positive attitude is repeated in the many medieval poems addressed to the fawn or gazelle (a popular form of endearment used in medieval Hebrew poetry).

Many medieval scholars claim that the Hebrew poets, far from being gay themselves, were simply emulating their contemporary Arab colleagues who wrote such poetry. There is no way of knowing who was gay and who wasn't. Nevertheless, if being gay were as abhorrent as we're led to believe, surely no heterosexual would wish to copy an overtly homosexual poetic form. The number of homosexual poems written by well-known poets is astounding. The proliferation of homosexual verse is proof positive that homosexuality, even to medieval Jewry, was not considered a significant problem.

Throughout Jewish history, until modern times, the voices one hears in Jewish history—the historians, poets, chroniclers—are overwhelmingly male voices. The few possible examples of lesbianism are filtered through male eyes. If images of gay males in Jewish history are obscured by homophobic bias, images of lesbians are even more obscured by the sexism of male-produced and male-oriented historiography.

One of the rare examples of a significant lesbian figure in earlier Jewish history is the Betula (or Maid) of Ludomir, Hannah Rochel

(1805–92).[18] Before her planned marriage, Hannah went into a trance and claimed to receive a "new and sublime soul." She broke her engagement and began acting like a man, wearing *tallit* and *tefillin* and studying and praying. Her synagogue was equipped with a special room for her own prayer and study, and from which, with the door open, she would deliver sermons to her followers in the next room. (Jewish law would not permit a woman to worship in the same room with men.) Due to her brilliance, and the belief that her new life was the result of a miracle, she became a well-known Chasidic leader whose followers were known as the Chasidim of the Betula of Ludomir.

The Zaddik of Chernobyl, a well-known Chasidic leader, finally convinced her to marry at the age of forty—a marriage she was unable to consummate. After her marriage her influence waned. She had previously been seen as a male *tzaddik* (righteous man) residing in the body of a woman. With her marriage, her identity as a woman was established, diminishing her credibility as a religious leader. The story is a sad one, full of repressed sexuality. Although there is no evidence that she ever was an active lesbian, her ambiguous sexuality was directly responsible for her influence as a Chasidic leader and her return to "normality" for the loss of her power.

These are just a few examples of gay role models from Jewish history. The search for gay Jewish role models will always be a difficult one. Obscured by time, by memoirs that are less than frank, by the hidden innuendos in the correspondence of Jewish leaders, by sexism of male recorders of history, and by the reluctance of Jewish scholarship to admit a gay presence within the scope of Jewish history, many positive images are lost to us. Although, strictly speaking, modern gay Jews don't *need* historical models from less open times, we can find considerable strength in positive images from times assumed to be even more repressive than our own. There *are* positive images, and with scholarship less afraid to focus on more unconventional views of history, perhaps we will uncover more than we could ever have imagined.

Gerry's Story: An Oral History

....

Jeffrey Shandler

I'm a seventy-nine-year-old great grandmother who also happens to be a lesbian.—GERRY FAIER, from a fund-raising letter for SAGE,[1] 1987

I MET GERRY FAIER LATE IN 1986 TO INTERVIEW HER FOR AN AN-thropology course on life histories given at the YIVO Institute for Jewish Research. At the conclusion of our second meeting, Gerry said to me, "My family's been after me to put my story down for years, but I haven't been able to do it. Now I've told you things I've never told anyone else. I feel like your surrogate grandmother." I welcomed her announcement; I had quickly come to feel that Gerry meant more to me than an informant for a scholarly study, and I was glad to learn that she saw me as something more than an intrusive student anthropologist. Gerry, now eighty years old, is in fact about the same age as my maternal grandmother; like her, Gerry has shared her life-lessons through her personal history. This has proven to be of great value not only for me, but, I believe, for Gerry as well, giving her an opportunity to formulate a meaningful understanding of her eighty years of experience.

I sought out Gerry because I was interested in studying the personal history of someone who is, like me, both Jewish and gay. This is both an intellectual interest and a personal one. I wonder what the concerns I face now, as a gay man and as a Jew, will look like if I live to be sixty, seventy, eighty, or even more. Unlike many of my straight contemporaries, I find that the almost exclusively heterosexual role models of people at the later stages of the life cycle found in American culture at large—and American-Jewish culture in particular—often have little to say to me as a gay person. On the other hand, the lesbian and gay subcultures' responses to such issues as community, family, and intergenerational continuity have only recently begun to show some sensitivity to ethnic identity and values. In a culture where the aged are ignored, lesbian and gay elders are even less sought out as resources. Thus, my decision to document Gerry's story is itself part of my personal response to the challenge of understanding both my gay and Jewish identities.

My first interview with Gerry took place in late October in her home, a small one-bedroom unit in a modern East Village apartment building for senior citizens run by a Jewish social service agency. She is a small, thin woman; her face is strong and alert, framed with short, grey hair, and her voice has a weathered edge to it. The tidy, uncluttered appearance of the apartment confirmed my sense that Gerry was an active person. I already knew that she was a busy woman; we'd had some difficulty arranging a time for our meeting that did not conflict with SAGE functions or other social activities.

During our first session, Gerry gave me an overview of her life, talking almost without interruption for nearly an hour. She was born in 1908 in Brooklyn, the third of eight children of East European Jewish immigrants. She remembers her father, who worked as a house painter, as being "like most Orthodox Jewish men of his day, very chauvinistic." Gerry describes her mother as a "hard-working" and "naive" woman who never fully adjusted to life in America. Gerry displayed an inquisitive mind during childhood, but, being a girl and a middle child in a large family, she reports receiving little intellectual support from her parents. This seems to have had a particularly negative effect on her attitudes about her Jewish identity, although it contributed at the same time to her independent-mindedness:

> Whenever it came to women or to women's roles [my father said,] "*Dos tor men nisht, un dos muz men nisht, un dos loz men nisht.*" [You're not allowed to do this, you mustn't do this, you can't do this.] And every time that my father went to shul, I wanted to go with him, but I wanted to sit downstairs; I didn't want to sit upstairs, behind a curtain. My life's ambition was to wear a *talis,* and my father said, "*A meydl trogt nisht a talis*" [A girl doesn't wear a prayer-shawl] . . . As time went on, I began to become estranged from Jewishness. . . . Without ever know-

ing anything about feminism, without ever knowing anything about the subjugated Jewish female role, I resented it. One day, we were walking along the street. There was a black Jewish family that lived on our block. My father and I were going to shul this day, and I said to him—I spoke to him in English, and he answered me in Yiddish—"Papa, if they're Jews, why can't we marry with them?" And he said, *"Fun azelkhe zakhn redt men nisht"* [People don't talk about such things]. This is the way that my father used to end all of my questions. That made me a very intelligent woman. I began to read a lot. I stopped depending on my father's answers. I would ask him questions, but I would have to find the answers for myself.

Gerry dropped out of high school at the age of fifteen and soon thereafter met Morris Faier, a young singer who worked as a housepainter. They married when Gerry was eighteen. Though their relationship did not last long, Gerry and Morris had a son and a daughter. At the beginning of the Great Depression, Gerry was an unsupported single parent in her early twenties. She applied to the Works Progress Administration (WPA), lying about her education, and was given a job as a social worker, and later on, a teacher. During the thirties, she became involved in the labor movement and radical politics. She joined the Communist Party and became a spokesperson for the New York Unemployment Council. At the beginning of World War II, Gerry applied for a civil service job as a tool inspector. Her application led to an interview with FBI agents, who interrogated her about her politics and asked if she knew whether certain of her acquaintances were Communists. Gerry did not incriminate herself or others in the course of the interview; nevertheless, she was turned down for the civil service job. Gerry left the Communist Party not long thereafter, disillusioned by the news of the Stalin-Hitler Pact of 1939.

After the war Gerry moved to Woodstock, New York, along with her children and Vasco, a man with whom she had become involved during her years working for the WPA. There they made the acquaintance of members of the local artists' community, which included many gay people. During these years, Gerry left Vasco and had her first lesbian relationship:

This particular weekend I was in the bar—not a gay bar, it was a social center of the town. The woman was on the opposite side of the bar—she looked at me, I looked at her—all of a sudden I find a beer in front of me, and I said to the bartender, "I didn't order this." He says, "No, the lady over there . . ." She sent me over a ten-cent beer—bigshot, right? So I thanked her for the beer, and I'm drinking the beer . . . Next thing I know, she's standing and talking to me. We became very, very friendly. The next morning—I went back home that night, of course—the next day she invited me to come to her home for breakfast, which I did. P.S.: I had my first love affair with a woman in Woodstock. It was a sudden entry into homosexuality. It wasn't even a matter of conscious choice—it happened. And then, in hindsight, I realized that most of my life was in that direction.

At the age of thirty-nine, her children grown and on their own, Gerry moved back to New York City and became involved in the lesbian subculture of Greenwich Village. Gerry has continued to live in New York City since the late 1940s, at times with lovers, at times by herself, as she does now. Her political activism led to her involvement in the gay liberation movement during the 1970s, and, most significantly, to her work with SAGE.

Gerry is among the organization's most industrious members, often writing or speaking in public on SAGE's behalf. She is currently SAGE's oldest active female member and serves on its executive board. In 1987, she was named SAGE's representative to Manhattan Borough President David Dinkins' Senior Citizens' Advisory Committee:

I'm one of twenty representatives of various senior citizen care givers . . . and when I had to introduce myself, I said, "My name is Gerry Faier, and I represent Senior Action in a Gay Environment"—I didn't [just] say "SAGE." I said it slow, and I looked at everyone—every one of them smiled, and one of them said, "Oh, it's good that you're here."

Later that year, Gerry received the Diego Lopez Community Service Award from the Human Rights Campaign Fund in recognition of her work on behalf of gay senior citizens.

Gerry knows well that others find her life story extraordinary and fascinating. "My daughter," she says, "thinks I'm one of the most interesting people she ever knew." Gerry relates her history with the skill of a gifted storyteller. Like any good author, she self-consciously selects elements from her personal history and puts the various pieces together in a way that for her makes sense out of her experience.

An essential aspect of this self-consciousness is Gerry's acute awareness of being different. As a female, a Jew, a poor person, a single parent, a labor organizer, a Communist, a lesbian, and now as a senior citizen, she has often been stigmatized as a member of a minority, as abnormal, deviant, or marginal. Throughout the course of her story, "not fitting in" emerges as a significant pattern: "Because I was third from the oldest," she explains, "I could never find a place for myself in the family." Gerry presents her sense of "otherness" as an important factor that shaped her identity: "[In school] I was discriminated against and lost, too. I never seemed to find a place for myself, I was always an outsider."

Ultimately, however, Gerry sees her otherness not only as deviance from or defiance of an establishment order, but as the fulfillment of her own pattern, of being true to the uniqueness of her life's course. As she tells her life story, Gerry transforms the adversities that attend her marginal status into virtues. In the end, being different emerges as a source of pride:

> [I was] a person who felt like such an outcast—because remember, in those days we [lesbians and gays] carried guilt, we carried embarrassment, we carried shame, we carried isolation, and all of the ugliness that society heaped on my kind of people—gay people—and we internalized it all to such a degree that it made us sneaky. . . . And my life was lived that way for a long time, until I realized . . . that I'm a person, I'm a wonderful person, I'm a very unique woman.

The most striking example of her transformation of apparent adversities into strengths is found in Gerry's story of her interview with the FBI. In relating this episode, Gerry vividly demonstrates how she has used her mind as a weapon in fighting the battle of "not fitting in":

> The very first question they asked me was, "On your application for the various jobs you've held on the WPA, you put down that you went to Hunter [College] for a year, and you got your B.A. . . . and then you took other courses. . . . But on your civil service application you said that you had only one year of high school—which is true?" I said, "Which was notarized?" "The

civil service application," they answered. I said, "Well, that was true." "Can you tell us why you found it necessary to do that?" I said, "The answer's very simple: I passed every test that was given to me for all of the jobs I held on the WPA. I just felt myself too qualified to clean toilets on the WPA." And that was my answer. Then they asked me, "Do you know Arnold Schwartz?" I said, "Oh yes, I know him very well." "Do you know that he's a member of the Communist Party?" I said, "Oh no, he can't be, he's such a nice man." They said, "Have you ever seen him with the *Daily Worker?*" I said, "Sure, we all read the *Daily Worker,* the *Daily News, The New York Times* . . ."

Despite the fact that the FBI succeeded in denying Gerry her much-needed civil service job, she tells the story as her triumph over the agents and the "establishment" world that they represent. It was a contest of wits, not of power, and she outwitted the FBI, avoiding incriminating either herself or others.

As I spent more time with Gerry, I learned that both her life story and her understanding of her experiences were more complex. When I met with Gerry again in January 1987, I was surprised to find her in a bad mood. She'd had a falling out with a former lover and friend of many years. She explained:

I'm glad you came, because [now] I have somebody to talk to. There's nobody in this house I could talk to about this. There's nobody in SAGE that this woman, Gerry Faier, who's liked and known by hundreds of people, is going to sit down with and say, "I'm lonely, I'm desperate, I need help . . ." I don't know. I just don't want to do it. It's a matter of personal conceit or something. It's a self-defeating position. But I can't bring myself to do that.

Loneliness was much on Gerry's mind that day. As she elaborated on the subject, it appeared to me that her loneliness was the darker consequence of her independence, of her having chosen to be true to her different, distinctive self. This choice has generated great strength and self-reliance, but it has also made for challenging relations with peers, friends, lovers, and family. Gerry observed:

[My friend and I] have grown so far apart, there is not even a reason for retaining a friendship, except the history we have together. And you know, I wouldn't be surprised if I'm not alone, if many men and women of my age find themselves in the same position, where they take different paths from the people that they have cared about and loved, they lose that common interest—and all of a sudden, they find themselves friendless. It doesn't seem to have any point to the story of my life, but I think that is the story of my life, Jeff. My children know about me, so they think I'm busy all the time, they don't bother me, I don't bother them. They don't even invite me to their affairs anymore. My daughter and I are just good acquaintances, my son claims to love me, but he's busy upstate . . . I love him very much, but *fun der vaytns* [from afar], I don't bother him too much.

Being a lesbian and a Jew figured prominently in our discussions about family relationships. Gerry experiences the problems of family fragmentation and assimilation that trouble many American Jews. In addition, she sees her being gay as a factor that has complicated her relationship with her family and played a role in her further estrangement from her Jewish identity. During our first session, she explained:

I was completely isolated [from my Jewishness], it had absolutely no part in my life at all. I put it behind me, my children were raised willy-nilly—no religion at all. They knew that their mother was Jewish, but my son was never bar mitzvahed. My daughter was in love and living with a *sheygets,* and I found myself in absolutely no position to tell my daughter that this is wrong—I'm a lesbian. How can I tell my daughter she can't live with the man she loves?

Gerry feels a sense of responsibility to be as tolerant of her children as they have been of her. She also has, however, a full awareness of her own feelings of frustration and guilt regarding her family's fate. She is anxious to have the story of her life documented for her great-grandchildren:

I want them to know that their great-grandmother was a lesbian, that she was a Jew. What if one of them is an anti-Semite? I feel that my sense of connection [to my Jewish past] stops with me somehow, because of the [children's] intermarriage. My son would ask me on Rosh Hashanah, "Is today some kind of a Jewish holiday?" And I tell him, "Yes." He's fifty-five years old, am I going to start educating him?

When I asked Gerry if she knew of any people from earlier generations who were homosexual, she told me a story about her father's cousin, Chaim, and another Jewish immigrant, nicknamed Potchiaye, who both worked as painters for her father. Gerry recalls that when she was a young girl the two men left their wives and children and "set up housekeeping" together. Years later, she remembers, the subject came up in a family discussion:

We were in my father's house, and we were talking about— we didn't call it "homosexuals" or "gay"—we were talking about "queers." I told them what I remembered of Chaim and Potchiaye. And my brother said, "That's right. Certainly, he was queer. That's right." A heated discussion ensued; my father came into the room and said, "What are you talking?" My brother said, "Poppa, is it true that Chaim was a fairy?" My father said, "A fairy, *vos meysntu* [what do you mean], a fairy?"—and my younger sister said, "*A timtam mit an oyringl* [a queer with an earring]." My father used to call them that. Well, my father stood up and spat; he said, "*Tfu!* In our family that never was," and he stormed out of the room. And my mother said, "Maybe, maybe *er is take geven* [he really was]." My mother was a socially and sexually naive woman. She had eleven kids, probably never found out where they came from. No one in my family knew about my being gay at the time. I was already living with Ginnie, the first woman in my life, and a sister of mine said, "You know, Mama, there are even women like that." "*Vos meynstu*, women like that?" "Well, there are women—you know, they live together as husband and wife. One goes to work, one stays home and does the cleaning, and one does this, and one does that—" And my mother, in all her naivete, said, "*Beser azoy. Beser* [Better that way. Better] than they should live with bums." So that's the story of my cousin Chaim, who was gay. You see, there's one in every family, and one in every generation. But I'll never forget my mother's interpretation—"Better they should live like that, than with bums." To my mother, you see, you were bums, you were tramps, if you lived with a person of the opposite sex out of marriage. I used to laugh about that, and I used to say—when I stood in a gay bar and looked in the mirror, with all these women dancing and standing around—"If my mother could see me now, she would say, *'Beser azoy*—rather than with a whole lot of bums around.'"

Gerry presents Chaim and Potchiaye as ancestors who prefigure and legitimate her gayness ("there's one in every family"). And in recalling her mother's verdict on such relationships—*"beser azoy"*—Gerry invokes a blessing on her life-style.

During this session Gerry and I also talked about the years after she came out and returned to New York City, a subject she did not discuss in any depth when we had first met:

Well, what I remember of that period—most of it is very uninteresting. I hung out in bars. I met women. I was never promiscuous; I was always very selective. I was never very popular. Selection was very easy, somehow—I mean, nobody ever broke my door down or came over to me and said, "What's your telephone number? You're a fascinating woman, I want to see you again—" That never happened. I would always have to make the first approach to anyone I wanted to get to know at these bars. I'll tell you the very first time I walked into a gay bar by myself . . . I came back to New York, and I knew the gay bars were on Thompson Street. Well, I wore brown shoes and a brown bag and gloves, I was dressed up like Astor's pet horse, and I tried to go into this gay bar where there were a whole lot of leather-jacketed dykes—in those days, if you were gay, you were either "butch" or "fem." Well, I wasn't either, because I didn't know what I was—"butch," "fem"—I didn't know from that; I still don't. I walked right in, without turning my eyes to the right or the left; I walked to the far end of the bar and I stood there—I was afraid to pick up my head, I was afraid to look around. I didn't know what to do, I was scared stiff . . .

Gerry also spoke of her politicization during the era of the gay liberation movement. Political activism, which had been an important part of her life during the Depression, has also played a critical role in Gerry's coming to terms with her lesbian identity, and, more generally, her sense of being different. She described the impact that the organized political activity of lesbians and gays during the late sixties and seventies had on her life:

> I was not a run-of-the-mill woman of sixty—I was unique, I was different. And that difference made me very, very proud, as soon as I realized I'd never really struggled against my gayness— I embraced it from the beginning.

New York's gay synagogue, Congregation Beth Simchat Torah, served as a catalyst for Gerry's personal reconciliation with her Jewish identity, though she is not a regular worshipper there:

> When I discovered the gay synagogue, I realized that these men who were performing the service were so knowledgeable in such a wonderful way, and they were able to bring . . . *yidishkeyt* back to me, a person who felt like an outcast. I have all this tremendous background, a whole lineage of people behind me, a knowledge of all these things that, when I have to solve a problem or tell somebody something, I realize [come from] my Jewish background.

Gerry's Jewish identity is not a conventional "religious" one, but a strong, personal devotion to her Jewish cultural heritage, embodied in Jewish books and the Yiddish language, as well as in its distinctive values—what she refers to as *yidishkeyt*.

Now Gerry herself has become a source of inspiration for others. She often invokes her life story when speaking publicly for SAGE about the needs of older lesbians and gay men. Telling her personal history has become a political act. Gerry is aware of the power that her personal experiences can have in a public forum, and she tailors her life story to suit different audiences. In doing so, she also continues to take life experiences that she initially saw as liabilities and transform them into assets, sources of power:

> When I speak for SAGE . . . I skim over the part of my life until the age of thirty-nine. And then I [tell people that] when I first realized that I was gay, the only place where I could meet friends and people like myself were in the gay bars. It was only later on, after Stonewall . . . that we began to feel some identification with people who had the "same sexual proclivities that you had." And it was only after that you began to realize that being

gay was a political thing, too. We have to fight that kind of discrimination and educate homophobic people . . .

If I speak in front of professional people, like social workers,
who are trying to learn more about homosexuality, I take a different vein. I show them—here, I'm a woman of seventy-eight.
Five, six years ago I was an old lady. I was aging rapidly, sitting
in a rocking chair, wondering where my next lover was coming
from. But now, six, seven years later, I'm sixty-five again, you
see?—with hope in my heart, my expectations are no longer
fantasies, they're expectations—but that can turn out to be a lot
of bullshit, too, you know. That is me only on certain days, let's
say, when I feel good, when I'm not constipated. When I feel
good, then my talk is optimistic and high, with a great deal of
promise and educational value for the people to whom I'm
speaking.

Gerry's story is a rich legacy—not only for her family and friends,
but for the many others to whom she has told it. For lesbian and gay
Jews it is especially valuable, offering a chronicle of one person's coming to terms with the complexities of these two identities. Gerry's life
gives those of us who are her spiritual grandchildren and great-grandchildren a sense of history, of ties that can cross generational lines.

I have been particularly moved by Gerry's courage to pursue her
life's challenges over these many years. It is a process in which she
continues to engage, sometimes accepting the possibility of desires
that may be unattainable and conflicts that may prove irreconcilable.
At the conclusion of one of our visits, Gerry observed that though her
political activism:

has turned me into a very proud, unembarrassed person, nevertheless I don't want the women in this building to know [that
I'm a lesbian]. So still, no matter what happens, no matter how
open we are, we will always be closeted. Except maybe, Jeff,
when you reach my age, maybe it will be a different world.

PART 3

....

Honoring Our Relationships

INTRODUCTION

LESBIAN AND GAY LIBERATION, ALONG WITH FEMINISM, HAS PERMA-
nently transformed our understanding of interpersonal relations. For
example, we no longer assume that two people of the same sex are
"just friends," or that it requires two people of the opposite sex related by marriage to parent. In the majority culture, as well as in the
Jewish, lesbian, and gay subcultures, the rules that govern interpersonal relationships of all kinds are now characterized by extraordinary flexibility and diversity.

Nowhere is this flexibility more apparent than in lesbian and gay
culture. The fact that laws and social conventions which govern heterosexual relationships don't also apply to lesbian and gay relationships has encouraged lesbians and gay men to rethink every aspect of
our relationships, from sexual monogamy to child rearing.

To begin this section, Martha Ackelsberg examines assumptions
about traditional Jewish family relations, including assumptions that
families are, and have always been, composed of two heterosexual
adults and their children by birth, that they last forever, and that they
meet the needs of all their members. Ackelsberg analyzes the ways in
which lesbian and gay relationships challenge traditional notions
about family life and contribute to the Jewish future.

Ackelsberg's essay provides a theoretical overview. Others in this
section offer highly personal accounts of changing relationships:
Agnes Herman writes about coming to terms with her son's gay identity; Paul Horowitz and Scott Klein describe their ceremony of commitment; and Linda Holtzman writes of life as a lesbian mother.

Finally, Judith Plaskow challenges readers to rethink Jewish views
of sexuality, traditionally based on assumptions of inequality between men and women, and on assumptions that sexuality is a force

that must be controlled by channeling it into procreation. Instead, she argues for a theology of sexuality based on values of mutuality, equality, and embodiment of the divine.

Each essay in this section represents a fundamental challenge to the primacy of biological definitions of sexual and family life. Each suggests new, more inclusive definitions of both. As we reconceptualize the family in more inclusive terms, we find many reasons for optimism.

Lesbian and gay Jews live in a variety of sexual and family arrangements, and we are enriched by this variety. In selecting essays for this section, we do not intend to assert the value of one form of relationship over others. Rather, we call readers' attention to the values typified by each.

Redefining Family:
Models for the Jewish Future

....

Martha A. Ackelsberg

If "Judaism" and "families" are often taken to be syn-onymous,[1] "gay families" or "lesbian families" are often taken to be inconceivable. If there is one thing that most heterosexual people think they know about gays and lesbians, it's that "they don't marry and have children"—a statement that presupposes that families are created by legal marriage, preferably followed by children. In fact, it is the presumed contradiction between homosexuality and "family life" that many liberal Jews point to as the chief obstacle to full acceptance of gays and lesbians in the Jewish community.[2]

The reality, of course, is that if we define families more flexibly, we find that lesbians and gays create and participate in a wide range of familial relationships. We think of families as fulfilling a number of specific functions—as the prime contexts in which people meet some basic human needs.[3] One thing we expect from families is compan-ionship and emotional intimacy: the common perception (both in the United States generally, and in the Jewish community more specifi-cally) is that "singleness" is a state of alienation and isolation to be overcome through marriage. In addition to providing for emotional intimacy, families are also the units that we expect to support us eco-nomically: mutual economic interdependence is presumed to be one of the core benefits of family life. Third, we look to families as con-texts for child-bearing and child-rearing, and, particularly within the Jewish community, as the contexts in and through which we fulfill our obligation to contribute to the continuity of the community and the tradition.

Like most people, Jewish lesbians and gay men seek relationships of intimacy, economic support, and ways to contribute to the continuity of our own and our people's traditions. Many seek to form intimacy constellations that look very much like heterosexual families—except that both adult partners are the same sex. Others have established more communal or collective living arrangements. Still others may be living alone, or at least not with any particular significant other on a committed basis, whether by choice or circumstance. In short—as is the case with heterosexual Jews—gay, lesbian, and bisexual Jews have found a variety of ways to live out personal and social commitments in the world. Nevertheless, because of relatively limited notions of what constitutes "a family" and of what place "families" hold in Jewish tradition, many Jews—and most of the major organizations and institutions of the Jewish community—either ignore the existence of gay and lesbian Jewish families or imply that to acknowledge our existence would be to undermine the long-term continuity of the community.

Interestingly, though consistent with this posture, most discussions in the Jewish community about the "crisis of the family" proceed without mention of lesbians and gays. The focus tends to be on late marriage, "singles," high levels of intermarriage, low levels of Jewish affiliation, high divorce rates, or some combination of the above. I believe that gay and lesbian Jews—and the variety of intimacy constellations we have created—have much to offer current thinking about the "Jewish family." In this essay, I explore the varieties of Jewish family life and the place of families in the Jewish tradition.[4] I look specifically at the politics of families—the nature and consequences of the ideological use of family in the Jewish community, what it might mean to open up that definition, and the potential contribution gay and lesbian families make to strengthening the Jewish community.

Changing Families: Demography and Ideology

There has been a great deal of discussion in recent years—both in the Jewish community and in the secular world—about changes in families and what those changes mean for the viability of "traditional values," for social stability, and for the future of the Jewish community. These discussions have taken place in response both to demographic changes affecting the society at large and to feminist critiques of power relations within traditional family structures. Political debates have often struck a fearful, if not hysterical tone—suggesting the dire consequences that may follow from the decline in "traditional family life and values." These fears have been as loudly, if not more loudly, voiced within the Jewish community, which has held to the notion that family is the center of our community and tradition. If traditional families are in danger, the future of Judaism, too, is under threat.[5]

Demographically, compared to the 1940s and 1950s (the most common benchmark of the "good old days"), Jewish families have changed along with other families in the culture, although at a somewhat slower rate. More people are marrying later or not at all. Many of those who do marry choose non-Jewish partners. A significant proportion of marriages are ending in divorce, and many children are growing up in other than two-parent households, or, at least, not with the two adults who are their biological parents. Poverty is on the increase, especially among women and their dependent children. Over half of all adult women are now part of the paid labor force. Taken together, what these changes mean is that a decreasing percentage of the U.S.population lives in a "traditional" heterosexually constructed nuclear family, where the father works outside the home and the mother stays home to tend the house and raise the children. In general, the trends for Jewish families are changing in directions similar to American families as a whole, although with some significant differences. Overall, Jews marry a bit later, have somewhat smaller families, and divorce somewhat less frequently than Protestants or Catholics of similar educational and social class backgrounds.[6]

At the same time that we are experiencing significant demographic change, we live in an era of important ideological change, characterized both by criticisms of the actual functioning of real families and, at the same time, by nostalgia for the "family that was." Many yearn for the family of "Father Knows Best" and "Leave It to Beaver" or, in the Jewish context, of *Life Is with People*[7] and "Fiddler on the Roof."

On one side of the ideological divide, many feminists point to the ways in which families restrain, limit, and disempower women and children, while masking the inequalities of power in the name of love. For love, women are supposed to deny their own aspirations; for love, women are supposed to accept economic dependence and the emotional and sometimes physical abuse that accompanies it. This is not to say that all families are abusive, nor is it to say that we don't need relationships of mutual interdependence. It is to suggest, however, that what is ideologically defined as a system of love and mutual interdependence is often lacking in true mutuality, to the particular detriment of women and children.[8] Further, this ideological use of the word "family" leads us to believe that the traditionally constructed nuclear family is the only context for meeting a variety of crucial economic, social, and interpersonal needs, and it blinds us to the ways other forms may achieve the same ends.[9]

On the other side of the ideological divide are those who maintain nostalgia for a past when relationships were simple and straightforward, and marriages were forever. That idealized past, however, never really existed. The differences between our current situation and that of the late nineteenth century, for example, are considerably less than might appear. Today we decry high rates of divorce and the large numbers of children growing up without both parents present; but rates of marital dissolution and the average length of marriage were almost identical 75 and 100 years ago—only then, the primary causes of dissolution were death of a partner, desertion, or the dislocations of emigration and immigration. In fact, as sociologist Andrew Cherlin has argued, the middle-class, single-earner, married-forever family of the 1950s, often taken as the benchmark for contemporary debates, is more a deviation from a trend than the representation of a timeless form.[10]

Finally, the ideology of families defines them excessively narrowly. When we hear the word "family," most U.S. citizens—regardless of the interpersonal constellation in which they are living—tend to think in terms of census definitions: two or more persons living together, related by blood or marriage. Large numbers of people, however, are living in constellations which they experience and define as "familial," but which do not fit this definition. Gay or lesbian couples living together—some of whom are raising children together—do not constitute families under this definition; nor do unmarried heterosexual couples living together, with or without children; and neither do elderly couples who may choose not to marry for reasons related to tax liabilities or Social Security benefits. Defining families in terms of the "two biological parents and kids" model marginalizes not only singles, single parents, and the divorced, but also an unknown number of people whose relationships of intimacy and community do not fit the normative stereotype. And it blinds us to the ways in which these relationships meet precisely the same needs that traditional families are supposed to meet.

Families, Intimacy, and Jewish Tradition

Families—of whatever sort—exist and function within a larger social, political, and economic context that can greatly affect their ability to fulfill the functions we assign to them: for intimacy, for economic support, and for passing on tradition. Both historical and contemporary evidence makes clear that, when they must rely completely on their own resources, a significant proportion of heterosexual nuclear families are unable to meet the needs of their members for emotional, physical, or economic support. The existence of *chevrei kadisha, hachnasat kallah* groups, and the myriad of other charitable Jewish communal organizations[11] that flourished in the shtetls of Eastern Europe or among immigrants to the United States serve as evidence of the Jewish community's recognition that families cannot always support their members. And they attest to the assumption of a *communal* responsibility to meet the needs of individual Jews.

In addition to noting that even traditional families cannot always provide for their members without considerable communal support, it is also important to recognize that intimacy constellations other than traditional families often meet very similar sorts of needs—especially given the appropriate communal context. Thus, many people find satisfying emotional relationships outside of marriage—in gay or lesbian relationships, by living together in unmarried heterosexual relationships, in collective living arrangements, or through relationships with close friends. Friends and/or communal groups may well help to sustain such relationships economically. And, of course, many people raise children without a legal spouse, or in the context of a gay or lesbian family. And many have found ways—other than by having children—to express their generativity and contribute to the vitality and continuity of the Jewish community as teachers, social workers, or youth group leaders, to name a few. In short, many of the values associated with families have been and continue to be realized in a variety of contexts other than the traditional nuclear family. I want to argue here, in fact, that there are specific resources that gay and lesbian relationships may offer to the Jewish community.

Jewish Families, Gay Families, and the Jewish Future

Gay and lesbian families come in all shapes and sizes. Some are constructed along the lines of heterosexual nuclear families—two adults in a committed relationship, and their associated children—except that the two adults are the same sex. Some may consist of an adult parent and her or his children, without an adult lover present. In other cases, because so many lesbians and gays have been married, had children in those marriages, and now "share" them with an ex-spouse in some form of joint custody, lesbian or gay households will sometimes have children present and sometimes not. In their variety, gay and lesbian families do not differ significantly from heterosexual families.

Nevertheless, some differences do exist, and many of these differences open new possibilities for the Jewish community at the same time that they challenge deeply held values and commitments.

Challenging Homophobia One difference is that gay and lesbian families do not share in heterosexual privilege, and family members are subject to homophobia. On the surface, one might argue that homophobia and heterosexism are not of great consequence to those already in relationships: If we have our love for one another, what difference does it make if that love is validated by others? But if that were so, if we could all live without social validation and recognition, why would so many go through the formalities of (heterosexual) marriage?

Of course, there are immediate benefits of marriage—and, conversely, disadvantages of being excluded from the category of legal family. Many of these are fairly obvious: the inability to claim and publicly celebrate those relationships most central to one's being; denial of "family memberships," whether in a museum or a synagogue; not being sure of having access to a partner in case he or she is hospitalized; fear of losing one's children in a custody battle, or of not being able to continue a relationship with the children of a lover, should the lover die.

But many of the consequences of living in a heterosexist society are much less obvious. Most significant, perhaps, is that the expectations and social supports that help to sustain many heterosexual families through the vagaries of interpersonal conflict and familial tension are largely absent for gay and lesbian households. In many areas of the country—and in most Jewish communities, in particular—few resources are available if a lesbian or gay couple runs into trouble and wishes to seek counseling. While there is a clear commitment on the part of most Jewish communal organizations to help families sustain themselves, that commitment has rarely—if ever—been extended, nor have resources knowingly been made available, to gay and lesbian families. When we are victims of homophobia on the streets, at work, in school, or in the synagogue, there are, in most cases, no Jewish communal organizations to come to our aid. And when our children have to confront homophobia, whether from their peers or from adults, there are no resources in the Jewish community to which they can turn. Homophobia saps the strength of gays and lesbians and makes the sustaining of long-term commitments, which are already extremely tenuous in our society, even more difficult. No matter how inadequate the social supports are for families in general (and there is much our communities need to be doing in this regard), they are even less available to lesbians and gays.

Homophobia and heterosexism affect heterosexuals as well as lesbians and gays, locking us all into confining sex-roles and behaviors out of fear that we might be labeled "queer." Addressing those issues head-on within the Jewish community would free up *all* members of the community to live in ways more expressive of their full selves. Further, it would mean making counseling and other support services available not only to those in gay or lesbian families, but also to those struggling with issues concerning sexual orientation, thus overcoming the isolation of many individuals and families within the community, and opening the community to many who now avoid it for fear of rejection. Heterosexual families as well as gay and lesbian families would benefit from the infusion of energy that attention to such issues could entail.

Sexual Equality A second way that gay and lesbian families differ from traditional heterosexual families is in the sexual equality built into their structure. We live in a male-dominant society, which means that, even with the best of egalitarian intentions, the average heterosexual family must continually struggle against male dominance and conventional sex-role definitions and expectations. It is the rare heterosexual family, for example, in which the woman does not feel some greater responsibility for child-rearing or for the administration of the home. But in a gay or lesbian family, everything is potentially "up for grabs"; all aspects of the relationship are on the table to be negotiated. That is not to say that there are no roles in gay or lesbian families. But it is to say that the organization of the relationship and of family life must be arranged more self-consciously: rather than beginning with a built-in *inequality* constructed by societal expectations, gay and lesbian relationships begin (at least potentially) from a position of relative *equality* between the partners. The implications of that difference are, conceivably, far-reaching.

In fact, without idealizing the realities of gay and lesbian families and relationships, the egalitarian aspects of these relationships provide important models for heterosexual families. One of the main components of the feminist critique of traditional families has been the way they participate in, and reinforce, the societal dominance of men over women. Much of the contemporary debate over families is constructed precisely around the issue of equality/inequality and of what happens when women insist on full equality with men in all aspects of familial life. The conservative position, of course, is that families will not be able to sustain the strain: that someone must be the head, and that, given the organization of our society, it makes sense for that someone to be the male. The spate of recent books on "women who love too much" suggests, even more specifically, that intimacy between men and women is possible only in a context of inequality (where the man does the economic work, and the woman does the emotional work). The existence of gay and lesbian families can serve as a useful corrective.

Fully incorporating lesbian and gay families into the community requires thinking clearly and creatively *as a community* about what it would take to sustain families and the community on a truly egalitarian basis. As I have suggested, many of the fears of gay and lesbian relationships—and, in fact, of the feminist critique of families and tradition—expressed within the Jewish community are rooted in the presumption that Judaism is based not just on families, but on families constructed on the basis of sexual inequality. Feminists have been challenging that presumption for years, demanding from the community that it provide what is necessary to support and sustain more egalitarian family constellations (e.g., communally sponsored day care, child care at synagogues, flextime schedules, and so forth). If Jewish communities began to meet these needs on a broad scale, the benefits would accrue to a very wide range of people, including single parents, lesbian and gay families, and feminists of whatever familial constellation, removing some of the major obstacles that have prevented women from full participation in the workforce or the community. In this area of concern, in particular, it seems to me, what is good for gays and lesbians is good for the Jewish community.

Intergenerational Continuity Third, although many gay and lesbian families consist of children as well as adults, many others do not. For those lesbians and gays who do not have children from heterosexual relationships, the decision about whether or how to become parents is much more complex than it is for the average heterosexual couple. Some lesbians and gays are attempting to construct families with children more or less on the nuclear family model: that is, by adopting children, becoming foster parents, or attempting to have children by "alternative methods"—lesbians, often through artificial insemination; gay men, by agreement with a woman who will bear a child for them.[12]

Here, again, I think that the experience and practices of gay and lesbian Jewish families can be a helpful model for others and can expand the range of alternatives and perceptions common in the heterosexual Jewish community. Judaism has long recognized that generativity comes in many forms and guises. As Susan Handelman has noted, "Jewish tradition holds that one who teaches another's child is as if s/he gave birth to that child."[13] Teachers, community leaders, those who care for the young, the old, the sick, all make their contribution to the vitality and continuity of the community. Gays and lesbians have long been active (although all-too-often closeted!), both in the Jewish community and in the larger secular world, as teachers, social service workers, and community supporters. They have made major contributions to culture and to religious life as rabbis, cantors, artists, songwriters, poets, writers, and critics. All of these are models for contributing to the continuity of the community—models that could be followed by heterosexual as well as nonheterosexual people, with or without children. Expanding our notion of what constitutes generativity can only benefit all of us.

Sexual Ethics Finally, another difference between heterosexual families and gay and lesbian families is the centrality of monogamy. "Sexual fidelity" (which tends to be interpreted to mean: no sex with anyone other than one's marital partner) is one of the cornerstones of heterosexual marriage, even though it may be a value honored more often in the breach than in the observance. However, as many critics pointed out in the early days of the feminist movement, the demand for sexual fidelity has its roots in male control of female sexuality—a control that feminists, as well as gays and lesbians, reject. Consequently, sexual fidelity has not always been a value in the gay or lesbian communities. Some gay men, for example, have argued that gay sexuality is positively antithetical to monogamy, though attitudes and sexual practices have been profoundly affected by the AIDS crisis. Much data on gay male relationships suggest that long-term commitments are not necessarily incompatible with short-term affairs. Lesbians who challenge monogamy do so in a rather different way, often blurring the lines between "friend" and "lover," and attempting to sustain more than one (sexually) intimate relationship at a time. And some people, of course, attempt to maintain both gay or lesbian and heterosexual relationships at the same time, whether as part of a single familial constellation, or in the context of two semi-independent relationships. The possibilities are manifold. While I am not arguing for non-monogamy, it is important to note that many gay familial relationships stand as a challenge to the conventional view that a long-term commitment to intimacy is incompatible with "sexual infidelity."

Many people (whether in the Jewish community or outside of it) find the explicit rejection of sexual monogamy on the part of some gays and lesbians very threatening. While I find fidelity and monogamy to be compelling values, I think the challenges posed by alternative ways of structuring relationships can be instructive and creative. They force us all to think about the meaning of sex and sexuality in our lives and in our relationships and also to explore the boundaries and intersections between friendship and love. While there are, no doubt, those within the gay or lesbian community who deny any significant moral component to these choices (as there are such people within the heterosexual community), my concern here is with those who recognize and value intimacy and commitment and, at the same time, insist that the forms we have to express them are not the only ones possible—or even desirable. Serious, respectful dialogue among people holding—and living out—different views on these issues might enable all of us to come to a deeper, and more self-conscious understanding of the strengths and limits of our own values and practices.

It is too early, at this point, to say just what full inclusion of gay and lesbian families would mean for the Jewish community. Obviously, before that vision becomes a reality, we have much work to do in reconceptualizing families and their place within the Jewish community. Although such a process might well strike fear in the hearts of many, the potential benefits—not just to gays and lesbians and their children, but to the community as a whole—are enormous. We have the potential not only to incorporate into the community thousands of people who have felt alienated or excluded, but to draw on the variety of our experiences to enrich the lives of each of us and of the Jewish community.

A Parent's Journey out of the Closet

....

Agnes G. Herman

WHEN WE AGREED TO ADOPT SEVEN-MONTH-OLD JEFF, WE KNEW that his life as a member of a Jewish family would begin the moment we brought him to our home. We celebrated that joyous homecoming with appropriate religious ritual, with blessings recited by Jeff's rabbi father as our gurgling, happy baby teethed on his infant kiddush cup and enjoyed his challah. There, in the warmth of our extended family circle of grandparents, an aunt, an uncle, and the Temple Board, our small son passed comfortably through his bris, his initial Jewish milestone. There would be many more.

By the time he was two, Jeff ate an ice cream cone without spilling a drop; his face came out of the sticky encounter clean. At five, he watched other kids play ball in the alley, standing aside because he had been told not to play there. Besides, he seemed more comfortable playing with the little girl next door. There were awkward moments as he began to grow up, such as the times when the baseball bat, which his father insisted upon, was not comfortable in his hands, but the rolling pin, which his father decried, was. His grandmother, whom he adored, remarked, "Jeff is too good."

I knew she was right, and privately I felt a nagging fear I could hardly express to myself. Was Jeff a "sissy"? That archaic term was the only one I dared whisper to myself. "Gay" only meant "lively and fun-loving"; "homosexual" was a label not to be used in polite society and certainly never to be mentioned in the same sentence with a child's name. Such a term would certainly stigmatize a youngster and humiliate a family.

Jeff continued to be an eager volunteer in the kitchen and a reluctant participant on the ballfield. We fought the former and pressed to correct the latter, frustrating our son while we all grew tense. As to our silent fears, we repressed them.

Jeff developed reading problems in school. We worried, but accepted the inappropriate assurance offered by his teacher: "He is such a good boy—don't confuse him with counseling." We bought it, for a while. As the reading problems continued, Jeff did enter therapy and was helped to become less anxious and learn how to read all over again. At our final parental consultation with the psychiatrist, I hesitantly asked, "Doctor, I often worry that Jeff is effeminate. What do you think?" I held my breath while he offered his reassurance: "There is nothing wrong with your son. He is a sensitive boy—not aggressive or competitive. So he likes girls! In a few years you will be worrying about that for other reasons."

Jeff looked forward eagerly to religious school. He accompanied his dad, helped around the temple, and received many kudos. He was quick, efficient, and willingly took instructions. In later years, even after his father was no longer in the pulpit, Jeff continued his role as a temple volunteer. He moved chairs and carried books; later, he changed fuses, focused spotlights, and handled sound equipment. Jeff was comfortable; it was "his" temple. Other children there shared his interests and became his friends, later forming the temple youth group.

Bar mitzvah class, however, was a difficult obstacle. When Hebrew became a daily family battle, we withdrew him from Hebrew school to be tutored instead by his father. He spent a substantial amount of time, which otherwise was not available, with his dad. As a result, a potential failure was transformed into another family milestone. Jeff yawned his way through formal bar mitzvah training, but when his big day arrived, he was prepared, and pleased even himself.

During confirmation and youth group years, Jeff seemed to be struggling to be like his peers. Temple became the center of his life. He worked and played there, dated, went steady, and attended meetings and dances. He shared with no one—not his parents, his friends, or his rabbi—his own feelings of being "different."

When Jeff was sixteen, we moved from New Rochelle to Los Angeles. It was a difficult move for him, cutting off relationships and sources of recognition and acceptance. As we settled into our new home, Jeff began to explore the San Fernando Valley, enrolled in high

school, and tried to make new friends. At our insistence, he attended
one meeting of the local temple youth group, but felt rejected by the
youngsters there. That marked the unfortunate beginning of Jeff's dis-
enchantment with synagogues and withdrawal from family religious
observances and celebrations.

Jeff gradually acclimated to his new environment. He took Amy, a
Jewish girl his own age, to the senior prom; he cruised Van Nuys Boulevard on Wednesdays with Ann. He was always on the move—coming home to eat, shower, change clothes, and zip out again. We blamed
it on the fast pace of California and the novelty of having his own
"wheels": first a motorcycle, and then a car. There were several acci-
dents—none serious, thank heavens! Again, in retrospect, the furious
struggle with his identity must have played a part in his fast-paced
behavior. At the time, though, we buried our heads in the sand, believing that Jeff was merely behaving like every other teenager.

After high school, the pace seemed to slow down a bit. So when Jeff
was nineteen and we decided to leave him in charge for the six months
of our sabbatical world tour, we had no hesitation. Conscientious and
cautious, he could handle the cars and the checkbook. He would continue in college and be available to his sister Judi, also attending college. We flew off to Europe and Israel, confident and secure.

When an overseas call came three months later in Jerusalem, my
heart beat fast, and my sense of well-being faltered slightly. "Everything is fine, no problem. I have quit college. Now don't get excited . . . I want to go to business school and study interior design. Jobs are plentiful; I know a guy who will hire me the minute I
graduate."

Jeff had always shown a creative flair for color and design. He constantly rearranged our furniture, changing one room after another.
All this raced through my mind as I held the phone, separated from
him by 9,000 miles. Erv and I looked at each other, wished Jeff luck,
and told him to write the check for his tuition.

When we finally returned home, Jeff was obviously depressed. His
answers to our questions were surly, clipped, and evasive. Behaving
unlike his usual loving self, he ran in and out of the house silently,
furtively, always in a hurry. He seemed uninterested in our trip and
was clearly trying to avoid us.

One day during Passover, Erv was searching for a favorite cantorial
record that Jeff often appropriated. He checked Jeff's record collection

and poked about among the torn jeans. Speechless and ashen, Erv returned to the breakfast room and dropped a book into my lap: *Homosexuality in Modern Society*. "This was hidden in Jeff's room." My heart raced and skipped. Confrontation was finally at hand, not only with Jeff, but with my own fears as well.

Then our son came through the front door on the run: "I'm late . . . can't stop . . . talk to you later."

The tone of our response and expressions on our faces stopped him mid-flight. "Son, stand still! Something is going on, you are not yourself! Are you in trouble? Drugs, maybe? Is one of your girlfriends pregnant? Or, are you, is it possible that you are . . . homosexual?"

I waited, trembling. The faces of my beloveds were creased with anger and worry. I could barely breathe.

"Yes, I am gay." A simple sentence, yet I did not understand. Nothing was "gay"!

We asked in unison, "What does that mean?"

"I am homosexual," he explained. After long minutes of uncomfortable conversation, we sent Jeff on his way with "we'll talk later." I ran from the room to what was to become my comfort zone, the cool tile of the bathroom floor, and I cried my eyes out. I guess Erv went to work. All we can recall now is that neither of us could face the reality right then.

That evening and the next, we did an enormous amount of soul-searching. What did I, a social worker, know about homosexuality? What did my husband, the rabbi, know? Our academic credentials were impressive—professionally we were both well-trained to help other people in pain. But in our personal distress, we felt helpless.

Everything I had ever heard about homosexuality destroyed all my dreams about our son's future. He would never marry and have children. His warmth, caring, good looks, and so many other wonderful traits would not be passed along to a son or daughter, a grandchild. We wondered whether we could keep him in our family circle, or would we lose him to "that other world" of homosexuality, a world that was foreign to us.

We wracked ourselves with self-blame—what did we do wrong? I accepted all the myths about homosexuality. First, the myth of the strong mother—I was a strong mother, but what mother doesn't over-exert her influence on her children? Second, the myth of the absent father—Erv spent so much time crisscrossing the country, berating

himself for not being at home enough. Third was the myth of seduc-
tion—had someone lured Jeff into this awful life-style? And then, finally, I believed the myth of "the cure"—that the right therapist could
change Jeff's sexual orientation.

We did seek help from a therapist. He was patient, caring, and accepting of Jeff and his life-style. He helped us begin to sort out myth
from reality and guided us through a tangled web of grief, pain, and
disappointment. He gently destroyed our unrealistic hope of "changing" Jeff. Our abiding love for our son was, of course, the key to this
difficult yet hopeful journey.

I did not like Jeff's life-style at that time, but that did not interfere
with my love for him. Understanding and acceptance gradually grew,
but the path to real comfort continued to be bumpy.

Jeff sought help, too. At nineteen, he admitted that there was much
that he wanted to know about himself. During that time, he offered a
comment that we gratefully accepted: "Please stop blaming your-
selves. It is not your fault that I have grown up gay." With those
words, Jeff erased our most devastating, yet unspoken, anxiety.

Time moved along for all of us. We grieved the loss of deeply held
expectations for our son's life. We experienced inner turmoil. Jeff
struggled to make peace with himself. We learned to support one
another.

Over time, we came to understand that a child who is homosexual
needs no less understanding, support, and acceptance than one who
is heterosexual. Clearly, our gay son has the same human needs that
his straight sister has: for empathy and patience, for security and success, for caring and love. Rejection is difficult for both our children,
yet perhaps more so for our gay child. Society has taught him that he
will experience less validation and more unnecessary pain. He, and
all of us who love him, are vulnerable to that pain.

It became clear that Jeff's sexual orientation was only one part of his
life. There remained the ordinary concerns and controversies intrinsic
to raising any child. Jeff rode the roller coaster of financial and voca-
tional problems. We provided advice, which he sometimes accepted,
and loans, which he often repaid. Jeff's married sister behaved in
much the same manner.

Jeff became ill and required the usual chicken soup and tender care
in his apartment. He preferred receiving that attention from friends,
but also expected Mother and Dad to stop by regularly with reas-

surance and love. His sister behaved the same way when she broke her leg and was living alone.

When a love affair went sour, Jeff became depressed and sad. We worried and tried to be especially sensitive to his pain. The same support was called for when his sister faced divorce with sadness and depression. We were happier when Jeff was living with a friend who cared about him and about whom he cared, and we felt the same way about his sister, now happily remarried.

During all this time, it never occurred to us to turn to the Jewish community for support, though we knew its resources well. We kept our concerns about Jeff's life-style to ourselves: we were in the closet. A child's homosexuality was not something one discussed in 1969 and throughout the 1970s. And sharing intimacies with others was not our way—these were matters we had to work out ourselves. We had decided alone, together, to marry each other; we decided alone, together, to have children. And we decided alone, together, to tough out our son's homosexuality, confront it, embrace him, and then face the world together.

I recall sitting with close friends one evening. Naturally, the conversation turned to our kids. At one point, someone said, "I think we have something in common." We all agreed, but even then, none of us could articulate it. In fact, on the way home, Erv asked, "Are you sure their oldest son is gay?"

Finally we came "halfway out," sharing only with family. We found almost unanimous acceptance; affection for Jeff did not falter. But it was seventeen long years before we went public in the Jewish community. Even during the years when my husband was deeply involved in supporting the establishment of a gay outreach synagogue in Los Angeles, when he was busy teaching others that Judaism must not turn its back on any of its children, we did not share our son's homosexuality with the Jewish public.

I "came out" for us, with Jeff's permission, in 1986, with an article in *The Reconstructionist*, a national Jewish magazine. The response was overwhelming. Support from rabbis, lay leaders, and friends poured in from around the country. Even at that late date, comfortable as we had become with Jeff's life-style, we found those messages heartwarming and reassuring.

Some of our friends were angry that we had not shared our pain with them. Perhaps we did not trust people to practice compassion and acceptance. Perhaps we did not trust them to understand that we are not failures as parents. We did not want our son to suffer rejection from those we loved. We did not want to be rejected by those we loved!

The pressure was greater on Jeff. Because he is a rabbi's child, he felt, correctly, that the expectations of him were high. Jeff was not alone in fearing the expectations of others; he had learned that sensitivity from us. Every family feels a need to be without flaws: a nonsensical, impossible attitude, but it is real. Among rabbis' families it is often exaggerated.

Should we have trusted our friends and colleagues from the beginning? Could we have dared to test the support of the synagogue leaders with whom Erv worked daily? Should we have risked our own self-image and left the closet earlier? Would any of that have made our son more comfortable at our seder table or at services? I do not have the answers. I believe we came out only when we were ready; getting ready took a long time.

There are Jewish parents who shut out their gay and lesbian children and erect a wall of alienation. There is little solace in that course of action, or in believing that their child can be "changed" to heterosexuality. Those who reject the person rather than accept the reality, or who chase fantasies rather than learning facts, deserve our compassion and understanding. It is difficult to face the disappointment, grief, and guilt that often precede true acceptance. Parents need to be helped to mourn broken dreams, to keep communication open, and to prevent love and parental devotion from being overwhelmed by pain and confusion.

Some parents actually chant Kaddish for their "wayward" children. For us, our Jewish dedication to family left no room for such behavior. Disappointment hurts, but is curable. Alienation, on the other hand, can kill relationships, love, and family. Thank God, our love—and our religious faith—did not falter.

We Jewish parents love our offspring, sometimes desperately. We can survive the shock of learning that a son is gay, or a daughter is lesbian. Eventually we can find that love will crumble the walls of alienation and that time is an ally. Our children, too, can learn to be patient with us as we grow.

Would we have done anything differently? Yes. We would have paid heed to the "flashing lights," the warnings of parenthood. We would have helped our son as early as possible to like himself and to make peace with himself. And when he did break the news to us in 1969, I wish we would have been wise enough to hug our beloved son and say, "We love you very much. Let's talk about it."

When strangers ask me today if our son is married, I do not hesitate to explain, "He is not. He is gay." We are out of the closet. It has been a long road, but well worth it.

A Ceremony of Commitment
....
Paul Horowitz and Scott Klein

ON JUNE 7, 1986, IN BROOKLYN, NEW YORK, OUR RELATIVES AND friends gathered with the two of us to honor our commitment to each other. We greeted them with the following words:

Welcome to our celebration! We're very happy you could be with us today.

This is a new experience for all of us. In preparing the ceremony that will commence the celebration, we were quite conscious both of its novelty and of how we might define what we are doing in relation to our received traditions.

The novelty, of course, arises because lesbians and gay men have rarely proclaimed their love or expressed their commitments before friends, let alone the families of their birth. On the contrary, gay people have lived in the closet, scorned alike by religion and state. We have suffered discrimination in the world of work and, all too often, rejection by family and community.

But in this century, especially since the Stonewall riot of 1969, lesbian and gay people have begun to say no to this oppression, and to affirm our self-worth, to demand the respect and recognition due us as human beings.

We believe our ceremony grows out of and contributes to this movement for self-affirmation and sexual liberation. Traditional forms can take on new meaning in a new historical and social context. As two gay men, our declaration of love before family and friends subverts the institution of marriage as it appropriates it for a new purpose.

Our own moral education began within the particular traditions, practices, and historical experience of the Jewish people, a heritage of which both of us are quite proud. In planning the ceremony, we have been especially inspired by the efforts of socialist secular Judaism and of the Reform movement to hold in dynamic tension the particular historical experience of the Jewish people on the one hand, and the imperatives of universal human liberation on the other. So we have chosen to stand under the *chuppah* and to break the glass. We have, furthermore, asked seven friends to contribute particular statements, inspired by the seven blessings in the traditional ceremony.

Our relationship is not an isolated phenomenon, but rather part of a larger social fabric, one that each of us has an obligation to sustain and nourish every day of our lives. So we want you to participate in this ceremony, as you have participated and, we hope, will continue to participate in our lives.

The Beginning

We first met in the spring of 1982. We had each been invited to a potluck dinner in a large Upper West Side Manhattan apartment. We reflected on our common Queens beginnings, our parents' ties to the secular Jewish Left, our upstate college education, and our current interests in lesbian and gay politics. We ran into each other once or twice more at these weekly dinners and then at a benefit movie screening.

On the day before New York's annual lesbian and gay pride march, we saw each other at the gay pride run in Central Park. By the time we met again on the morning of the parade, it was clear there was mutual interest. After each of us finished marching separately with our respective parents, we found each other at the post-march rally. Soon after our sexual and emotional relationship began.

At first we commuted between Manhattan and Brooklyn. A short time later we found an apartment for the two of us and faced the joys and challenges of living together.

In any relationship, gay or straight, learning to live with another person is an ongoing process of give and take, of struggle and compromise. We soon discovered that Paul was more fastidious and Scott more laid back when it came to maintaining the apartment. Scott was more committed to Jewish religious life, while Paul was more excited about holiday gatherings with family. We continued to learn about each other, to merge our possessions, and to build our lives together.

In some respects the challenge of creating a loving and thriving relationship is different for lesbians and gay men. Our generation did not grow up with visible role models of long-term gay relationships. But to our advantage, we enter our own relationships without the baggage of preordained gender roles, as each of us (in our case) is male. We had the wonderful challenge of creating our own household arrangements from scratch, and we found it easier than most straight couples to rely more on personal preferences and skills when establishing the division of labor at home. Paul does more of the cooking, Scott cleans the bathroom, and we continue to figure it out as we go along.

As we built our life together, we entertained at home and became active in the local lesbian and gay Democratic club, as well as in other political projects. We expanded each other's cultural horizons, as Paul exposed Scott to dance, and Scott exposed Paul to theater. We traveled, taking each other to our old favorite haunts while discovering new ones together.

Our friends, gay and straight, treasured getting to know us as mates. As we attended relatives' weddings, bar mitzvahs, Passover seders, and Rosh Hashanah dinners, the nature of our relationship became clear to all. Nearly all our aunts, uncles, and cousins were loving and supportive. But we wondered about the nature and depth of their apparent "acceptance." How did all these people really conceive of our relationship?

The Ceremony

We decided that a ceremony defining and declaring our relationship before family and friends would answer such questions, while giving us an unequaled opportunity to reflect on our love and commitment to each other.

We began to develop the shape of our public ritual. There are a thousand ways to be Jewish and at least a thousand more ways to be gay. We had to choose our models, invent what could not be claimed from the past, and weave it all together into some form that would be coherent to all present. Since all public ritual is at least half theater, we had the challenge of writing a play that would appeal to the matinee crowd we imagined many in our parents' generation belonged to, and would also inspire our friends in the political and cultural avant-garde. So we mixed and matched, stitching together our own ritual.

We both knew from the start that we did not want to call our ritual a "wedding." We did not want any association with an institution that was rooted in concepts of property, an institution that had oppressed women for centuries, and that still today can imply stultifying possessiveness and confining gender roles. Ironically, our involuntary position outside the law was an opportunity to stand apart from "marriage"; we took that opportunity with relish.

We immediately confronted the issue of how our ceremony would be a recognizably Jewish ritual. We knew we wished to affirm our identity as Jews as well as our identity as gay men in a loving relationship. But why proclaim our Jewishness while proclaiming our gay love for each other? Why did we want any connection at all with a tradition that is, in part, homophobic, sexist, and antisexual?

While the tradition is all of those things, it is clearly much more. For each of us, being Jewish has been crucial to the development of our ethical beliefs and our sensitivity to other human beings. For Scott, in addition, Jewish ritual has helped him to develop his sense of spirituality. Ironically, being Jewish has also made it easier for us to come to grips with some of the difficulties of being gay: being scorned and rejected, being outside the mainstream, knowing that collective cultural and political action is required to change that condition. So it was quite consistent with our understanding of our own histories and commitments that our ceremony would be Jewish.

We further recognized that our families' lingua franca for life cycle events is Judaism. Choosing to make our ceremony Jewish would make it easier for many of those present to recognize the purpose of our endeavor, especially those for whom the formal equality of gay people is still an open question.

Such questions did not apply to our immediate families, who had unhesitatingly accepted us with love and dignity. But just as the two of us continually go through a process of coming out to the world about who we are and what we mean to each other, so, too, our parents go through a process of coming out as parents of gay men. With some of their contemporaries, the Jewishness of our ceremony would help them understand the full meaning of our relationship. Our parents wanted that for us: the same public recognition and support as we would receive if each of us were straight and marrying a woman.

Another important component of our ceremony was the symbolic joining together of our two families. Traditionally weddings are occasions to make such recognition official, with both families affirming the significance of the relationship as well as affirming their willingness to support the couple through life's many problems. Both our immediate families were enthusiastic about taking on these responsibilities.

As we worked to create our ceremony, we also dealt with the many practical details faced by any other couple. We reserved a renovated space near our home, in Prospect Park, where many others had held weddings and other special events. We went through the chores of finding a caterer, picking out suits, choosing invitations and putting together a guest list. We arranged for our friend, Rabbi Yoel Kahn, to officiate at our ceremony, after he discussed our relationship with us and confirmed that it was one of love and commitment.

As the time approached, friends and family came from near and far to be with us: two friends from Mexico, Paul's brother and sister-in-law from London, an old friend from Germany. Others joined us from San Francisco, Seattle, and New Orleans. The night before the ceremony, close friends, immediate family and far-away travelers trekked to suburban New Jersey for a dinner held in our honor by Paul's sister and brother-in-law.

The day of the ceremony finally arrived. Nearly 150 relatives and friends gathered, filling the space with their presence. Some in the older generation and the extended families looked curious and ill at ease, seemingly unclear about the meaning of this ritual. On the other hand, our friends, especially our lesbian and gay friends, were already beaming with pride and anticipation, with many reflecting on whether they would ever do something like this, and how their own families would respond.

We began with the New York City Gay Men's Chorus recording of a Stephen Sondheim song, "Our Time," which speaks of the important role of those who work to change their world. Our parents and siblings entered with us, two sets of four to hold the four corners of the simple *chuppah* made from a colorful piece of fabric fastened to four wooden poles.

After brief words of welcome from Rabbi Kahn, we asked everyone to join in responsive reading woven together from the words of Walt Whitman, Harvey Milk, and the Song of Songs. The assembled throng began to read aloud:

I have perceived that to be with those I like is enough,
To stop in company with the rest at evening is enough,
To be surrounded by beautiful, curious, breathing,
    laughing flesh is enough . . .

A man's body is sacred and the woman's body is sacred,
No matter who it is, it is sacred. . . .

                              [Whitman, *Leaves of Grass*]

The voices grew stronger, and those who were comfortable from the start seemed to give strength to those who began more tentatively. By the time we reached these closing words from Harvey Milk, all discomfort and distance seemed to dissipate:

If you are not personally free to be yourself in that most important of human activities—the expression of love—then life itself loses its meaning.

Then we each spoke, recalling our meeting, the four years we had lived together and the special qualities we treasured in each other. When all the generations laughed at these words from Scott, we were warmed by the feeling that everyone was there for us, and that everyone would be there for us in the years ahead: "When we first moved in together, it was a compromise. I lived with Karl Marx and you lived with Ralph Lauren. I guess we have reached a synthesis, as I consider myself a democratic socialist and you worship Giorgio Armani."

Seven friends shared personal reflections and favorite poems with us. We shared wine, expressed our appreciation for our family and friends, and sang an old civil rights song with everyone. We remembered Paul's father and Scott's Aunt Rose, two people we loved who did not live to celebrate this special occasion with us.

When it was all over, we were mobbed by family and friends. There were tears of joy and lots of hugs. The mood was positively electric.

We had arranged for the disc jockey to play a hora, figuring that Paul and his sister Susan would dance a little, and that would be that. But to our surprise, first two, then four, then ten others joined in, until practically all 150 people were on their feet. (A photo of the two of us, lifted up in chairs by friends and dancing with the traditional napkin joining our hands in the air, appeared in the special gay pride issue of the *Village Voice* a few weeks later.) It was a wonderful feeling: everyone dancing the hora together, young and old, Jewish and gentile, gay and straight, black and white and Latino. We were high for weeks.

Later Reflections

Our relationship has continued to grow during the past three years. We have learned that a ceremony is one special moment in time which cannot possibly solve all the problems in any relationship. We have struggled not to get locked into narrow roles as a couple, and to continue to grow as individuals and be willing to allow our relationship to change, too. After such a public ceremony, we have experienced pressure to be "the perfect couple" in everyone else's eyes. We try to remain honest about our difficulties in the face of such expectations.

While our relationship is now recognized by our family and friends, we are still denied such recognition by most legal, religious, and social service institutions. Barred from the privileges usually taken for granted by heterosexual couples, we cannot include each other on employer-provided health insurance. If one of us were sick, we could not assume that the hospital would grant us family visitation rights. (It is difficult to comprehend the pain that must be experienced by someone who has sacrificed and endured hours of agony in caring for a partner with AIDS, and who is then not accorded the dignity the relationship deserves because their tie is not recognized by law.) On issues of child rearing and adoption, our home would be assumed by many to be an unacceptable environment, without any examination of who we are and how we live. And when one of us dies, the other partner cannot be assured, even with a will, that he will receive property meant to remain with that partner.

Today, when filling out routine forms that require basic personal information, we can only describe ourselves as "single" or "married." It makes each of us, and so many others, feel angry to check "single," since that is clearly not the case. We are comforted in knowing that in the eyes of our families, friends, and community, we are regarded as committed partners, our relationship sanctified by ceremony. We look forward to the day, though, when our relationship, along with the relationships of others in all their variety, will be acknowledged and celebrated by all.

Jewish Lesbian Parenting

....

Linda J. Holtzman

I SAT DOWN TO START WRITING ABOUT MY EXPERIENCES AS A JEWISH
lesbian mother, thinking that I had a few quiet moments to begin to
organize my thoughts. Then Jordan, our two-year-old son, ran in
screaming that someone had put his favorite toy too high up for him
to reach. Two minutes later, Zachary, our three-week-old son, began
crying, demanding to be fed, stopping me from writing for the hun-
dredth time. I realized again that in most ways, life as a Jewish lesbian
mother is like life as any mother: chaotic, wonderful, and terribly exhausting. But there are differences, ways in which having a child as a
Jewish lesbian is not just like having a child as any other Jew or any
other lesbian.

When I first told my mother that I wanted to give birth to a baby,
she was outraged. How could I do that to an innocent baby? Me, a
rabbi yet, a committed Jew! How could I be so insensitive? We had
this conversation months after my life-partner Betsy had given birth
to Jordan, a baby who was (of course) sweet and lovable. Both my
parents loved Jordan, but *my* doing the same thing? God forbid!

Betsy and I had spent years debating whether or not we could raise
a child together in a world that was far from accepting of lesbian parents. I was then serving a small synagogue near Philadelphia. I had
been their rabbi for six years and had decided that I'd like to be there a
few more years, even if this meant living a fairly closeted life. When I
told the congregation that I would need two weeks of co-parenting
leave to "help my housemate when she gave birth" written into my
next contract, the board of directors was shocked. One by one they
came into my office and let me know that they could never consider
the possibility.

Eventually I left the synagogue, promising myself that my next job would be different. Somehow I'd find a way to work for the Jewish community and be open about my relationship and about any children we might have together. I've always hated secrets, and I knew that young children are generally incapable of keeping them anyway. I couldn't imagine placing the burden of a large family secret on our children. In my next job, I'd be open.

Easy to say—but for me, as a rabbi, this decision meant tackling the Jewish community head-on. First was my work, but beyond that was the rest of our life. Could there be a place for our family in the Jewish community? I found a job where I could be open at the rabbinical college where I was ordained, so my short-term career problems were solved, but other issues remained. I needed to find a way to sort out the complications involved with potential parenting.

Betsy and I began our decision-making process by joining a "baby group." Several women, mostly lesbian, none in a heterosexual marriage, met monthly to discuss our thoughts and feelings about having children. After talking at great length about all the possible means of having children, Betsy and I decided to use alternative insemination by an anonymous donor. Our sons will never know who their fathers are, and we know this is a great loss. But for us, adding a third adult to our household seemed impossible, and having a donor who did not share parenting felt confusing and potentially painful for our children. A man who randomly came and went would not give very solid parenting. Our hope is that the men with whom we are close will be significant people in our sons' lives. We worry about there not being access to male role models in our household, but we hope that our children will have men who are significant in many other aspects of their lives.

Both Betsy and I wanted to give birth to a child, so we took turns, she having our first child, I, the second. When Jordan was born, we consulted a lawyer to determine my legal rights concerning him. We discovered that I have virtually no rights, other than the medical power of attorney that we both signed for. I am named as Jordan's guardian in Betsy's will, but it is unclear whether a lesbian could ever gain custody of her partner's child if the will were contested by the child's biological grandparents. This is frustrating and frightening, and it is clear that as a community, all gay and lesbian people, whether parents or not, need to stand up and fight against such unjust laws, which undermine the strength of lesbian parents regardless of whether they're enforced. It is hard enough to build a household under any circumstances. When there is constant invalidation by the law, it is even harder.

Despite the negative laws, despite the fears underlying our decision, it still seemed possible for us to parent children. We had hoped for daughters; it seemed easier to raise girls; we know what girls' lives are like; we could provide reasonable role models for girls; somehow, it just seemed safer. How could we help a boy to find his place in the world? Were we ready for that challenge? When we found out that Jordan was going to be a boy (through amniocentesis), we worried. Could we overcome the many negative male role models that he would meet? Could we love him enough to give him all that he'd need in life? Would our community of women be an awkward place to bring a boy?

The minute that Jordan was born, we knew the answer. Of course we could love him enough; we adored him instantly. He felt like so much more than just "a male child"; he was a marvelously complex being. And there were so many ways that we could respond to the full person of Jordan that went far beyond our femaleness. Blending of male and female roles has always been important to both of us: in Jewish life and in all of life. The birth of our sons convinced us that we could transmit to the next generation the philosophy that we both believed. Jordan and Zach see us, two women, doing everything, "male" and "female" things: women light the Shabbat candles and say the *kiddush;* women do the laundry and mow the lawn. Women cook the dinner and pay the bills. In Jordan and Zach's minds no specific roles belong to either men or women. As much as society tries to invalidate this message, it is at least a clear one in our home life. Hopefully, our sons will incorporate it into their lives.

Before our sons were born we debated at great length what they should call us. We both wanted titles, yet nothing seemed exactly right. Finally, we settled on mommy and *ima,* Hebrew for mommy. I like the sound and feeling of the Hebrew word while Betsy is more comfortable with the English.

The first question for our family arose immediately after Jordan was born. How should we welcome him into the community? Ritual circumcision felt to both of us like an exclusive male initiation rite; we'd be symbolically bringing our son into a world that excluded us and limited his horizons. If we were creating new welcoming rituals for baby boys, they certainly would not include the cutting of the penis. Yet, we were very sensitive to the fact that as the child of lesbians, our son would be different from most other Jewish boys; did he need one more difference?

We reluctantly decided on *brit milah*, ritual circumcision, for our son, and found a very accommodating *mohel*. He assented to our naming our child "son of Esther Miriam (Betsy) and Liba (me)," and he was open to our both saying the blessing after the circumcision traditionally reserved for fathers (or at times both parents). Only immediate family were invited to the *brit*; all of our friends were invited to a second ceremony when Jordan was a month old. This ceremony welcomed him into our community gently and lovingly, with a ritual foot washing, music, poetry, and other soft, warm words of welcome.

We were pleased with what we had done with Jordan, but chose to do it differently for Zachary, who was born in July 1988. We decided to have only one ceremony, since we thought that many people would be away on vacation. The same *mohel*, the same ritual circumcision, the same anxiety and misgivings were present. But so were at least seventy-five friends and family members, all singing and smiling and helping us relax. The pressure of having a circumcision held in the presence of so many people was great, but so was the outpouring of love and support. We felt the weight of Jewish tradition as the *mohel* performed the rite, and we felt our own ambivalence about *brit milah* very strongly.

The lengthy decision-making process about the *brit* for both our sons was symbolic of the struggles that we knew we would face for the entire length of our parenting careers. The Jewish community is a difficult place for children with a family that is very different from most others. Though divorced parents and blended families are now the norm, two women committed to each other and raising children together are still a rarity. Traditional Judaism is so negative in its teachings about homosexuality that homophobia has found a hospitable environment in the Jewish community. It is not easy to gain legitimacy for a gay or lesbian family in the eyes of the official Jewish world.

Finding a preschool program came next. Relentlessly we quizzed uneasy principals and teachers about how they would accept our son and our family: would they list us both as parents? How would they respond to questions posed by other parents and children? How is "family" taught in their curriculum? Does every book they read have a mommy, daddy, and child?

We wanted to be certain that Jordan's preschool teachers would not only respect our choice of titles, but would also help Jordan feel comfortable as perhaps the only one in class with a mommy and an *ima*. Would his teachers use these terms along with mommy and daddy, when describing families? In as many ways as possible we wanted our son to be fully at peace with himself, with his classmates, with his first plunge into the educational establishment and, as it turned out, the Jewish establishment. Jordan is enrolled in a Jewish preschool program which, much to our pleasant surprise, has met all our criteria.

As we began this process with a preschool program, we both realized that educating our children's teachers and other role models about the special needs of our family will be an ongoing process. Will there possibly be a Jewish day school or a good Hebrew school that does not teach, even in subtle ways, that our family was not formed in an acceptable model? We both want to be acknowledged as parents when our sons become b'nai mitzvah; we both want to *kvel* openly when they have parts in the Purim play or lead a prayer at services. We want their religious educations to be backed up by a solid synagogue base, one that accepts us as women, as feminists, and as lesbians. I had such warm feelings about Jewish life when I was a child because I felt as if I fully belonged in our synagogue. I hope that Jordan and Zachary can have the same warm, comfortable feelings.

There may not be an established synagogue that fully meets our needs, but there certainly are many lesbians, gay men, and others searching along with us for a more inclusive Jewish base. I will not compromise my integrity or values to be part of a Jewish establishment, but I will not give up my Judaism because of an unbending, unaccepting community.

The Jewish community often feels like family, and confronting it often feels as painful as confronting my own biological family. The issues that both "families" raise are linked. My parents were initially so negative about my decision to have children in part because of their sense of what a "good Jew" did and did not do. Certainly, violating a law that has been expressed so unequivocally throughout Jewish tradition cannot be okay; it is simply not acceptable to be a lesbian. Having children as a lesbian is out of the question. We dare not inflict our own shame on the next generation.

In my parents' eyes a Jewish family looks a certain way and behaves a certain way; there is little room for diversity. Yet a very interesting change has taken place in my parents. When I first told them that I was thinking about having a baby, they planned on moving to Florida to escape the shame that I would heap upon them. Yet my parents were actually present at my son's birth; my mother cut Zachary's umbilical cord. And at his *brit*, they both stood up next to Betsy and Jordan and me. They recited a grandparents' blessing with pride, and I overheard my mother joking about how quickly she'd started "talking like a grandmother" as she declared the new baby "absolutely gorgeous." The change is dramatic, and it is largely based on my parents' realization that this is the only way they'd ever be grandparents (I'm an only child). Yet the change is incomplete.

My parents will accept Zachary as their daughter's son. I'm thirty-six years old, and I am (in their eyes) unmarried and am unlikely to be married soon. It's unusual but certainly understandable that I would want to find a way to parent a child. Insemination by an anonymous donor also seems strange to them but is safer than "sleeping around." This picture is a good one for my parents to present to their friends and relatives.

There's just one problem: in my eyes they already have a grandson, and I am in essence married. I am not, as they present to people, a single parent. When Jordan calls my parents Grandmom and Pop-pop, it's because he sees them as his second set of grandparents. Yet, as much as my parents seem to love Jordan, he is not quite a grandchild; as much as they like and respect Betsy, she is still my housemate and not my life-partner.

As both of our sons grow up, there will be some confusion and pain as our biological families struggle with questions of how to accept these nonbiological nonlegal relatives. What should Betsy's siblings tell their children when they ask how two mommies can have babies? How do our parents explain these two children who call themselves brothers, who call us parents and who see them as grandparents?

It's hard to resist an adorable baby, but as the babies grow, the questions multiply. We will always be honest with our sons about their biological and nonbiological families. We will tell them whenever they ask about the way that they were conceived. And we will teach them that family does not only mean biologically linked people. They will know that people who love each other and who are committed to supporting and caring for each other are family. (That is also a lesson I hope our biological families are able to learn.)

While the traditional definition of family is exclusive and must be broadened, I still believe that family is at the heart of Judaism. To grow up Jewish, our children need to experience the two: family and Judaism, linked together. We need to celebrate holidays, be together for life-cycle events, share these events with our families. Biological or nonbiological, our families create our Jewish memories and our Jewish life experiences. When I saw our extended families reach out to us during the births of our sons, I knew that if we kept working at building solid nonbiological family relationships, our sons would feel the warmth they deserve.

Facing the Jewish community is not easy and dealing with our biological families is even more difficult, but the most difficult aspect of having children for me has been facing ourselves and each other. Betsy and I began questioning the feasibility of our having children several years ago. We made a formal commitment to spend our lives together with the understanding that we would begin the process of decision making. If we decided to have a child, could we iron out our personal differences so that our children would have a consistent upbringing in a stable home? Could our very different approaches to Judaism and religious observance be life-enhancing and not confusing for a child? Betsy and I are very different people in almost every way. I talk incessantly and she is somewhat quiet; I like taking my time and doing things slowly and Betsy is quick and efficient; I love doing public speaking and sharing my life with groups of people while Betsy is a very private person; I love Judaism and the Jewish community passionately, while living a Jewish life is not one of Betsy's goals. Some of our differences feel healthy when presented to children; after all, two differing role models only expand one's sense of possibilities in life. It's okay to be talkative or quiet, public or private. But it is not possible to have a home that is both kosher and not kosher. Either a child is enrolled in a Hebrew school or not enrolled.

Before Jordan and Zach were born, Betsy and I could experiment with as many Jewish options as we wanted. I could do one thing and she could do another. Our house could be "loosely kosher," and we could vary our Shabbat and holiday observances on the basis of our current needs. Children changed our attitudes and limited our flexibility. I want Jordan and Zach to see candles lit, to taste wine and challah every Shabbat. I want them to know how to observe holidays, how to sing Hebrew songs and to know Jewish stories, to incorporate Jewish values into their lives. Betsy knows how important this is to me and has been willing to compromise in many ways: we have a Shabbat dinner together most weeks; I take our children to shul when it's feasible; we build a *sukkah*, light a menorah, bake *homentashn*, have a seder. Our sons will live Jewish lives. But I also compromise. Our home is only a modified form of kosher; our Shabbat observance is limited; our conversation rarely revolves around Judaism. We have both become more adept at compromise.

As Jordan and Zach grow and develop so do we: together and individually. We bend in ways we didn't know possible and we see new aspects in each other that increase our love and our respect for each other. We also push each other in new directions. Betsy never thought she'd help build a *sukkah* or light Shabbat candles; I never thought I'd be concerned about my astrology chart. We have incorporated respect for each other's values and enriched our own lives in the process. When I see Betsy sitting down with our two-year-old son to discuss his feelings with him, I am impressed and touched. When I hear her singing tunelessly and happily as she puts Jordan to bed, I feel a fresh surge of love for her. And when we argue with each other about the clothes our sons wear or the food they eat or the other ways we express ourselves through them, I feel exasperated, angry and deeply grateful—grateful that our sons have two parents who love them enough to care so passionately about the details of their lives.

Having children as a Jewish lesbian has meant a new closeness with my parents, an ever-deepening relationship with my partner, and a sense of connection to both past and future. It has meant finding strengths I barely knew I had and using them: to struggle with the Jewish community, to assert myself with my parents, to work with Betsy to find ways to raise our sons in a difficult, complex world. It means learning that as a lesbian and a Jew I have much to give my sons. My values and ideas can be a source of strength and nourishment to a new generation. Most of all, having children has meant learning to love deeply and fully and to bind my life to the lives of these members of the next generation. All of us need to find a way of learning just how much we have to offer, how valuable our contribution to the world can be. All of us must feel free to decide whether or not to use our abilities to raise children, and society must open up to let us make honest, clear decisions. Then, whether or not we decide to, our decisions will be worthy of celebration.

Toward a New Theology of Sexuality

....

Judith Plaskow

JEWISH ATTITUDES TOWARD SEXUALITY ARE COMPLEX AND OFTEN
confusing and conflicting. Both historical changes and developments,
and contradictions within particular historical movements and periods yield an array of views on sexuality from the freest to the most
inhibited.[1] From a feminist standpoint, there are three aspects of Jewish attitudes toward sexuality particularly in need of exploration and
change: the centrality of an "energy/control" paradigm of sexuality;
the assumption that all sexuality is the same, namely marital and exclusively heterosexual; and the special place of women in the econ-
omy of sexual control. While each of these topics might be the subject
of a separate essay, I will consider them only briefly as background for
setting out an alternative, feminist perspective on sexuality.

An emphasis on control is central to Jewish understandings of sexuality. From the viewpoint of the tradition's "energy/control" model,
sexuality is an independent and sometimes alien energy that must be
held in check through personal discipline and religious constraints.[2]
While the sexual impulse is given by God and thus is a normal and
healthy part of human life, sanctified within its proper framework,
sexuality also requires careful, sometimes rigorous control in order
that it not violate the boundaries assigned it. Conflicts between affirming sexuality and enforcing restraint emerge in the tradition in a
number of forms, in part through the very naming of the sexual impulse. The rabbis called this impulse the *yetzer hara*, the evil impulse,
and yet at the same time acknowledged its necessity to the creation
and sustenance of the world. "Were it not for the evil impulse," said
Rabbi Nahman B. Samuel, "man would not build a house, or take a
wife, or beget a child, or engage in business."[3]

Assuming that sexuality must be controlled, the tradition under-
stands heterosexual marriage as the proper framework for taming and
enjoying the sexual impulse. Even within marriage, sex is forbidden
during menstruation and for seven days thereafter. Outside the boundaries of marriage lies a whole realm of licentiousness and transgres-
sion that must be carefully guarded against with well-defined re-
straints. Legal prohibitions, moral standards, and social expectations
all serve to delineate certain periods within a marriage as the sole
realm of the sexually permitted. So pervasive is the assumption that
sex is properly marital and heterosexual that homosexuality gets
short shrift, even by way of interdiction. Male homosexuality is a
major offense (to'evah, an abomination), but it is assumed by the
rabbis to be so rare in Israel that there is little need for safeguards
against it.

While moral norms concerning sexuality generally apply both to
men and women, women play a special role in the Jewish understanding of sexuality. They are the ubiquitous temptations, the sources
and symbols of illicit desire, the ones whose sexuality threatens even
their husbands/possessors with the possibility of illegal action. To
speak of control is necessarily to speak of women—of the need to
cover them, avoid them, and contain them in proper (patriarchal) families where their threat is minimized if it cannot be overcome. Laws
concerning marriage and divorce decrease the danger of women's
sexuality by providing for the acquisition and relinquishment of male
rights to that sexuality. Marriage brings the "wild and unruly poten-
tialities of female sexuality" under control[4] by designating a woman's
sexuality as a particular man's possession.

The control of women's sexuality and its role in the institution of
the family, the normativeness of heterosexuality, and the energy/con-
trol paradigm of sexuality are all connected pieces of a patriarchal
understanding of sexuality. Where women's sexuality is seen as an
object to be possessed, and sexuality is confined to heterosexual marriage and perceived as an impulse that can take possession of the self,
the central issues surrounding sexuality will necessarily be issues of
control. The question then becomes how a positive Jewish feminist
discourse about sexuality can move beyond this patriarchal framework, not only rejecting its ethical implications but defining sexuality
in fundamentally different terms.

In the past twenty years, feminists have reconceptualized the nature and functions of human sexuality, generating alternatives to the energy/control model that potentially establish our thinking about sexuality on new foundations. Rather than seeing sexuality as a separate and alien energy that can engulf the self, feminists have described it as part of a continuum of embodied self-expression, or as part of a spectrum of erotic energy that ideally suffuses all activities in our lives.[5] Audre Lorde, in her brilliant essay, "Uses of the Erotic: The Erotic as Power," describes the erotic as the life force, the capacity for feeling, the capacity for joy, a power we are taught to fear and ignore by a society that "defines the good in terms of profit rather than in terms of human need." The erotic is a source of empowerment, a "lens through which we [can] scrutinize all aspects of our existence," evaluating them "honestly in terms of their relative meaning within our lives."[6] Ethicist Beverly Harrison similarly interprets sexuality as a reality rooted in "our bodies, our selves." Setting out the base points for a feminist moral theology, Harrison argues that "all our knowledge, including our moral knowledge, is body-mediated knowledge." Our sensuality or our capacity for feeling is the foundation stone of our connection to the world, the prerequisite without which we would lose all ability to act or to value. Our sexuality, as an aspect of our embodiedness and inherent in it, is one especially intense dimension of our body-mediated power, of the body space that is "literally the ground of our personhood."[7]

This view of sexuality as part of a spectrum of body/life energy rather than a special force or evil inclination has at least two important implications for understanding the place of sexuality in human life. First of all, it challenges the value of control by suggesting that we cannot suppress sexual feelings without suppressing our capacity for feeling in general. If sexuality is one dimension of our ability to live passionately in the world, then in cutting off our sexuality, we diminish our overall power to feel, know, and value deeply. While the connection between sexuality and feeling does not compel us to act out all our sexual feelings, it does mean we must honor and make room for feelings—including sexual ones—as "the basic ingredient in our relational transaction with the world."[8] Second, insofar as sexuality is an element in the embodiment that mediates our relation to reality, an aspect of the life energy that enables us to connect with others in creativity and joy, sexuality is profoundly connected to spirituality, indeed is inseparable from it. Sexuality is that part of us through which we reach out to other persons and to God, expressing the need for relationship, for the sharing of self and of meaning.[9] When we touch that place in our lives where sexuality and spirituality come together, we touch our wholeness and the fullness of our power, and at the same time our connection with a power larger than ourselves.[10]

Feminist reconceptualizations of the energy/control model of sexuality and affirmation of the profound connection between sexuality and spirituality provide directions for rethinking the ambivalent attitudes toward sexuality within Judaism. Acceptance and avowal of a link between sex and spirit is by no means foreign to Jewish experience. In the mysteries of the marriage bed on Sabbath night, in the sanctity of the Song of Songs, for mysticism, in the very nature and dynamics of the Godhead, sexual expression is an image of and path to the holy.[11] Yet again and again in theology and practice, Judaism turns away from and undermines this acknowledged connection by defining sexuality in terms of patriarchal possession and control. Since such categories are inimical to the mutuality, openness, and vulnerability in sexual relations that tie sexuality to the sacred, a feminist approach to sexuality must reconstruct both the institutional and conceptual bases for linking sexuality with the spiritual.

It is striking that one of the most profound images of freedom and mutuality in sexual relations that the Jewish tradition has to offer is at the same time its central image of the connection between sexuality and spirituality. Unlike the Garden of Eden, where Eve and Adam are ashamed of their nakedness and women's subordination is the punishment for sin, the Garden of the Song of Songs is a place of sensual delight and sexual equality. Unabashed by their desire, the man and woman of these poems delight in their own embodiment and the beauty surrounding them, each seeking the other out to inaugurate their meetings, each rejoicing in the love without dominion that is also the love of God.[12] Since this book offers a vision of delight that is easier to achieve in a sacred garden than in the midst of daily demands, it is perhaps no criticism of the institution of marriage that the couple in the Song of Songs is not married. Yet the picture of mutuality and the sacredness of mutuality offered by this book stand in fundamental tension with the structures of marriage as Judaism defines them. When the central rituals of marriage and divorce celebrate or enact the male possession and release of female sexuality and exclude the possibility of loving same-sex relationships, what are the supports and resources for the true reciprocity of intimate exchange that marks the holiness of the Song of Songs? The achievement of mutuality in the marriage bed is extremely difficult in the absence of justice in those institutions that legitimate and surround it.

A first concrete task, then, of the feminist reconstruction of Jewish attitudes toward sexuality is the radical transformation of the institutional, legal framework within which sexual relations are supposed to take place. Insofar as Judaism maintains its interest in the establishment of enduring relationships outside a patriarchal framework, these relationships will be entered into and dissolved by mutual initiative and consent. "Marriage" will not be about the transfer of women or the sanctification of potential disorder through the firm establishment of women in the patriarchal family, but the decision of two adults—any two adults—to make their lives together, lives which include the sharing of sexuality. In the modern West, it is generally assumed that such a decision constitutes a central meaning of marriage, but this assumption is contradicted by a religious (and secular) legal system that outlaws homosexual marriage and institutionalizes inequality in its basic definitions of marriage and divorce.

This redefinition of the legal framework of marriage is based both on rejection of the institutionalization of heterosexuality and on the important principle that sexuality is not something we can acquire or possess in another. We are each the possessor of our own sexuality—in Adrienne Rich's phrase, the "presiding genius" of our own bodies.[13] The sharing of sexuality with another is something that should happen only by mutual consent, a consent that is not a blanket permission, but that is continually renewed in the actual rhythms of particular relationships. This principle, simple as it seems, challenges both the fundamental assumptions of Jewish marriage law and the Jewish understanding of what women's sexuality is "about." It defines as immoral legal regulations concerning the possession, control, and exchange of women's sexuality, and it disputes the perspective that a woman's sexuality is her contribution to the family rather than the expression of her own embodiment.

If one firm principle for feminist thinking about sexuality is that no one can possess the sexuality of another, a second principle is that sexuality is not something that pertains only or primarily to the self. Indeed, our sexuality is fundamentally about moving out beyond ourselves. The connecting, communicative nature of sexuality is not something we can experience or look for only in sexual encounters narrowly defined, but in all real relationships in our lives. We live in the world as sexual beings. As Audre Lorde argues, our sexuality is a current that flows through all activities that are important to us, in which we invest our selves. True intellectual exchange, common work, shared experience are laced with sexual energy that animates and enlivens them. The bonds of community are erotic bonds. The power that is generated by real community, that gives us access to a greater power that grounds and embraces us, is in part the power of our own sexual, life energy that flows through community and enlarges and seals it. We are all, women and men, embodied, sexual persons who respond sexually to the women and men among whom we live.

This erotic nature of community is by no means lost on Judaism; indeed, it is the subject of profound ambivalence in both the midrash and law. Extensive rabbinic legislation enforcing the separation of the sexes tries to protect against the feelings it recognizes, even as it acknowledges the sexual power of community. If the energy of community is erotic, there are no guarantees that eroticism will stay within prescribed legal boundaries rather than breaking out and disrupting communal sanctity. The strict "fence around the law" that is necessary when it comes to sexual behavior is itself testimony to the power of sexuality.

A feminist account of sexuality will not deny the power of sexuality to overturn rules and threaten boundaries; it rather embraces this power as a possible ally. There is no question that the empowerment that comes from owning the erotic in our lives can disturb community and undermine familiar structures. On the level of sexual behavior, if we allow ourselves to perceive and acknowledge sexual feelings, there is always the danger we may act on them, and they may not correspond to group consensus about whom we may desire and when. And when we understand the erotic not simply as sexual feeling in the narrow sense but as our fundamental life energy, owning this power in our lives is even more threatening to established structures.

In Audre Lorde's terms, if we allow the erotic to become a lens through which we evaluate all aspects of our existence, we can no longer "settle for the convenient, the shoddy, the conventionally expected, nor the merely safe." [14] Having glimpsed the possibility of genuine satisfaction in work well done, we are less likely to settle for work that is alienating and meaningless. Having experienced the power and legitimacy of our own sexual desire, we are less likely to subscribe to a system that closely and absolutely prescribes and proscribes the channels of that desire. Having experienced our capacity for creative and joyful action, we are less likely to accept hierarchical power relationships that deny or restrict our ability to bring that creativity and joy to other aspects of our lives. It may be that the ability of women to live within the patriarchal family and the larger patriarchal structures that govern Jewish life depends on our suppression of the erotic, on our numbing ourselves to the sources of vision and power that fuel meaningful resistance. Obviously, from a patriarchal perspective, then, erotic empowerment is dangerous. That is why, in Lorde's words, "we are taught to separate the erotic demand from most vital areas of our lives other than sex,"[15] and that is why we are also taught to restrain our sexuality, so that it too fits the parameters of hierarchical control that govern the rest of our lives.

From a feminist perspective, however, the power and danger of the erotic are not reasons to fear and suppress it but to nurture it as a profound personal and communal resource in the struggle for change. When "we begin to demand from ourselves and from our life-pursuits that they feel in accordance with that joy which we know ourselves to be capable of," we carry with us an inner knowledge of the kind of world we are seeking to create.[16] If we repress this knowledge because it also makes us sexually alive, then we repress the clarity and creative energy that is the basis of our capacity to envision and work toward a more just social order.

This understanding of the power of the erotic is a particularly crucial corrective to rabbinic attitudes toward sexual control. The rabbis recognized the connection between the sexual impulse and human creativity. "The bigger the man, the bigger the *yetzer*," they said, and advised, "Hold him [the *yetzer hara*] off with the left hand and draw him nigh with the right."[17] Yet at the same time they acknowledged the role of sexuality as an ingredient in all activity, they apparently believed one could constantly guard against sexuality without damaging the larger capacity to act and to feel. To love God with all the heart meant to love God with the good *and evil* impulses, and yet it was imagined one could rein in the evil impulse without diminishing the love of God.[18] If we take sexuality seriously, however, as an expression of our embodiment that cannot be disconnected from our wider ability to interact feelingly with the world, then to learn fear and shame of our own bodies and those of others—even when these feelings are intermixed with other conflicting attitudes—is to learn suspicion of feeling as a basic way of valuing and knowing. We should not expect, then, to be able to block out our sexual feelings without blocking out the longing for social relations rooted in mutuality rather than hierarchy, without blocking out the anger that warns us that something is amiss in our present social arrangements, without blocking and distorting the fullness of our love for God.[19]

I am not arguing here for free sex or for more sexual expression, quantitatively speaking. I am arguing for living dangerously, for choosing to take responsibility for working through the possible consequences of sexual feeling rather than repressing sexual feeling and thus repressing feeling in general. I am arguing that our capacity to transform Judaism and the world is rooted in our capacity to be alive to the pain and anger that is caused by relationships of domination, and to the joy that awaits us on the other side. I am arguing that to be alive is to be sexually alive, and that in suppressing one sort of vitality, we suppress the other. The question becomes, then: can we affirm our sexuality as the gift it is, making it sacred not by cordoning off pieces of it, but by increasing our awareness of the ways in which it connects us to all things? Can we stop evicting our sexuality from the synagogue, hiding it behind a *mechitzah* or praying with our heads, and instead bring it in, offering it to God in the experience of full spiritual/physical connection? Dare we trust our capacity for joy—knowing it is related to our sexuality—to point the direction toward new and different ways of structuring communal life?

Obviously, I am suggesting that the implications of a changed conception of sexuality go well beyond the sexual sphere, and yet it is also the case, of course, that they shape that sphere as well. The ability to feel deeply in the whole of our lives affects what we want and are willing to accept in the bedroom, just as what we experience in the bedroom prepares us for mutuality or domination in the rest of our lives. A new understanding of sexuality and a transformed institutional context for sexual relationships will have significant impact on personal sexual norms. If the traditional models and categories for understanding sexuality are no longer morally acceptable from a feminist perspective, but sexuality is fundamentally about relationships with others, what values might govern sexual behavior for modern Jews?

To see sexuality as an aspect of our life energy, as part of a continuum with other ways of relating to the world and other persons, is to insist that the norms of mutuality, respect for difference, and joint empowerment that characterize the larger feminist vision of community apply also—indeed especially—to the area of sexuality. If in our general communal life, we seek to be present with each other in such a way that we can touch the greater power of being in which all communities dwell, how much more should this be true in those relationships that are potentially the most open, intimate, and vulnerable in our lives?

The unification of sexuality and spirituality provides an ideal of what a sexual relationship can be, an ideal that is more a measure of the possible than the continuing reality of every day. What keeps this ideal alive as a recurring possibility is the exercise of respect, responsibility, and honesty—commensurate with the nature and depth of the particular relationship—as basic values in any sexual connection. In terms of concrete life choices, I believe that radical mutuality is most fully possible in the context of an ongoing, committed relationship in which sexual expression is one dimension of a shared life. Long-term partnerships may be the richest setting for negotiating and living out the meanings of mutuality, responsibility, and honesty amid the distractions, problems, and pleasures of every day. Such partnerships are not, however, a choice for all adults who want them, and not all adults would choose them, given the possibility. To respond within a feminist framework to the realities of different life decisions and at the same time affirm the importance of sexual well-being as an aspect of our total well-being, we need to apply certain fundamental values to a range of sexual styles and choices. While honesty, responsibility, and respect are goods that pertain to any relationship, the concrete meaning of these values will vary considerably depending on the duration and significance of the connection involved. In one relationship, honesty may mean complete and open sharing of feelings and experiences; in another, it may mean clarity about intent for that encounter. In the context of a committed partnership, responsibility may signify lifelong presence, trust, and exchange; in a brief encounter, it may signify discussion of birth control, condoms, and AIDS. At its fullest, respect may mean regard for another as a total person; at a minimum, it may mean absence of pressure or coercion, and a commitment, in Lorde's words, not to "look away as we come together." [20] If we need to look away, then we should walk away: the same choices about whether and how to act on our feelings that pertain to any area of moral decision-making are open to us in relation to our sexuality.

The same norms that apply to heterosexual relationships also apply to gay and lesbian relationships. While other essays in this book re-evaluate various facets of the traditional Jewish rejection of homosex-uality, the central issue that requires rethinking in the context of a feminist reconceptualization of sexuality is the relationship between homosexual choice and the continuity between sexual energy and embodied life energy. If we see sexuality as part of what enables us to reach out beyond ourselves, and thus as a fundamental ingredient in our spirituality, then the issue of homosexuality must be placed in a different context from those in which it is most often discussed. The question of the morality of homosexuality becomes one not of Jewish law, or the right to privacy, or freedom of choice, but a question of the affirmation of the value to the individual and society of each of us being able to find that place within ourselves where sexuality and spirituality come together.[21] It is possible that some or many of us for whom the connections between sexuality and deeper sources of per-sonal and spiritual power emerge most richly, or only, with those of the same sex could choose to lead heterosexual lives for the sake of conformity to Jewish law or wider social pressures and values. But this choice would then be a violation of the deeper vision offered by the Jewish tradition that sexuality can be a medium for the experience and reunification of God. Although historically, this vision has been expressed entirely in heterosexual terms, the reality is that for some Jews, it has been realized in relationships with both men and women, while for others it is realized only in relationships between members of the same sex. Thus what calls itself the Jewish path to holiness in sexual relations is for some a cutting off of holiness—a sacrifice that comes at high cost for both the individual and community.

Potential acceptance of gays and lesbians by the Jewish community raises the issue of children—for Judaism a primary warrant for sexual relations, and the facade that prejudice often stands behind in reject-ing homosexuality as a Jewish choice. Again to place this issue in the context of a feminist paradigm for understanding sexuality, procrea-tion is a dimension of our sexuality, just as sexuality itself is a dimen-sion of our embodied personhood. If sexuality allows us to reach out to others, having children is a way of reaching out beyond our own generation, affirming the biological continuity of life and the continuity of Jewish community and communal values. Insofar as Jewish communities have an important stake in the rearing of Jewish children, it is in their interest to structure communal institutions to support in concrete ways all Jews who choose to raise children, including increasing numbers of lesbians and gay men.[22] But, just as Judaism has always recognized that procreation does not exhaust the meaning of sexuality, so having children does not exhaust the ways in which Jews can contribute to future generations.[23] Recognition of the continuities between sexuality and personal empowerment strengthens the conviction of the inherent value of sexuality as an expression of our personhood and of our connection with and love for others. The sense of integrity and self-worth that a loving sexual relationship can foster enhances the capacity to make commitments to the future, whether this takes the form of bearing and raising children or nurturing communal continuity in other ways.

Lastly, but underlying all that I have said, sexuality as an aspect of our life energy and power connects us with God as the sustaining source of energy and power in the universe. In reaching out to another sexually with the total self, the boundaries between self and other can dissolve, and we may feel ourselves united with larger currents of energy and sustenance. It is also the case, however, that even in ordinary, daily reachings out to others, we reach toward the God who is present in connection, in the web of relation with a wider world. On the one hand, the wholeness, the "all-embracing quality of sexual expression" that includes body, mind, and feeling, is for many people the closest we can come in this life to experiencing the embracing wholeness of God.[24] On the other hand, the everyday bonds of community are also erotic bonds through which we touch the God of community. In recognizing the continuity between our own sexual energy and the greater currents that nourish and renew it, we affirm our sexuality as a source of energy and power that, schooled in the values of respect and mutuality, can lead us to the related, and therefore sexual, God.

PART 4

Creating Lesbian and Gay Jewish Community

INTRODUCTION

....

As an increasing number of lesbian and gay Jews have come out to ourselves and each other, we have developed various forms of community. Many small groups have drawn from the models of feminist consciousness-raising groups and from *chavurot*, creating contexts for personal support, spiritual exploration, cultural expression, and political action. Some larger groups have evolved into congregations. While most gay and lesbian Jews remain unaffiliated with any of these groups, they play a crucial role in creating a culture that enables us to envision "living as all of who we are," to paraphrase the title of Eric Rofes's essay.

Aliza Maggid chronicles the development of the World Congress of Gay and Lesbian Jewish Organizations, known as the "gay synagogue movement." She describes its origins, its growth, its accomplishments, and the challenges it faces. Lesbian and gay synagogues are often our most visible institutions and are important to study as they continue to grow. Maggid addresses the question of "why a gay synagogue," and she looks to the way these congregations welcome those who are not necessarily lesbian or gay.

Evelyn Torton Beck discusses developments among Jewish lesbian-feminist groups, especially since her landmark anthology, *Nice Jewish Girls*, was first published in 1982. Beck stresses the importance of naming all of one's identities, understanding and valuing the intersections among them. She addresses the complexities of building community on this basis. Beck describes Jewish lesbian-feminists as "the new prophetic minority" in the Jewish community.

Yoel Kahn writes about the liturgy that has evolved in lesbian and gay congregations. Starting with the decision to eliminate sexism in the prayerbook, as well as the need to express our unique experience, congregants have created new prayers and rituals, while also infusing old ones with new meaning. Kahn discusses *kiddushin* ceremonies for same-sex couples, shabbat observances during lesbian and gay pride week, and the many issues presented by the AIDS crisis.

Unlike other essays in this volume, Eric Rofes discusses his experiences as a Jew in the gay community, rather than as a gay person in the Jewish community. He acknowledges the ways his experience as a Jew strengthened and prepared him for life as a gay man. He also talks about instances of overt anti-Semitism he has encountered, as well as the more elusive difficulties of not fitting in with the majority culture, or even the subculture of the gay community.

Clearly, lesbian and gay Jews are building community in many ways already, and this will only increase over time. As options for integration and inclusion open up in more mainstream Jewish contexts, the shapes of those institutions are bound to change. Meanwhile, we will continue to build and strengthen our own.

Joining Together:
Building a Worldwide Movement[1]

Aliza Maggid

IN BOSTON, A GROUP OF MEN AND WOMEN FROM AM TIKVA ARE BUSY wrapping *homentashn*, fruit and candy in small Purim gift packages to deliver to elderly Jews in nursing homes.

In Los Angeles, a joyful couple stands under the *chuppah*, surrounded by family and friends, as the rabbi of Beth Chayim Chadashim leads them in the exchange of their vows.

After completing a successful fund-raising campaign, a very proud Congregation Sha'ar Zahav in San Francisco gathers to dedicate their new synagogue building. The city's mayor has sent a proclamation of good wishes.

Many diverse organizations from the Amsterdam Jewish community join the evening candlelight march and rally in support of Soviet Jews. Sjalhomo's members join the crowd.

A lively Purim party and dance draws a big crowd at Bet Haverim in Paris.

Tikva Chadashah in Seattle plans the purchase of a wooden chest to house the Torah scrolls they will receive under permanent loan from a neighboring synagogue.

In New York, the leaders of Beit Simcha Torah announce the fall educational program to their congregation of several hundred people. Classes will include Hebrew, Yiddish, Talmud, and other Judaic studies.

These scenes depict activities that represent the very fiber of Jewish communal life. They could be found in synagogues and Jewish groups throughout the world. None of this would seem out of the ordinary, except that all of the groups mentioned above are groups of gay men and lesbians.

During the 1970s and 1980s, Jewish lesbians, gay men, and bisexuals in over twenty U.S. cities, Canada, England, Belgium, the Netherlands, France, Israel, Australia, and other countries have organized a variety of dynamic organizations and congregations. Our groups vary greatly, reflecting local conditions and the needs of members. Some have established synagogues with a building, a rabbi, weekly services, and religious education programs. Others fill a primarily social and cultural function, bringing men and women together in a Jewish atmosphere for friendship, support, and education. Many groups have a *havurah* structure with a religious component, but not all the functions of a synagogue. In addition, our groups promote social and political action, acting as a gay voice in the Jewish community and a Jewish voice in the gay community. And in Israel, the group fulfills the role of a national gay social and civil rights organization, given the need there for an affirming environment for lesbians and gay men, rather than a place to affirm one's Jewish identity.

These diverse groups have joined together to form the World Congress of Gay and Lesbian Jewish Organizations. The Congress sponsors international and regional conferences, promotes public education, and supports the growth of new and existing lesbian and gay Jewish organizations.

At the time of the Stonewall riot in 1969, many gay and lesbian Jews lived with their homosexual identities concealed, even as they filled such roles as rabbi, communal worker, or active congregant. Important parts of their lives remained invisible; for example, not feeling able to bring a same-sex partner to synagogue, and if they did, consciously refraining from sharing warmth and affection, while nongay couples or friends felt free to extend Sabbath or *Yom Tov* greetings in the form of a hug or kiss. The recognition awarded only to heterosexual couples on the occasion of an engagement, anniversary, or sanctification of a new home further heightened the alienation experienced by Jewish lesbians and gay men. Often identified as "single," these gay and lesbian Jews reluctantly tolerated offers of social introductions or invitations to "singles" events.

Other gay and lesbian Jews refrained from active participation in

the Jewish community, largely because of the discomfort of concealing identities or from the pain of feeling rejected by one's community.
Many denied or ignored their Jewish identities, while some may have
found each other gathering informally in homes and at bars and
dance clubs.

Many of us who were just entering adulthood in 1969 were deeply
affected by the climate of social change and experimentation of our
era. The influences of feminism were taking root everywhere across
the country. Ignited by the early women's movement, the tenet that
"the personal is political" shaped much of my own thinking and that
of many men and women who would later join a gay and lesbian congregation. I remember the time in 1974 when lesbian friends invited
me to a Hanukkah party, which for most of us was the first in many
years. It seemed courageous then to raise issues of Jewish identity in
the women's and lesbian community even though so many of us were
Jews. And once we began exploring these issues, we became hungry
for more opportunities to do so.

In the early 1970s, a small but significant number of lesbian and gay
Jews began to show up in various congregations of the Metropolitan
Community Church (MCC), an international gay and lesbian Protes-
tant denomination. These women and men sought a comfortable
framework for their religious lives, and though they felt attached to
Judaism, they felt unwelcome as gays in the synagogue. In several
cities throughout the country, MCC became a spiritual home for Jews
seeking camaraderie and support.

In 1972 in Los Angeles, three years after the Stonewall Riot, a group
of gay and lesbian Jews attending MCC began to recognize that the
time was ripe to create a specifically Jewish alternative. They first
called themselves the Metropolitan Community Temple, then continued on to found Beth Chayim Chadashim (BCC), "the House of
New Life," a place where Jewish lesbians and gay men could shape
their own ritual life and social environment.

The founders of BCC began to announce the existence of this bold
new option for gay and lesbian Jews. They published advertisements
in local gay newspapers, and the group began to grow, attracting
others who were glad to find each other. They cautiously approached
the local office of the Union of American Hebrew Congregations
(UAHC), the Reform movement, and were warmly greeted with assis-
tance and support. Arrangements were quickly made for prayer books

and for meeting space. A regular schedule of worship services was established, and BCC was on its way. That same year a gay Jewish group was formed in London, and between 1972 and 1975 at least ten more lesbian and gay Jewish groups were established in the United States and abroad.

Of particular significance during this period was the early decision by BCC's founders to build on their ties with the UAHC and begin discussions about obtaining membership in that body. The application for membership of a "gay outreach" congregation caused discussion throughout the entire Reform movement. There was controversy and debate at many levels, but by the end of 1973 BCC was voted into membership in a historic action that cracked open the door of mainstream Judaism to gay and lesbian Jews.

In 1974 and 1975, a handful of gay Jews attended the annual MCC convention, sharing experiences, and offering one another moral support in their efforts to sustain their fledgling groups. They were also planting the seeds of a gay and lesbian Jewish network. It wasn't long before these seeds began to grow. When members of Congregation Beit Simchat Torah, New York's gay and lesbian synagogue, found themselves in a heated discussion about the 1975 UN resolution condemning Zionism as racism, they sent out a call for a meeting to develop strategies for combatting anti-Semitism. So, on the weekend of December 5–7, 1975, representatives from Los Angeles, Philadelphia, Boston, and Washington, D.C., traveled to New York for the first meeting of gay and lesbian Jewish groups. We were finally together at an official gathering, giving us a taste of possibilities for a broader and stronger network in the future.

During the historic 1975 meeting, we laid the groundwork for our first international conference in Washington, D.C., in 1976, when gay and lesbian Jews from Toronto, Montreal, and London traveled to join the U.S. participants. (A delegate from Israel was unable to attend, but sent a proxy.) We then moved forward to conferences in New York in 1977 and Los Angeles in 1978.

These conferences were filled with the exuberance of coming together in a setting that most delegates had never before experienced. We felt proud together, and we were able to share our concerns in a completely accepting atmosphere. Warm and lasting friendships grew quickly and easily. We attended dozens of workshops on gay and Jewish subjects, ranging from Yiddish culture to Jewish/Gentile

couples, to Middle East peace. Business meetings were filled with debate and enlivened by the camaraderie developing among delegates
from all over the world. We sang, danced, conducted religious services in many alternative forms, and of course enjoyed lots of eating
and festivities.

We took a big step toward building a truly international movement
in 1979, with the decision to hold the conference in Israel and to recruit more delegates from outside the United States. Our movement
matured by handling crisis conditions that arose when the Orthodox
rabbinic authorities threatened to revoke the kashruth license, a necessity for doing business in Israel, from the kibbutz where the conference was to be held. The Israeli organizers showed great determination and creativity as they scrambled for alternate arrangements.
The delegates showed similar determination as they flew in from
around the world, unsure at the moment of their departure that any
conference would be held at all. The conference was held, and the Israeli hosts, the Society for the Protection of Personal Rights, welcomed registrants from France, England, Australia, Bermuda, Canada, West Germany, Holland, Mexico, Portugal, South Africa, and
the United States.

After several days, delegates gathered in the city of Lahav and were
shocked to learn that the Jewish National Fund (JNF) had cancelled
our dedication of a grove of 3,000 trees that was to serve as a memorial
to gay and lesbian Jews throughout the ages. Nearly $9,000 had been
raised to pay for the woodland through a joint tree project of the gay
and lesbian Jewish organizations. The JNF decided it would not in-
scribe the words "gay and lesbian" on the customary dedication
plaque, and it offered to return the money. The conference leadership
knew it would be impossible to return the contributions to the mostly
anonymous donors. The delegates knew even more deeply that those
trees had been donated in honor of births, deaths, celebrations, and
sorrows of their families and loved ones. One of our eldest delegates,
Henry, a man in his sixties from New York City, spoke strongly to our
group about what our response should be. Henry had been advised
by his doctors that he was too ill to make the trip to Israel but had
come anyway out of his great desire to see the Jewish homeland for
the first time. We regained our determination when he insisted that
"we had come much too far and could not be denied a dedication
ceremony."

When the bus arrived at the forest land in Lahav, delegates convinced a sympathetic worker to allow the planting of a symbolic tree,
and they created a joyful dedication ceremony on the spot, complete
with prayers and dancing and singing. The only thing missing was
the recognition of the JNF.

During the conference week, delegates were filled with anger at the
prejudice we encountered, but were also filled with feelings of warmth
and solidarity for our Israeli brothers and sisters. En masse, we descended on Tel Aviv's Independence Park for Israel's first gay rights
demonstration. Many curious onlookers engaged in animated discussion with the demonstrators, eager to question and to learn about gay
people. Television cameras and reporters recorded the event for posterity. Later that night as we relaxed at an outdoor cafe, we gathered
around the television on the counter as Israel's first program on gay
and lesbian rights filled the airwaves.

Out of the deep bonds among people and the strength gained by
handling these experiences grew a desire to create a more formal and
lasting international structure that could serve as a link between
conferences and provide a unified public voice. The following year,
the sixteen groups attending the Conference in San Francisco officially founded the World Congress of Gay and Lesbian Jewish
Organizations.

The structure provided by the Congress spurred a period of substantial growth. Established congregations grew more stable and began to give support and guidance to newer groups. Regional networks emerged in the United States and in Europe. The Congress
began to publish and circulate a newsletter and to network with other
organizations. We produced an educational pamphlet dispelling some
of the major misconceptions about gay and lesbian Jews and mailed it
to thousands of synagogues and Jewish communal institutions.

The Congress also gave guidance to local organizations, which
hosted annual conferences in Philadelphia in 1981, Los Angeles in
1982, and Miami in 1983, and then our first biennial conference in
Washington, D.C., in 1985. These conferences continued to enable us
joyfully to explore and express our gay and lesbian Jewish identities,
while providing a forum for addressing such topics as creating liturgy,
recruiting new members, and increasing our ability to fulfill our Jewish responsibilities of social action and *bikkur cholim* (the traditional
mitzvah of visiting the sick). Conferences have also given us tremen-

dous opportunities to reach out and educate our host Jewish communities, where major Reform congregations sometimes welcomed the delegates for Shabbat worship. Our conferences customarily receive a proclamation or welcoming remarks from the host city's mayor, and in Washington, D.C., a U.S. congressman addressed the group.

In 1987 we took another big step toward solidifying our international character, with Sjalhomo, our affiliated organization in the Netherlands, hosting the conference in Amsterdam. Our plenary sessions were translated into Dutch, English, Hebrew, and French to accommodate the needs of the most nationally diverse group of people ever attending one of our conferences. Our Dutch hosts designed the conference to introduce people from around the world to the experience of being a European Jew. For many, stories of Jewish wartime experiences came to life in a new way upon hearing them from gay counterparts with whom they closely identified. A memorial for Holocaust victims was held in a location that had been a holding space for Dutch Jews being deported to concentration camps. In addition to Dutch speakers, we listened to one of our San Francisco delegates, formerly a refugee, who spoke of the time when he had been held for deportation in that very building. He expressed great joy in being able to return there as a free and proud gay Jew.

The memorial and other experiences left us with tears in our eyes, but we also had many occasions of celebration. The lobby of the Grand Hotel Krasnapolsky, which sits on a main square in Amsterdam, was filled with delegates from early morning to late in the evening, eager to use every moment to meet each other and share experiences. The closing session in the grand ballroom ran an hour over schedule as several hundred people danced round and round the hall, singing a Dutch song that has become popular there as a gay pride anthem. No one could bear to go home.

Our groups have grown to fill the same needs that congregations provide for any Jew: religious services, pastoral care, education for ourselves and our children, a context in which to mark life-cycle observances and *simkhes,* and an avenue for contributing *tzedakah* and good works to our community. In addition to these functions, our groups also strive to meet the special needs of our members.

Members often comment that their group is like a family to them. Many gay people have become alienated from their families of origin over the issue of their homosexuality. For lesbian and gay Jews, membership in one of our organizations is often a helpful antidote to this alienation, providing the warmth, support, and acceptance that all of us need in order to thrive.

It is a rare Shabbat when parents, siblings, or former spouses aren't in attendance in our congregations, and we are glad to provide contexts for reconciliation. But sometimes families just will not accept the fact that a loved one is gay, and alienation becomes permanent. In those situations, the congregation often becomes a substitute *mishpacha*.

Many gay men and lesbians are parents, mostly as a result of heterosexual marriage. Now, an increasing number of lesbians and gay men are choosing to parent, and many who are Jews want a Jewish education for their children. Some gay and lesbian congregations have begun to establish family *chavurot* and religious schools, bringing new vitality and commitment to synagogue life.

While communal and pastoral concern for the sick and dying is a very traditional function for a congregation, the AIDS epidemic has required much from us. We have learned to be care givers for the sick and comforters of the bereaved, especially as established Jewish congregations and agencies have only recently begun to acknowledge the need for services to people with AIDS and their families.

The joys and benefits of joining together with gay and Jewish sisters and brothers have always strongly outweighed disagreements and differences in philosophy, style, and background of participants. But these disagreements and differences are real. Because gays and lesbians seeking to join one of these organizations seldom have more than one choice in their geographic area, a much more diverse group of people are drawn together than in the traditional congregation, where members often self-select on the basis of religious orientation or other affinities.

Typically, our groups are founded by people who identify as Orthodox, Conservative, Reform, Reconstructionist, and secular or cultural Jews. Nearly all groups currently include men and women, though some have been predominantly male or female, especially in earlier years. Members range in age from their early twenties to their seventies and older, though most have been primarily from the "Stonewall generation," in their thirties and forties. Occupations range from blue-collar jobs to highly paid professional positions. The political

perspectives of members constitute another current of diversity, varying on such important issues as feminism, the Middle East conflict,
and relations between Jews and other groups of people. The views of
those who were radicalized by the social movements of the sixties
have not necessarily been shared by other members.

One of the most central and long-lasting areas of conflict has been
about feminism and the role of women. Many gay and lesbian people
have made their closest bonds with people of the same sex. Many
who participated in the women's movement and gay movement of the
seventies became accustomed to same-sex consciousness-raising, political, or social groups. Some felt a sense of relief when they joined a
gay and lesbian Jewish group and were able to share warmth and
friendship with people of the opposite sex. But inevitably conflicts related to sexism and feminist philosophy colored day-to-day interac-
tions and organizational decisions.

Almost every group had an early struggle regarding traditional sex-
differentiated language and roles in Judaism. Many groups decided to
write original prayerbooks for a variety of reasons, but primarily to
remove gender references to God. Groups were usually quick to make
ritual participation and leadership equally open to men and women.

While the majority of members approved of these changes, sometimes with some initial discomfort, others equated the changes with
destroying Judaism or rendering it unidentifiable to their senses.
Arguments would break out during or after a service when a de-
genderized liturgy was introduced. The international organization
debated resolutions to mandate nonsexist language in religious texts.
Workshops were held on reworking liturgy where members debated
how far to go in this process. Men bristled at strong women leading
from the *bima,* and women seethed when men, who often had much
more extensive childhood training in religious practice and Hebrew,
dominated leadership in this important area.

There was also friction outside the religious realm, much of it similar to what was happening in groups of men and women everywhere.
Women expected men to show more sensitivity to the subtle dynamics of sexism and had waning patience when men dominated conversations or overlooked women's points of view. This problem was com-
pounded by the tendency in gay men's culture to play loosely with
gender stereotypes, such as using female-like gestures or in other
ways identifying as female. The annual Purim party or talent show

might start as a fun occasion but end in an argument if women felt that some men had gone too far in the manner in which they masqueraded as the opposite sex.

Men also tended to be more open than most women in their joking about sexual matters. While this openness in gay men's culture is often a virtue, it sometimes led to women being offended or alienated. Some men, in response, characterized women as overly sensitive. To compound the matter, not all men or women agreed with the majority of their respective group. Some women, especially those who did not identify strongly with the women's movement, were angered by the issues other women raised. Some men, newly sensitized to their role in perpetuating sexism, were particularly critical of their brothers.

Groups handled these issues in different ways and sometimes lost members. One or two groups split apart over these issues and more than one international conference witnessed a walk-out by women offended by entertainment or programming we saw as unbearably sexist. Congregations sponsored workshops to help men and women work together. Our shared affection motivated us to try and try again to understand each other, despite many hurt feelings.

At one conference, the Saturday evening comedy act caused a group of twenty women and a few men to leave the ballroom in disgust over the typically sexist nightclub-style jokes. The women stayed up most of the night caucusing. When our caucus rose to speak at the plenary session the next day, the atmosphere in the room grew tense. The men, expecting to be lectured about sexism, felt tremendous relief when we surprised them by singing a parody of the entertainer, making our point by leaving everyone laughing, rather than angry and defensive.

Our groups have made a variety of choices about joining or working with other Jewish organizations and about adopting elements of traditional congregational life, such as a building, a rabbi, and a significant operating budget. On the whole, our groups have moved toward more recognition in the mainstream of the Jewish community, partly because of the influence, resources, and support it affords us. For example, BCC invested a great deal of energy in the Reform movement and eventually paved the way for more gay congregations to follow. In 1977, they successfully lobbied to reverse the rejection of a gay rights resolution, and by the mid-1980s they were able to co-sponsor a workshop with three more of our groups (San Francisco,

Chicago, and Miami), attracting a standing-room-only crowd who came to learn how to support gay and lesbian Jews. While such mainstream affiliations have afforded us valuable opportunities, they have sometimes moved us in a more conservative direction, in style and sometimes in politics.

Some of our groups have also begun to raise substantial sums of money, signing long-term leases or buying buildings of our own. Membership dues and the level of contributions have become comparable to those of neighboring congregations. An increasing share of our groups' energies have gone toward fund-raising, a reflection of our pride in our institutions and a step toward taking ourselves seriously.

Of course, money is a difficult issue. Some people don't want to pay dues or participate regularly. They may come to High Holy Day services, but can't imagine themselves affiliated with something that despite its gay membership, so closely resembles the congregation of their childhood. Some people have difficulty affording dues and are uncomfortable asking for a reduced rate, let alone socializing with a crowd that is increasingly professional.

In addition to economic issues, many women have tried our groups but found themselves more at home in a women-only Jewish lesbian group. Also, an increasing number of people who identify as bisexual are questioning whether the definition of the organization as gay and lesbian includes them as well.

Of particular interest has been the issue of hiring a rabbi or other professional staff. Some congregations have hired one or a succession of rabbis, while others just as big and able to afford a professional have steadfastly decided to leave liturgical leadership in the hands of their members. The relatively recent grass-roots origins of all our groups leads to dynamic tension in this area. Each group struggles to maintain accessibility, informality, and a strikingly high level of enthusiastic participation, while being open to what sensitive rabbinic leadership can offer to us.

While the trend toward religion and a synagogue style of organization has predominated in the United States and England, our groups in Canada, Europe, and Israel have not affiliated with a major religious movement or hired professional staff, nor have they made religious ceremony a major focus. Some of these groups are smaller or less stable, or their members just don't have the money that their U.S.

counterparts have. Some actively relate to the Jewish community and government of their country, but religion is not of major interest to them. The Dutch group, for example, proudly displays a very progressive political orientation, and, as postwar European Jews, have a distinct set of feelings about synagogue affiliation. The Israeli group reflects a largely secular interest in Judaism, just like most other Jews in Israel, and it finds its allies among nonreligious civil rights forces. Even in the United States, we have reached out to include noncongregational groups, such as a recently affiliated organization, the Jewish Lesbian Daughters of Holocaust Survivors.

Because religion and a sense of community have been key foci in most of our organizations, political action, with its potential for divisiveness, has often taken a much lower place on the priority list. The desire to offer an inclusive atmosphere for as many gay and lesbian Jews as possible has led to attempts to accept each other's political differences and to focus on activities that do not highlight these differences. With the exception of our active involvement in gay civil rights struggles, we often lack consensus on social and political issues.

Our history regarding Israel and Middle East peace issues illustrates this point. Over the years, the majority of our leaders and probably our members have held views on Israel very similar to those of mainstream Jewish community institutions, with the exception being our strong disagreement with Israeli society's discriminatory attitudes toward lesbians and gay men. At the same time there have always been other voices, although a minority, speaking for Palestinian self-determination and negotiations with Arab nations and representatives. These views have been the subject of many workshops, heated debates and resolutions brought to the plenary sessions of many early conferences. But the essential purpose of our organizations, building a gay Jewish community, included no framework for taking these issues beyond the discussion level. Like other Jews, our members often talk about Israel's situation and some take action through other organizations. But within the World Congress, the topic of the Middle East has almost slipped from sight.

Clearly, an international movement of gay and lesbian congregations and groups will continue, and the World Congress has reached a secure status as an organization. We expect to continue growing, with a larger and more involved membership base on the local and regional level, and more groups starting in places where they don't now exist. We hope for greater growth in Europe and outreach to other parts of the world, despite the fact that most of our activity, membership, and leadership are still centered in the United States, with our policies and activities reflecting U.S. perspectives. We are considering membership in international organizations that exist for both Jews and gays, including the UN's nongovernmental organizations for human rights.

We are often asked if a time will come when our groups will cease to be necessary. If heterosexual Jews understood and accepted us as gay people, would we want to join existing congregations and dissolve the organizations we have developed? Though we originally developed largely in response to our exclusion from the Jewish community, we have grown and flourished as positive alternatives alongside other Jewish organizations and movements. More likely than our dissolution is the possible integration of heterosexuals into our organizations. Some of our groups have designated themselves "gay outreach groups," with this phrase denoting that all are welcome, with a particular sensitivity to gay concerns and empowerment. Many of our groups include heterosexual members who are friends and allies or who are partners of bisexual members.

We have much to be proud of in our fifteen years of development. We have built dozens of strong, vibrant organizations that serve as a spiritual and communal home for their members. An international organization weaves our groups together and facilitates the sharing of resources. We have contributed to the Jewish community, the gay community, and to the world beyond these communities.

We have provided an avenue for thousands of Jews to find a proud and satisfying way to return to Judaism. Our existence and presence in the Jewish community has made it more possible for gay and lesbian Jews to belong to and contribute to other segments of the Jewish community.

We are contributing significantly to the Jewish dialogue about the family and about men's and women's roles. Our struggles to create egalitarian modes of spiritual and organizational leadership have taught us a great deal. The respectful closeness between gay men and lesbians in our groups is a rare model for friendships between men and women.

We are an organized voice influencing the rest of the Jewish community to change its attitudes toward gay people. Our member organizations played a key role in getting liberal Jewish organizations and community service providers to begin their involvement in the AIDS crisis. In times when the level of antigay oppression in society intensifies, we will continue to mobilize a significant segment of the Jewish community on behalf of gay rights, as we have already. As we work to educate other Jews, we strengthen the Jewish community in its ability to deal with others who have often been stigmatized and excluded.

We have created an energetic grass roots movement of Jews learning about, writing, and revising liturgy. Most of our groups have prepared their own Shabbat prayerbook, and some have developed many other pieces of liturgy for High Holy Days, gay pride day, and individual *simkhes*, like baby-naming. We have also added to the treasure of material created by women who are bringing female images and concepts into Jewish worship. These rich contributions are shared among our groups and, in some cases, much more widely.

In the early 1980s, the World Congress placed ads in several U.S. gay and women's publications just before Rosh Hashanah, to help local groups recruit new members. We planned to respond to every inquiry with a form letter and a printed list of our local organizations. As a staff member at that time, I answered many of these letters and repeatedly found myself writing personal responses. Letter after letter came from individuals in small towns, rural areas, and states with low Jewish populations. Occasionally a letter came from Brooklyn or Los Angeles where someone sat a few miles from us, but was unaware of our existence. Their stories of isolation, fear, and loneliness touched me and renewed my vision that our organization, our newsletter, our speaking engagements, our public education project, and even a newspaper reference to us could change a person's life.

The following year, an Orthodox rabbi called me repeatedly asking for resource materials. Only after the third phone call did he slowly begin to hint that he was gay. Imagine my deep satisfaction when a man took me aside at the international conference later that year and indicated that he was that rabbi: our phone calls had given him the courage to attend.

For this man and for so many others, we have helped to break their isolation as gay and lesbian Jews. Such connections are of profound importance to the human beings we have reached, and they are surely our greatest accomplishment.

Naming Is Not a Simple Act:
Jewish Lesbian-Feminist Community
in the 1980s

....

Evelyn Torton Beck

IT IS PROBABLY NOT AN ACCIDENT THAT I CANNOT FIND THE WRIT OF excommunication I received in 1982 from a Supreme Rabbinical Court of America, located in Silver Spring, Maryland, in the midst of celebrations heralding the publication of *Nice Jewish Girls: A Lesbian Anthology,*[1] which I edited. In that same year, speaking at a University of Wisconsin—Madison Hillel symposium on gay and lesbian Jews, I was ordered by a young male guardian of the faith to "Get out of *my* Judaism!" Though I cannot now physically put my hands on that letter of expulsion, I have no difficulty locating the pain inflicted by these assaults.

My reasons for repeating these stories are not simply to tell us what we already know. Until today it had not occurred to me that they were indeed Jewish forms of spiritual rape. I tell these stories because I want publicly to shame those groups and individuals who have hurt me as a Jew; I want other Jews to know that this *does* happen within Judaism, even in the 1980s. I want to pronounce the pain publicly because it can best be healed communally. I want to remind us that while we are working for the full acceptance of lesbian and gay Jews in the Jewish community, there are still Jews who actively reject gay and lesbian Jews *as Jews* and probably also as human beings.

These stories are also useful because they illustrate the underlying tension that comes to the surface whenever the needs of the individual Jew come into conflict with those who believe they are empowered to speak in the name of the *community.* I was not surprised to discover that the *Washington Jewish Week* recently featured a discussion focusing on "The Centrality of Community in Judaism," which singled out Rabbi Hillel's admonition, *"Separate not from the community"* as one of the most important "pillars of practical Jewish ethics."[2] Tellingly, the formulation of this precept places the burden of separation entirely on the individual and places no responsibility on the community to maintain its constituency. There is no parallel admonition to the community, "Separate not from those who challenge you by their difference." Historically, this valorizing of the community over the individual is as deeply embedded in Jewish secular as in religious life, as is made evident in a ground-breaking study of traditional Eastern European shtetl culture, which takes its title from the folk wisdom, *Life is with People.*[3]

Appealing as the ideal of cohesiveness is to a people perpetually at risk in the dominant culture, an unexamined celebration of Jewish "community" inevitably leads to the kinds of painful experiences with which I began this essay. While Jews the world over share much, we have never been a unified community. For this reason, it is vital to understand contemporary Jewish lesbian-feminists as simply *one* grouping among a multiplicity of Jewish communities which, when taken together, constitute "the Jewish People." Like any other people we are one and many at the same time.

In a highly imaginative scholarly study entitled *Another Mother Tongue: Gay Words, Gay Worlds,* lesbian-feminist poet-activist Judy Grahn discusses the history of gay/lesbian culture in ways that make a compelling parallel to Jewish culture. Like Jewish culture, gay culture is both old and continuous, with traditions that survive even as they are transformed. Like Jewish culture, gay/lesbian culture is marked by rhythms of resistance and survival against great odds. Because we challenge the hegemony of Christianity and heterosexuality, members of both Jewish and gay and lesbian groups have been subject to physical and verbal abuse simply for *being* who they are.[4] Epithets like "dyke," "queer," and "faggot," parallel the insults *kike, yid,* and most recently, "JAP."[5] Members of both groups have developed particular ways of seeing and experiencing the world and have made major contributions to the dominant and minority cultures in which they live.[6]

Grahn attributes that continuity to the fact that "members teach each other so that the characteristics are repeated era after era."[7] In this description, I am struck by the resemblance to the Jewish command to pass on the teachings and history of our people across the generations. "And thou shalt teach them to thy children"[8] and by implication, "to thy children's children." If Jews could learn to value the passing of culture across generations *without at the same time* insisting on biological continuity as the only form of cultural transmission, then the parallel between the two cultures would be even stronger, and more poignant, since each group contains some "hidden ones" of the other.

In both cultures, at times the meanings behind particular religious or social practices (which serve as reminders of history) are lost. For example, many descendants of Marranos[9] no longer know the meaning or origin of the Friday evening candle lighting ritual in which they participate; similarly, many gay and lesbian people have no idea why it is customary for them to wear pinky rings or why purple is their color. Grahn continues, "I have found that Gay culture has its traditionalists, its core group, that it is worldwide, and that it has tribal and spiritual roots. Gay culture is sometimes underground, sometimes aboveground, and often both."[10] This sounds very much like a description of Jewish culture if we think in global and historic terms.

Each culture identifies itself by means of special colors that have ancient roots. As noted above, purple is the color of gay male culture and the Lesbian Nation.[11] Blue and white are the colors of the ancient *talis;* these were adopted by modern Jews as symbolic of the Jewish people and thus became the colors of the flag of Israel.[12] Language is also an important unifier. Grahn shows how gay/lesbian life relies on a special vocabulary that helps the culture remain cohesive. The "Jewish" languages (ancient and modern Hebrew, Yiddish, and Ladino) carry significant symbolic weight and have provided an essential means of communication across time and national boundaries. If normative Judaism were not so threatened by the idea of gay/lesbian life, and normative gay culture didn't reflect the dominant culture's Christian assumptions, the parallels between the two cultures could provide points of communication and a mutual recognition, perhaps even alliance. Such an understanding is particularly important to Jewish lesbian-feminists who live in the intersection where these two cultures meet, a place that feminist psychologist Lee Knefelkamp refers to as "living in the in-between."[13] Precisely because Jewish lesbian-feminists live in this place, insisting on the power to name ourselves is crucial.

Naming is not a simple act. Naming is a public declaration of identity, a statement that becomes a responsibility both to oneself and to the group. Naming separates one group from another, but at the same time, creates a space where others like you can join. In a lesbian-feminist context, naming oneself is a way of speaking truth, and a way of claiming power that challenges the traditional owners of the name. As my opening stories make clear—and as my experiences of Jewish invisibility in the lesbian-feminist movement make evident—there are those in both communities who would *take away my name.*

Exactly *who* owns the name of any group is a critical issue that needs to be further developed, for the power to name is nothing less than the power to *include* and to *exclude.*[14] The heat surrounding the question of "authenticity" and the determination of exactly who has the right to bestow or deny the name *Jew* or *lesbian* leads one to wonder *who* has *what* at stake in keeping people out.[15] In this context, naming becomes one way of "bothering the world."[16]

Naming can also become a catalyst for bringing to the surface a kind of tacit knowledge that resides within an individual or is shared by a group—what the philosopher Michael Polanyi describes as knowing viscerally, "with and through the body."[17] Naming does not necessarily happen all at once and can come in stages; it can mark the beginning or the end of a learning process.[18] Further, it can be a statement of expectation, a declaration of hope, a promise. But it can also be dangerous, since the meaning of our namings does not remain within our control. As I take the risk of naming myself, I expect that this naming will do something *for* me, perhaps solidify a sense of who I *am* or reconcile warring contradictions within.

The naming "Jew" held more surprises for me than the naming "lesbian." For me, "Jew" was about history, culture, and shared identity; in practice, it led me to become immersed in patriarchal world politics more than I wished to, and it involved me in an ongoing struggle with Jewish ritual. In the last few years I have had to face the fact that when Jewish rituals in a gay/lesbian synagogue are relatively untransformed by feminism, they do not give me any greater spiritual satisfaction than those in the average enlightened traditional (i.e., heterosexual) congregation. I have found that I must seek Jewish spiritual nourishment outside the synagogue, and I have been surprised to discover that it may not be in the exclusive company of gay/lesbian Jews.[19]

Perhaps most risky of all, I cannot predict what my namings will evoke *in* me. Internalized anti-Semitism in combination with homophobia may catch me by surprise and may surface together with enthusiasm, relief, and joy. These internalizations may lead me to impose limitations on how I now conceive of myself; they can determine behavior and constrict possibilities from within and without, as much as naming can provide new openings. Given these dangers, it is essential to understand that naming is not a singular act, but a daily and continual process of affirmation.

Ironically, because Jewish identity takes so many different forms, even so small and seemingly unified a group as those who name themselves "Jewish Lesbian Feminists" displays all the elements of diversity that characterize Jewish life in the United States. Yet, to say that Jewish lesbian-feminists do not constitute a community of any kind would be as false as if we were to make such a statement about Jews.

In a thought-provoking book which discusses the meaning of Jewish community (without, however, discussing gay/lesbian Jews), Leonard Fein poses the question, "What does it mean that we are Jews? Odds are the answer will not be about belief, or about ritual, or about shared language or shared culture or even shared history. Odds are the answer will one way or another focus on *our shared fate*. . . ." [20] I believe that this is probably also the most accurate answer to the parallel question, "What does it mean that we are Jewish lesbian-feminists?" It is the intersection of our shared fate as Jews *and* lesbians that gives us our most common ground, while feminism provides us tools of analysis and a politics. But we are probably in far greater agreement about who our enemies are than about how to proceed, or on which fronts to fight first. Like Jews everywhere, Jewish lesbian-feminists are both one and many.

Some historical perspective might prove useful here. This is not what I would have written (or did write) in the early 1980s, when grass roots Jewish lesbian-feminist communities first sprang into existence in dozens of small and large cities across the United States and in Europe to serve as support, study, and action groups. [21] In those years, merely declaring our existence and claiming our identities both as Jews and as lesbians was cause for celebration. Bringing the two cultures together created a sense of solidarity and provided a strong sense of community, which we did not question. I use the term community here as defined by Lee Knefelkamp in her "Community of

Scholars" speech: "Community is a place where individual differences are respected and heard, and where common values are affirmed and can serve as a basis for recognition."[22]

When Jewish lesbian-feminists first came together in the late 1970s, we viewed ourselves as communities that were built on common interests, common identities, and common histories. For a time, these were the safest spaces we had created for ourselves, and they served to nurture and protect us. They also provided the safety in which we could explore our differences, which proved to be many and treacherous. As our explorations of commonalities deepened, it became apparent that differences in class backgrounds, Jewish education and religious training, knowledge and political opinions about Israel, as well as crucial differences in our ages, memories, experiences of the Holocaust, together with all the other differences that divide Jews, also marked our groups, no matter how small our groupings were.

Perceiving these differences, we still wanted to be together. But beyond the initial thrill provided by simply being together and in response to the familiarity these groups evoked, we did not always know what we wanted from each other, since shared identities do not necessarily result in affinities or friendships. More serious yet, these resemblances to our Jewish families of origin also brought with them some of the unhealthy patterns and tensions that seem inevitably to reside in family units. (In this connection, it strikes me as possible that the strong familial resonances Jewish lesbians set up in one another may explain, at least in part, the apparently high incidence of non-Jewish partners among Jewish lesbians. The smaller pool of available Jewish partners, especially in certain areas of the country, is of course another factor.) Nonetheless, for many years Jewish lesbian groups were "home" to Jewish lesbian feminists, even as most of us continued to do political work in other arenas as well. A few such groups still exist as communities; most have lost their identities as discrete groups, usually after a long and reluctant loosening process.[23]

These groups were a parallel to the consciousness-raising groups that were critical to the development of the second wave of the women's movement in the early 1970s—with one essential difference. These groups were composed of Jewish lesbian-feminists, many of whom had been active for years in lesbian-feminist organizing. While some Jewish lesbians had never really given any thought to what it meant to be Jewish, others had not, as lesbians or as feminists, been able to find a welcoming context in which to nurture their Jewish identities. Thus, this shift toward Jewish consciousness was for some a return home, for others, a new discovery. But for all, it was part of an evolutionary process, in which the personal really became political and one form of feminist work gave rise to yet other layers of personal/political activism.

Jewish awareness was also spurred by the unexpected anti-Semitism Jewish lesbians encountered in the women's movement, including among lesbian-feminists.[24] Anti-Semitism within the women's movement was far less virulent than the rising tide of anti-Semitism in the United States and around the world, where right-wing Christian fundamentalists and neo-Nazis fomented overt acts of racism, anti-Semitism, and homophobia. Nonetheless the lesbian-feminist movement mirrored some of the attitudes of the dominant culture, particularly stereotypes of Jews, and anti-Israel sentiments which easily elided into anti-Semitism. That the women's movement was not entirely immune to the prejudices of the dominant culture was a sharp disappointment to many, not only to Jewish lesbians.

It was out of this political ferment that *Nice Jewish Girls* developed; its publication in 1982 was thus a culmination and a new beginning. I can still easily tap into the intensely pleasurable feelings of joy, surprise, elation, and liberation that were released at the first "official" public gathering of Jewish lesbians that I attended.[25] In the excitement of giving name to the identities that had been hidden, we were at first more than willing to overlook the differences among us, because one fact remained clear: we wanted to be *Jewish* as lesbian-feminists. And we needed each other to affirm ourselves.

We began by sharing our stories, creating an even more intense bonding among us. We also poured our energies into analyzing contemporary issues from Jewish lesbian-feminist perspectives; we learned to identify anti-Semitism and developed strategies to cope with and interrupt it. We also created Jewish lesbian-feminist cultural events in order to introduce Jewish themes to the larger lesbian community;[26] we held conferences and other educational programs, and of course, celebrated Jewish holidays as a community.

In many communities the Passover seder quickly became the major event of the year.[27] Because it is a celebration of freedom, the seder provided a unique opportunity to reconceptualize the traditional ritual, especially as there exists within modern Jewish tradition the precedent of transforming the seder by rewriting the Haggadah and making it inclusive of contemporary issues.[28] While dozens of texts were written for use at all-women's seders, many Jewish lesbians felt the need to create specifically Jewish lesbian-feminist Haggadahs to be read at lesbian-feminist seders.[29]

Though harder to transform, Hanukkah also attracted lesbian-feminists, since it provided an effective buffer against the pervasive emphasis on Christmas that mars the winter season for Jews.

Both holidays have their limitations (especially for nonreligious Jews) in giving meaning to Jewish lesbian-feminist identity. In most groups it became clear that the celebrations were not sufficiently rooted in a deeper and more ongoing connection to what it meant to be a specifically "Jewish" lesbian-feminist.

Many Jewish lesbians expected the simple act of naming themselves "Jewish" to be sufficient to activate changes within themselves for which they did not even know they were yearning. Some hoped to find new political direction and answers to unresolved personal and professional life decisions; others expected never again to feel isolated or alone, to find perfect security. Because such unrealistic expectations could not be fulfilled, many groups that had formed with high hopes and much enthusiasm did not remain alive as identifiable communities. While individual clusters of friendships within groups remained strong (and even evolved into extended families) most Jewish lesbian-feminists evolved patterns of activism that can best be described as "a web of overlapping group affiliations."[30] Jewish lesbian-feminists subsequently chose different means of living out their (for some, newly activated) Jewish identities. Some chose to do lesbian-feminist work within previously existing Jewish institutions like the *chavurah* movement, New Jewish Agenda, The National Council of Jewish Women (whose New York chapter formed a Jewish lesbian-feminist support group in 1986); others chose to put energy into the gay/lesbian synagogue movement, or Jewish feminist spirituality groups not limited to lesbians; or to work with Jewish groups fighting AIDS, or to enter Jewish communal professions as rabbis, cantors, teachers, and counselors (few in this group could risk being "out" in their jobs; for obvious reasons, most still remain closeted). Many Jewish lesbian-feminists in academe also chose to work within the strong Jewish caucus of the National Women's Studies Association, which was founded by a core group that included lesbian-feminists. Still others turned their energy toward writing and publishing; in recent years a vast number of works by Jewish lesbians have appeared in print. In at least one city, a small group of Jewish lesbian-feminists began a dialoguing group with heterosexual Jewish feminists; together they addressed the issue of homophobia at the National Hillel Directors conference in 1986.

Though I am still not active in any established Jewish community, I spend many hours doing educational outreach on Jewish feminist and lesbian-feminist issues within many different kinds of Jewish community groups and within the Women's Studies community.

In addition to the activities described above, Jewish lesbian feminists are deciding to parent or co-parent in large numbers. It may seem strange to include the choice to parent as part of the activism of Jewish lesbian-feminists, but this choice is widely interpreted as a political one, though it obviously also meets deep emotional needs. It is also made possible by the availability of insemination and the willingness of adoption agencies to place babies with "single" parents. (Adoption by two same-sex parents is not yet possible in most places.) This trend is probably also a reflection of inherited Jewish survival strategies which place enormous emphasis on childbearing as a means of perpetuating the Jewish people. Like other Jewish women, Jewish lesbians respond to that internal pressure;[31] most of these Jewish lesbian mothers are determined to raise their children with nonsexist Jewish consciousness. As the children of Jewish lesbians grow older and are perhaps sent to Jewish schools, they will pose a real challenge to those Jews who continue to oppose same-sex relationships because they "produce no (Jewish) children." It would be nice to speculate (and hope) that the presence of these children will spur the development of specifically Jewish nonsexist and nonhomophobic teaching materials that will lead to a Jewish history inclusive of "the world of our mothers."

There are yet other namings to which we have not paid sufficient attention. Jewish lesbian-feminist converts[32] to Judaism are naming themselves within Jewish lesbian contexts, and in so doing are challenging the widespread assumption that "one is born a Jew." My partner, Lee Knefelkamp, who lived Jewishly for many years before her formal conversion, helps us extend our concept of naming when she insists that naming "is an interactive process between the individual and the community." She continues, "One cannot name oneself a Jew

apart from the community's recognition, any more than the community can annex an individual without her consent."[33] Knefelkamp and
other converts to Judaism report having been met with disbelief
("*Why* do it?") or painful silence when they have "come out" as converts in Jewish lesbian-feminist circles, a response that resembles the
silence that all too often greets lesbians who come out in predominantly heterosexual groups. Such experiences are deeply disappoint-
ing and leave the lesbian convert feeling that she is not accepted as "a
real Jew." She thus remains isolated even in the one community in
which she might expect differences to be affirmed.[34]

Another group that has recently claimed a voice and its own space
is the international network known as Jewish Lesbian Daughters of
Holocaust Survivors (JLDHS), who have organized an annual conference and have developed networks for communication.[35] Important
questions concerning women's bonding in the concentration camps
and lesbian relationships among the inmates (whose presence has
only recently been acknowledged) also need to be further researched.[36]

As we see from these examples, Jewish lesbian-feminism provides
a multiple axis along which Jewish and lesbian histories should be
studied: there is the axis of Jewish history, literature, and learning; the
axis of gay and lesbian culture; and the axis of feminism; taken together, they offer a new way of approaching (and appreciating) the
complexity of our work and our lives. In an evolutionary process, we
can expect new groupings of Jewish lesbian-feminists (Sephardim, Is-
raelis, working class, disabled, old, and others yet to be named) to
make their presence known, offering the hope that *none* of us is made
invisible.

It is not an exaggeration to say that the fabric of feminism is laced
with, and in some significant ways held together by, lesbian-feminist
theory and practice. In a parallel analysis, Jewish feminism has been
enormously energized by the activism of Jewish lesbian-feminists
who have challenged patriarchal norms within Judaism from a particularly radical vantage point.

Historians have noted that Jews participated in radical movements
in the modern era in disproportionately large numbers.[37] In our time,
Jewish lesbian-feminists represent a new "prophetic minority"
among Jews who are carrying on the legacy of our radical foremothers
and fathers. It seems that no matter how little some of us actually

know of Torah and Talmud, we still live by what historian Gerald Sorin calls "the messianic belief system," which supports traditions of *righteousness, justice,* as well as *mutual aid* and *communal responsibility.*[38] I believe that the work of the Jewish lesbian-feminist community represents a continuation of *mentshlikhkayt*—humanitarian values that were honed in the *shtetl,* from which many American Jews stem. I believe that Jewish lesbian-feminist activism reflects the *shtetl* value of *yidishkayt,* which embodies a way of being Jewish in the world and "a yearning for an end to dispersion and a reintegration of Jewish life."[39] It also reflects a yearning for an end to all the oppressions within Jewish life and the surrounding world, that keep us divided within ourselves and from each other.

The Liturgy of
Gay and Lesbian Jews

·······························

Yoel H. Kahn

Hinei Mah Tov! How good it is to gather, in a rainbow of affec-
tions and sexual preferences, in the house of a God who loves
each of us as we are created, who loves without limit and forever.
How sweet it is to gather, women and men together, in the house
of a God who transcends human limits and categories.

THIS INVOCATION, WHICH OPENS THE HIGH HOLY DAY SERVICES AT
Congregation Sha'ar Zahav in San Francisco, conveys to the wor-
shiper not only that lesbian and gay people are welcome in this community but that the liturgy—and the congregation—embraces all of
us. This passage is also a theological statement: God loves each one of
us, not *despite* our sexuality but *because* of it. This prayer celebrates the
diversity of human sexuality as part of creation itself. If religious language and symbols have been used historically as tools of oppression
against lesbian and gay Jews, then we use the liturgy today to express
an affirmative message of God's acceptance and love. Liturgy, like
other religious symbols, tells us who we are and conveys a vision of
what we and the world might be. The liturgy of lesbian and gay Jews
affirms who we are and reflects a vision of our highest selves as individuals and as a community. The examples in this essay are drawn
from the liturgy of the lesbian and gay outreach synagogues, primarily from the texts and customs of Congregation Sha'ar Zahav in
San Francisco.[1]

Like the invocation quoted above, the liturgy of lesbian and gay
Jews includes many new texts composed over the last fifteen years,
but also draws from and is grounded in the traditional Jewish liturgy.
"Lesbian and gay Jewish liturgy" consists of the texts, customs and

traditions lesbian and gay Jews use in circumstances in which they identify themselves as Jews and as lesbian and gay people.[2] We bring the books, customs, and practices of our families of origin, synagogues, youth movements, and summer camps to the synagogue or religious community we join as adults, where the language of the traditional prayers often assumes new meaning in a gay-affirmative environment. We often borrow liturgical materials that were not necessarily composed with gays and lesbians in mind, but which use inclusive language and therefore speak to us. A major source has been the creative work of the Jewish women's movement. Also, in recent years the Reform and Reconstructionist movements began to publish nonsexist liturgical texts. In 1987, the Union of American Hebrew Congregations (Reform) endorsed a resolution on "Inclusion of Gay and Lesbian Jews," which calls for inclusiveness in liturgy.

Liturgy, however, is not limited to words. The meaning of the prayers we say is shaped by the context in which they are said, as the staging of a play affects how a playwright's words are understood. The seating arrangements in a room, wearing name tags, the style of service leadership, and the choice of music are all part of the "liturgical message."[3]

Acceptance and Integration

The overarching message that our liturgy communicates is acceptance and integration. The worshiping community at lesbian and gay-outreach synagogues is a community of choice; having been pushed away from Judaism because of their sexuality, the members have actively chosen to build or seek out a place where they are truly at home. Most congregations take specific steps to foster the building of community. At Sha'ar Zahav, we end every service by standing, linking arms, and singing "Oseh Shalom." Bernard Pechter, one of the synagogue's founders, explains that this is one of several customs emphasized in the earliest days of Sha'ar Zahav that were intended to bring people physically together and develop a sense of community.

In addition to joining our lesbian, gay, and Jewish values, our liturgy expresses our feminism. Historically, lesbian and gay groups were among the first in the Jewish community to make a commitment to egalitarianism between men and women. The insistence on gender-neutral language, in reference to humanity and to God, has been a symbol and expression of this commitment. The unacceptability of male God-language (Lord, His, Master, King, etc.) to the worshiping community has been an impetus to retype—and then rewrite—the traditional liturgy.

This commitment to replace sexist language has been a distinctive characteristic of our liturgical innovation. How best to accomplish this goal has also been a matter of controversy over the years and remains so today: What about the sexism inherent in the Hebrew? If the Creator truly includes and transcends human categories, why is "God" more acceptable than "Goddess"?

The earliest "prayerbooks" produced by lesbian and gay groups consisted of photocopied versions of a traditional prayerbook with the sexist references "whited-out" and replaced by hand. The service leaders, many of whom grew up using the Conservative or Orthodox prayerbook, sought to retain as much of the traditional Hebrew liturgy's format and texts as possible. The result was usually a liturgy readily recognizable as "conservative," accompanied by a progressive English text.[4]

Another meaningful distinction of our liturgy has been the widespread commitment in lesbian and gay Jewish organizations to rotating ritual leadership. The diversity in service-leadership styles—from neo-traditional to classical Reform to experimental (such as dance or meditation services)—reflects the diversity of our membership. Sharing ritual leadership emphasizes the spiritual democracy of the community and represents a further step in the empowerment of lesbian and gay Jews. Even those congregations now served by rabbis continue to share the leadership of worship between the rabbi and lay members. Yet the experimentation and diversity that characterized the early years has gradually given way to a more permanent liturgy as each congregation has developed its own traditions and customs. The published prayerbooks, however, typically include a variety of interpretations of each prayer. The options printed in the prayerbook, along with supplementary handouts and a diverse pool of service leaders, together ensure the continuing renewal and diversity of spiritual leadership.

The Question of Authenticity

Early in the nineteenth century, the first Reform Jews instituted changes in the liturgy by altering words, music, and themes of "the" prayerbook. Their detractors condemned these replacements as "inauthentic" substitutes. This criticism has been heard over the centuries whenever a group of Jews has wished to make changes in the liturgy. What one generation considers an innovation is defended by succeeding generations as wholly authentic. In truth, the standard of authentic Jewish prayer is whatever the Jewish community values over time. The authenticity of the new traditions being developed in our communities today will be fully validated only when succeeding generations decide whether they are meaningful and resonant for them.

In the meantime, it is important for us to let go of the idea of a monolithic "traditional liturgy." Most American Jews grew up in synagogues influenced by the liturgical customs of East European Jewry, and when we speak of the "traditional liturgy" it is these texts and traditions to which we refer. In fact, there has always been pluralism in Jewish prayer and liturgical custom. Local communities have always had special holidays, variations in the prayer service, special melodies, and other distinctive customs. The creation of a new set of customs and prayer rituals that reflect our generation and our community is the most authentic Jewish act of all.

Gay and lesbian Jews are sometimes excessively concerned with this question of authenticity. Having been told for so long that we are not valid members of the community, we go out of our way to show that we are "correct" in every other respect. This internalized oppression is expressed, I believe, in an excessive concern for doing things "the right way"—which is often equivalent with what we remember from our youth or our first explorations of Judaism.[5] An important part of coming out as lesbian and gay Jews is claiming our inheritance—the Jewish tradition—as our own and authorizing ourselves to contribute to its evolution and growth.

Rewriting the Prayerbook[6]

Until we created our own congregations, lesbian and gay Jews were invisible in the liturgy of the synagogue. A gay or lesbian couple was never invited to light the candles together or to receive an aliyah on their anniversary; gay martyrs were not recalled during Holocaust commemorations nor was Lesbian/Gay Freedom Day acknowledged from the pulpit. The first changes we made to the liturgy redrew the community's boundaries to include us. Sometimes this was as simple as replacing "husband" or "wife" in the Yizkor memorial prayers with "lover" or "spouse." Often the opening reading of a Shabbat or holiday service emphasizes the gay/lesbian context in which the service occurs. Though the rest of the service may remain unchanged from the traditional liturgy, the specialness of this service is acknowledged and validated. If lesbian and gay Jews have felt themselves invisible in the synagogue, the explicit recognition that lesbian and gay Jews are present begins to compensate for the years of exclusion.

The celebration of diversity is an important motif in the liturgy of lesbian and gay Jews. In response to the societal message of rejection or marginality because we are different, our liturgy emphasizes the unique contribution each person can offer. The Silent Prayer, below, concludes the Morning Blessings section in the Shabbat morning service and is based on a passage written by Martin Buber. Buber gives a religious humanist interpretation to what is originally a mystical concept—every soul is unique because it has a particular task or role to perform. The editor of this prayer expands Buber's general passage into an explicit affirmation of gay and lesbian Jewish personhood. Coming out, this text suggests, is a redemptive act, furthering the individual's own redemption and also helping to bring about "the coming of the Messiah":

> My God, I thank You for my life and my soul and my body; for my name, for my sexual and affectional nature, for my way of thinking and talking. Help me realize that in my qualities I am unique in the world, and that no one like me has ever lived: for if there had ever before been someone like me, I would not have needed to exist. Help me make perfect my own ways of love and caring, that by becoming perfect in my own way, I can honor Your name, and help bring about the coming of the Messiah.[7]

Lesbian and gay Jews identify the oppression of the Jewish people over history with our own oppression as lesbians and gay people. One of the earliest additions to the liturgy was adapted from a reading that focuses on Shabbat as the day of rest from the pace and pressures of modern life. The insertion of two new sentences emphasizes the Shabbat—and the synagogue—as the time and place of sanctuary from the pressures of passing as heterosexual in the weekday world:

> We have left the office, the store, the plant and the university, and we have eagerly prepared ourselves to greet the Shabbat, to begin our moment of rest.

We have come here for Shabbat, for rest not only from bread-winning, but also, for some of us, from the effort of appearing straight in a straight world, to rest from the effort of pretending to be what we are not.[8]

Many lesbian and gay Jews are spiritually and emotionally drained by the need to lie or to take other steps to pass as heterosexual. Having come out in order to make ourselves whole, many of us are once again fragmented by the need to hide. Like so many Jews before us, in our hour of worship we seek to affirm and strengthen our true identity. The following prayer is from the Friday evening service of Congregation Beth Simchat Torah in New York City:

O God of truth and justice, the evasions and deceits we practice upon others and upon ourselves are many.

We long only to speak and to hear the truth, yet time and again, from fear of loss or hope of gain, from dull habit or from cruel deliberation, we speak half-truths, we twist facts, we are silent when others lie, and we lie to ourselves.

As gays, we often feel forced to pretend to be that which we are not, to present ourselves in ways which are not truthful, and sometimes with outright lies.

But as we stand before You, our words and our thoughts speed to One who knows them before we utter them. We do not have to tell untruths to You as we are often forced to do in the straight world. We know we cannot lie in Your presence.

May our worship help us to practice truth in speech and in thought before You, to ourselves, and before one another; and may we finally complete our liberation so that we no longer feel the need to practice evasions and deceits.

This passage was originally written for use as a High Holy Day meditation on the importance of truth in our lives. The editors of the prayerbook inserted a single sentence ("As gays, we often . . .") into the middle of the reading and slightly modified two other lines. These additions transform the entire prayer into a challenging reading about coming out. Do we remain closeted "from fear of loss" or "hope of gain"? Without making judgment, the first half of the prayer acknowledges the real-life circumstances of most gay and lesbian Jews.

The second half affirms the acceptance of lesbian and gay Jews before God and points to the contrast between inner truth and external appearances. The text reminds us that the lies which many lesbian and gay Jews are forced to live are a consequence of our oppression: "We do not have to tell untruths to You as we are often forced to do in the straight world." The closing sentence is a statement of messianic hope, emphasizing that a more perfect divine service can occur only in a liberated world.[9]

Many Jews say Kaddish in memory of those who died in the Holocaust because "they have none to remember them but us." This custom has inspired gay and lesbian Jews to recite kaddish for our gay and lesbian brothers and sisters throughout the ages. At Beth Chayim Chadashim in Los Angeles, for example, before kaddish is said, the service leader asks the congregation to remember "those who died wearing the yellow star or the pink triangle," along with those who have died from AIDS. The High Holy Day Yizkor (memorial) service at Sha'ar Zahav includes this passage:

> Sister that I never held near
> Comrade that I never embraced
> Your memory is almost lost:
>
> The one we don't talk about.
> The loving one who never married.
> The one for whom no Kaddish is said.
>
> Your loneliness calls out to me:
> I know of your struggles; we are not strangers,
> And if my path is easier, I will not forget who walked it
>   first.
>
> We call you to mind, but did you not sometimes think of
>   us,
> Your children, lovers across the years,
> Those who would follow and would think of you
> And bless your memory, and call you to mind.
>
> With David and Jonathan, we will not forget you,
> With Ruth and Naomi, we will not forget you,
> In the name of God you are our sisters and our brothers,
> And we ask that you be remembered for peace.

In the traditional liturgy, a special prayer is read at Yizkor services and on certain Sabbaths in memory of Jewish martyrs. This custom began in the years following the Jewish massacres during the Crusades. The theme of the traditional prayer, which calls upon God to remember the sacrifice of those who died, is reflected in this introduction to the kaddish:

> O God, remember today our gay sisters and brothers who were martyred in years past: those murdered by fanatics in the Middle Ages, those who perished in the Holocaust, and those struck down in our own city, in our own time. Remember also those who took their own lives, driven to despair by a world that hated them because of their love. And in mercy remember those who lived lives of loneliness, repressing their true nature and refraining from sharing their love with one another. O God, remember the sacrifice of these martyrs, and help us bring an end to hate and oppression of every kind.[10]

Like "O God of truth and justice," this prayer acknowledges the external sources of gay oppression. By locating gay oppression in a social context, this prayer helps channel our anger about our historical oppression into the work of *tikkun olam* ("making the world whole"), thereby giving religious meaning to our political struggle.

Lesbian and Gay Pride Shabbat

The examples we have looked at so far have been individual prayers. The English translations in the Shabbat evening prayerbook of Congregation Beth Simchat Torah in New York, *B'chol Levavcha*, illustrate how a Jewish lesbian/gay sensibility can enter into the interpretation of every prayer. The editors use the word "liberation" to emphasize the connection between the liberation of gay and lesbian people and Jewish messianic hope in all its dimensions. Throughout the *siddur*, the Hebrew word *"yeshu'a"* is translated "liberation," instead of the customary "salvation" or "redemption." The use of "liberation" is faithful to the spirit of the Hebrew while resonating with the imagery and language of gay liberation.

The struggle for gay liberation is identified as another stage in the struggle for freedom that began with the first Exodus/Coming Out. The Jewish religious tradition, in turn, speaks directly to the life-circumstances of lesbians and gay men. This process of integration is fully realized on the Shabbat before Lesbian/Gay Pride Day, which Beth Simchat Torah celebrates as "Gay Pride Shabbat" and observes as a festival. Hallel, the group of psalms that are read at the festivals and other holidays, is sung. Thus, we add a religious dimension to the otherwise secular holiday which celebrates gay pride and liberation. Through the use of the Hallel, Lesbian/Gay Pride Day is equated with the other pilgrimage festivals and the celebration of this new holiday becomes, through its observance as a Jewish religious event, "a reminder of the Exodus from Egypt." The opening words of Psalm 118, a section of the Hallel, *Kol rinah v'yeshu'ah*, are brilliantly translated: "Hear the gay shouts of liberation/from the tents of the just." [11]

Influenced by Beth Simchat Torah's example, we at Sha'ar Zahav have begun to observe the weekend of our Lesbian/Gay Freedom Day as Shabbat Freedom. The observance of Gay Pride Shabbat or Shabbat Freedom will be enhanced by choosing a *haftarah* for the festival. Every Jewish holiday has a special scriptural reading assigned to it. After the founding of the State of Israel, the Jewish community agreed on a special *haftarah* for Israel Independence Day. We can look to the prophetic voices of our historical tradition or to those of our own generation for a special *haftarah* reading, appropriate for the day and season. This ritual reading could become a shared tradition among lesbian and gay Jews and their supporters around the world. [12]

Siddur B'chol Levavcha's "Prayer For the Congregation and The Community" connects the continuing oppression of Jews and of gay people through complementary calls for liberation:

> Bless all gay people with liberation—men and women, young and old, those fully open as well as those deeply in hiding. May we all be granted Your blessings of freedom, liberation and equality. . .
>
> Bless the household of Israel wherever they dwell. Be with us here, where we worship You in freedom and liberation. May those who live under oppressive rule find release and liberty speedily, in our own day. . .

The closing line refers back to both groups: "As we cherish the freedom that is ours, so do we pray that those of our brothers and sisters who live in oppression, may find liberation."

In contrast to the claim that lesbian and gay people are "sinners before God," the liturgy of lesbian and gay Jews teaches that God's acceptance and love transcend human categories. Truly, in the words of the 118th Psalm, "The stone which the builders rejected has become the chief cornerstone." This idea is expressed in the following interpretation of the *Aleinu* prayer. The traditional *Aleinu* emphasizes the special destiny of the Jewish people and our messianic hope for the day when all the world will be one.[13] Using universalistic language, this version celebrates the unique destiny of all people:

> We are called to praise the Ruler of all things, and to magnify the Creator of all beginnings, who has made all people different, and has given us each a special destiny; who has led our souls to worship the one God of all creation, and who has formed our hearts to love in our own unique way.
>
> It is before the God who created us, who transcends human power and human judgments, that we bow down, worship and praise. . .

The closing paragraph of this passage is directly based on the traditional Hebrew text, echoing its call for an end to idolatry. The prayer assumes contemporary significance by equating religious bigotry with blasphemy:

> And so our hope . . . is that all peoples abandon their empty worship of human bigotry, and cease the blasphemy of calling on Your Name to justify oppression and hatred. Speedily turn all hearts to you . . .

The *Aleinu* has been a controversial prayer over history because of its emphasis on the "chosenness" of the Jewish people. An earlier interpretation of the traditional *Aleinu* identifies the "chosenness" of the Jewish people with the "chosenness" of lesbian and gay people:

> Let us give praise to the Ruler of the Universe . . . who did not make us like other nations, who created us different from other people, and set us on a separate path toward a special destiny.
>
> As gay and lesbian Jews we sometimes are forced to hide the qualities that distinguish us from others, our love for each other, our heritage of creativity spanning the millennia, our unique attributes with which we, in God's image, were created.
>
> But this cannot affect our inner resolve to honor and fulfill our special purpose, to live out this wonderful and unknowable design, in which each of us has a part to play.
>
> And so we bow in reverence . . .

These two parallel texts show how our theology of Judaism influences how we imagine our lesbian and gay identity. The second text emphasizes difference: "who created us different [sic] from other people" is a literal translation of the Hebrew original. Its second paragraph assumes a lesbian and gay "character" which, presumably, all lesbian and gay people share. The more recent interpretation, consistent with a universalizing trend in Jewish liturgy today, is more individualistic. Each nation's "special destiny" replaces Jewish "chosenness." Instead of focusing on gays and lesbians exclusively, this prayer thanks God who "formed our hearts to love in our own unique way." This passage, both inclusive and subtle, could be used at any Jewish service.[14]

A new *Mi sheberach* prayer, which appears below, reflects the impact of AIDS on our communities. The traditional prayerbook includes a public prayer for a person who is ill, which is recited after the reading of the Torah. The name *Mi sheberach* comes from the formulaic opening: "May the One who blessed our ancestors." Since 1985, we at Sha'ar Zahav have been reciting a *Mi sheberach* at every service for those affected by AIDS. Recently we have begun to pause in the middle of the prayer so that the congregation can say out loud the names of friends and lovers who are ill. The traditional closing of the prayer is, "May God soon send [the person who is ill] a complete healing, a healing of the body and a healing of the spirit." These words conflicted both with our theology of partnership and with the reality of the epidemic in which so many are dying. We have modified the traditional language to reflect a collective and messianic—if more distant—hope:

> May the One who blessed our ancestors, Sarah and Abraham, Rebecca and Isaac, Leah, Rachel and Jacob, bless [——— along with] all who are touched by AIDS and related illnesses. Grant insight to those who bring healing, courage and faith to those who are sick, love and strength to us and all who love them. God, let your spirit rest upon all who are ill and comfort them. May they and we soon know a time of complete healing, a healing of the body and a healing of the spirit, and let us say: Amen.[15]

Our Relationship with God

The use of nonsexist and gender-neutral language began as something which we changed from the traditional liturgy. Today the standard pioneered by Jewish women and adopted by lesbian and gay Jewish communities is increasingly becoming the "authentic norm" for a large portion of the Jewish people as a whole. It is not enough, some lesbian and gay Jews hold, to simply match each male reference with a female or neutral replacement—substituting "Ruler" for "Lord" or alternating "King" with "Queen." [16] The models of relationship they represent—sovereign and subject, master and servant—reflect neither our experience nor our ideal of our own relationship with God. While they were once meaningful and powerful images, today these terms often interfere with prayer and may actually reinforce oppression. We empower ourselves by replacing the passive language of the traditional liturgy, such as "Blessed are You," with language of reciprocity, "We bless You and we invoke Your blessing." The closing sentence of the prayer for gay and lesbian martyrs, discussed above, illustrates this change. The original version of the prayer said: "O God accept the holy sacrifice of these martyrs, and *call an end* to the hate and oppression that we have known for so long." The revised version now reads: "O God, accept the sacrifice of these martyrs, and *help us bring an end* to hate and oppression of every kind."

In wrestling with the existing categories and language of Hebrew prayer, poet and liturgist Marcia Falk has composed entirely new blessings in Hebrew and English in a rich and modern voice. These texts, though not explicitly gay/lesbian, are inclusive and feminist. Falk's carefully worded and spiritually moving prayers challenge and invite the entire Jewish community to re-envision both the form and the content of our liturgy so that it more accurately reflects who we are today and our highest visions of what might be. [17]

A New Canon

Another valuable source of empowerment is the work of gay and lesbian writers, and especially lesbian and gay Jews. The process of including these previously excluded voices is twofold. First, we must seek out the texts and sources that have been overlooked or never considered "religious" before. Then we must come to value them as authentic expressions of Jewish spirituality, as valid as any text in the "official" liturgical canon.

Judah Ha-Levi and many other medieval Jewish poets whose *piyyutim* are in the prayerbook also wrote homoerotic verse; some of their poems are appropriate for use in the Kabbalat Shabbat service, in union ceremonies, and in other liturgical settings.[18] We often incorporate the poetry of modern Hebrew poets, such as C. N. Bialik or Rachel, or read a story by I. B. Singer in a service; we consider their literary work as part of the Jewish spiritual heritage. Our lesbian and gay past is also rich. Drawing on our heritage gives us a greater appreciation of our history, strengthens our identity, and enriches us by expanding our vision. The possibilities are vast: Audre Lorde, James Baldwin, Mary Daly, Judy Grahn, Walt Whitman, Stephen Spender, and many others. Congregation Beth Chayim Chadashim, for example, uses a selection from Whitman's *Song of Myself* as an interpretive setting of the *Ma'ariv Aravim* prayer, whose theme is God's presence in nature.[19]

Our most valuable resource is the lives and legacy of lesbian and gay Jews, from David and Jonathan to Harvey Milk and the prophetic voices of our community today. Novelist Alice Bloch has written new readings for the High Holy Days, which are included in the liturgy of Beth Chayim Chadashim. The poems and prose of Adrienne Rich are infused with a Jewish-lesbian consciousness. At a memorial for the martyrs of the Holocaust or in memory of those who died of AIDS, the closing lines from Rich's poem, "Natural Resources," sum up the pain of our history, our choice to claim our identity, and our commitment to the future:

> My heart is moved by all I cannot save:
> so much has been destroyed.
>
> I have to cast my lot with those
> who age after age,
>
> with no extraordinary power, perversely,
> reconstitute the world.[20]

Rituals for the Cycle of Life

Many gay and lesbian Jews desire a union ceremony that is equivalent to a heterosexual marriage ceremony. Since lesbian and gay people are denied the social and legal privileges of marriage, the purpose of the ceremony is more personal: to create a ritual and spiritual context that affirms the sanctity and commitment of two people's relationship. Designing a ceremony that is authentic for us as Jews and as gay and lesbian people presents a special challenge. On the one hand, we do not need to imitate exactly what heterosexual people do; on the other hand, our relationships and our ceremonies deserve to be granted the same validity and seriousness.

In my role as rabbi, I do not call lesbian and gay union ceremonies "weddings." Weddings are licensed by the state and require a marriage license provided by the civil authorities. Avoiding the term "wedding" points out the social and legal marginality of our lives and unions.[21] Instead, I call these ceremonies by the traditional Hebrew name for a marriage, *kiddushin. Kiddushin* means "sanctification" and accurately describes the ceremony: a declaration before the community and before God that this union is a sanctified relationship, and an invocation of the blessings of both upon it.[22]

Most lesbian and gay Jews want their ceremony to include the central rituals and themes of the traditional Jewish *kiddushin* ceremony: kiddush, *chuppah* (canopy), rings, *sheva berachot* (seven blessings), *ketubah* (contract), and breaking of the glass. Some of these need no reinterpretation to be used in a lesbian and gay context; the symbolism of the *chuppah* as the couple's home and of God's *sukkah* is equally meaningful for all Jews. The seven blessings parallel the seven days of creation. They represent the idea that this union is a "completion," as "natural" for these two lives as the creation itself, which was finished on the seventh day. The text of the seven blessings is slightly modified, substituting *rai-im ha-ahuvim* or *rai-ot ha-ahuvot* ("beloved companions") or *b'nai ahavah* or *b'not ahavah* (literally, "children of love") for "the bride and the groom."[23]

The exchange of rings, and the accompanying legal formula, is the climax of the traditional ceremony. The traditional language, "you are consecrated unto me *according to the law of Moses and Israel,*" is replaced with *"lifnei Elohim v'adam b'ru'ach ameinu Yisrael"* ("before God and humanity in the spirit of our people Israel"). This change acknowledges that the ceremony is not a halakhically valid one.[24] Instead, the new wording affirmatively states what this ceremony is: the invocation of God's and the community's recognition and blessing of the seriousness and sanctity of the union, a statement of commitment by the two partners, and the conscious linking of their relationship and the home they establish with the historical Covenant of the Jewish people.

There are other rituals and new forms of liturgy that are either being created today or will be created in the near future. There is a great need for a ritual of "coming out," the act of claiming one's identity, of assuming responsibility, and of choosing to cast one's lot with one's people. Coming out as lesbian or gay can be considered as complementary to the place which bat/bar mitzvah has assumed in contemporary Judaism. Perhaps the obvious parallels in purpose will guide the form such a ritual would assume.

Gay and lesbian Jews need new mourning customs. Often parents or family members die and are buried in a distant city. Gay men and lesbians participate in the mourning rituals with their families of origin and then return to their extended family and community. How can the extended family and community express their support? When do the mourners share their grief with those closest to them when none were able to attend the "official" rites? We have had a special night of *shiva* when a mourner returns home so that the local community can gather. On other occasions, we have used the conclusion of *sheloshim*, the thirty-day period of mourning for an immediate relative, as an occasion for a memorial service and communal coming-together. The AIDS epidemic requires new rituals of healing and mourning whose form we are only now beginning to shape.

Since 1987, family and friends have been memorializing people who died of AIDS by making a panel for the Names Project Quilt. First unveiled during the October 1987 National March on Washington for Lesbian and Gay Rights, the quilt is the largest folk art project in history. The Names Project Quilt, its thousands of panels inscribed with the names of people who have died of AIDS, has become a *yizkor* memorial in thread and canvas. It is surely appropriate to recite kaddish when visiting the quilt; I believe that we can find Jewish meaning and consolation through creating a special kaddish or an added ritual for this occasion.

The Hebrew essayist Achad Ha-Am (Asher Ginzberg) described the task of spiritual renewal as: *"L'chadesh et ha-yashan u'l'kadesh et ha-chadash"* (To renew the old and to sanctify the new). The need to reclaim our history, redefine community, and re-envision our future is not the exclusive task of gay and lesbian Jews. We are fortunate to have many allies who are also laboring to create an inclusive, feminist- and gay-affirmative liturgy that all Jews can share.[25] For lesbian and gay Jews, this process is both the outcome and fulfillment of our coming out. Our vision is reflected in this passage by Judy Chicago:

> And then all that has divided us will merge
> And then compassion will be wedded to power
> And then softness will come to a world that is harsh and
> unkind
> And then both men and women will be gentle
> And then both women and men will be strong
>
> And then all will live in harmony with each other and the
> earth
> And then everywhere will be called Eden once again.[26]

Living as All of Who I Am: Being Jewish in the Lesbian/Gay Community

Eric E. Rofes

NOTHING PREPARED ME BETTER FOR MY LIFE AS A GAY ACTIVIST than growing up as a Jew in America.

My Long Island middle-class Jewish family provided me with three primary skills that have enabled me to feel at home in the world. They taught me pride in being who I am, even when that identity seemed to conflict with mainstream American culture. They helped me learn to value education, analysis, and issue-oriented debate. Finally, they impressed upon me the critical importance of building and sustaining community, as well as the responsibility to serve that community.

While these skills were intended to aid my survival as a Jewish boy in an Italian/Irish suburb, they have proven indispensable to me as a gay man living in a world that often prefers that I not exist. During my years of activism in the gay community, I have frequently been aware that my values are closely aligned with those of my parents. My efforts as an organizer focus on what I learned to value in my parents' home and at our Jewish community center: community, family, security, and justice.

Growing up, I experienced several occasions when other kids would single me out for anti-Semitic taunts, seizing on characteristics that placed me outside the accepted mainstream of American culture: my inability to throw "like a boy," my refusal to fistfight, my studiousness, my glasses, or my nose. While these were all identified as "kike" traits, most are strikingly linked to cultural definitions of masculinity. While I was overtly being targeted as a Jew, I was also being labeled as "queer." This was hard but useful preparation for later experiences of being much more overtly targeted as gay.

Style and Assimilation

After graduating from college in 1976, I became involved in Boston's lesbian and gay community through working in several organizing projects—a gay youth support group, a men's child care collective, and the weekly paper, *Gay Community News*. My attempts to enter my new community met with mixed success. I found it difficult to sustain friendships and often felt at odds with the culture of the community. While I initially ascribed these problems to my jitters over coming out, it soon became apparent that people were put off by my "style": my openness, my anger, my passion, my rough edges. I seemed to lack the ability to "tone it down." People wanted me to speak less emphatically, to acknowledge my vulnerability, and to be less direct and confrontational. I was stunned that in my own community, I was hearing some of the same critiques I had heard from gentiles at Harvard.

At this point I felt isolated as a gay Jew. While there were certainly other Jews involved in key positions in the gay community, we did not acknowledge our shared identities, and we rarely challenged anti-Semitism. Frankly, I found myself confused as I attempted to understand how my personal style affected others. The level of anger seething within me did not seem at all unusual in the Jewish community in which I was raised, where shouting and kvetching and direct confrontation were part of normal human interaction. Yet after several years among people with different styles of communication and very different ways of responding to anger—particularly the nonconfrontational "polite" style prevalent among WASP New Englanders—I questioned myself and sought to explore the sources of rage within me. I wondered whether Jews were simply angrier than others, or whether some of us just feel more comfortable expressing it.

I was well aware that I needed my new community—I needed to feel at home somewhere in the world. I made a conscious effort to change, to assimilate. I found myself attempting to say difficult things in collective meetings without really saying them. I worked to de-

velop techniques that would mute anger and blunt the harsh edges of
criticism. Initially this felt odd to me, and I experienced conflict between my desire for acceptance and feelings of disloyalty to myself
and my ethnic heritage. I wondered whether the traits I was attempting to blot out were real Jewish characteristics or Jewish stereotypes.
Communication style felt like such a strong basis of my ethnic identity. I often felt sad and exasperated: did claiming my identity as a gay
man necessitate giving up my Jewishness?

Through the pain of assimilation I grew, and over the years I have
established a balance, in large measure due to support from other lesbian and gay Jews and the growing discussion of anti-Semitism
within our community and among ourselves. But this process of bal-
ancing is ongoing. Shortly after moving to Los Angeles in 1985, word
got back to me once again that my "style" was not going over well
with certain other activists. I was told that people were categorizing
me as "too East Coast." I was warned that my manner of confronting
issues directly and failing to couch my language in niceties would
cause problems for me. One woman asserted openly that I was a
"typical pushy New York Jew," a remark that apparently went un-
challenged in a group of a dozen lesbians.

To deny that I continue to struggle with these issues would be to
deny that I continue to want to live as all of who I am in the gay and
lesbian community. I have had to examine my personal characteristics
and manner of communication, as well as my energy level and inten-
sity, and decide which were worth preserving. I continue to value
traits that I ascribe to my Jewishness. For example, I value the ability
some of us have to release rage through humor or verbal sparring.
However, these days I choose my sparring partners carefully and
don't assume that all gay and lesbian activists will share this predilec-
tion with me.

Understanding my cultural characteristics as a Jew and the traditions of Jewish culture—and experiencing the tensions surrounding
assimilation and maintaining cultural integrity—has moved me to relate personally to the concerns voiced by people of color seeking to
create a multicultural gay and lesbian community. A melting pot
where we would all simmer together and slowly lose our ethnic and
cultural characteristics, blending into a singular American identity, is
not what I want for our community. The quilt or the rainbow are images I prefer: a community united in its diversity.

Anti-Semitism in the Gay Community

In addition to the insistence on the primacy of WASP culture and style, I have encountered several overt examples of anti-Semitism in my work in the lesbian and gay community. Many of these revolve around stereotypes about Jews and money, such as a committee member once suggesting that I manage the finances at a fund-raising event because "Jews know how to handle these things." I have also encountered oppressive perceptions of Jews as martyrs, having been accused of this complex by another activist who simplistically explained my psychological makeup as being similar to "the Jews who let the Holocaust happen." I have heard "JAP" comments bantered about at gay bars and meetings, with participants seemingly unaware of the inherent sexism, racism, and anti-Semitism in these remarks.

Obviously, these examples are very common to many other settings, and may even be less frequently encountered in the gay and lesbian community, certain sectors of which appear to be more sensitive than most communities to issues of difference, oppression, and assimilation. I expect more from the gay and lesbian community, and perhaps that is what makes anti-Semitism so painful to me when it is encountered.

Once, at a fund-raising dinner for a gay political group, a speaker was passionately discussing the impact of AIDS on the gay community and engaging in rapidly escalating hyperbole. At one point, he insisted that gay people not go silently to their deaths, "like six million Jews did in the Holocaust." This ignorant and offensive revision of history cut me sharply and I sat stunned, unable to move. I felt tears start to well in my eyes. Suddenly I felt a hand on my shoulder. Standing behind me was a friend—a friend who is not Jewish—who bent down to whisper, "I saw you flinch with that outrageous statement about the Holocaust." As his hand kneaded my neck and shoulders, he continued, "Before you go crazy and start screaming, I just wanted to let you know that someone else thought it was outrageous, too." I felt comfort and solidarity. This is what I need from my community.

My responses to these overt anti-Semitic actions have changed over the years. Initially, my own self-hatred and my fear of confronting the dominant culture kept me a silent co-conspirator to anti-Semitism. As my own consciousness developed, and as other gay and lesbian Jews began to create spaces for support, as well as analysis and critique of the gay and lesbian community, I felt able to speak up. I am particularly grateful to leadership from the lesbian-feminist community and from gay and lesbian synagogues across the country for spearheading the resistance to anti-Semitism among gay men and lesbians.

Perhaps most difficult for me have been incidents in which other gay and lesbian Jews have made anti-Semitic remarks in a "mixed" gay setting. I have heard one prominent Jewish businessman regularly make comments such as, "The Board treasurer should be a Jew." I have listened to Jewish gay and lesbian entertainers make deeply anti-Semitic "jokes." And, while expressing my outrage or my amazement at the lack of outcry from others, I have been told that I was "too sensitive." While I initially expressed my concerns angrily, I have learned to approach people in a gentler way, trying to help my Jewish sisters and brothers gain more awareness and comfort with their own Jewish identities. I am well aware that, were it not for my exposure to certain individuals over the past decade, I could be the one making these offensive remarks.

Physical Appearances and Internalized Oppression

I am a Jew of Eastern European background. From my earliest years, dark hairy men—Eastern European or Sephardic—have been my primary erotic interest. Such men have seldom adorned the pages of gay male porn magazines or, more recently, erotic videos. The blond "surfer boy" look appears to reign as America's accepted cultural ideal. This bias has often made me feel invisible as a Jewish man and has made me ponder my own erotic feelings.

I have gone through different phases in attempting to analyze my erotic preferences. Early on, I resented the narrow focus of my fantasies and felt as if I were limiting myself. I imagined that my early sexual feelings—which I remember occurring in Jewish settings such as Sabbath services, Hebrew school, or at my Jewish Federation summer camp—were shaped by the characteristics of the boys and men in close proximity. I therefore felt no erotic interest in blond, hairless men. I recall feeling a bit arrogant later, assuming my attraction to men of my own ilk (and other similarly ethnic-looking men, such as some Italians) somehow proved that I accepted myself. At that time, I felt that Jewish men who turned on to the blond "All-American boy" look were self-hating Jews. In more recent years, I have relaxed my judgments, although my attraction for traditionally Jewish-looking men has not wavered. Big noses, curly hair, and balding men may never appear on the cover of *Advocate Men*, but they continue to make me happy.

Many times, I have felt conflict regarding the preference many gay men appear to have for "uncut" (uncircumcised) men. On one hand, I resent activists who are quick to judge as "politically incorrect" gay men and lesbians who have preferences for particular body types, races or ethnicities, or physical appearances. I believe erotic desire is too complex to analyze and judge quickly, and I don't want to beat down all of us who have worked so hard to get to the point where we could experience and enjoy our desire for others of our gender. On the other hand, I believe our erotic preferences are culturally formed, and that desire for uncircumcised men sometimes reflects the anti-Semitism of our culture.

My relationships with Jewish men have always interested me, as I have attempted to understand my diverse feelings of erotic attraction, brotherhood, competition, and rivalry. While I have dated and slept with many Jewish men, I have been surprised that my two long-term relationships have been with gentiles. My shorter-term experiences with Jewish men have often been confusing to me. I often feel an immediate identification and sexual charge, enhanced by intellectual exchange. The banter may remind me of my childhood friendships or my rivalry with my brother. Yet, for a variety of reasons—including intense competitiveness—these relationships have never taken hold and developed. I am aware that as I find myself dating certain Jewish men, my own anti-Semitism intensifies. I would like to pretend that such feelings have not crept inside me—that I am a proud, self-affirming gay Jew at all times. I know now that part of me is and part of me is not. Rooting out self-hatred and messages from the dominant culture is a lifelong process.

When I first became seriously involved with one particular Jewish man, Jay, I began to have some very uncomfortable feelings and realizations. I was very attracted to him, especially when we were either alone or at the gay synagogue. But when we were out in public as a couple, I felt glaringly gay and, surprisingly, glaringly Jewish, as if there were a sign around my neck saying both "queer" and "Jew." My

feelings about Jay focused on my assessment that he looked more traditionally Jewish and more "effeminate" than I did. I am not sure he
actually did, but I felt this way at the time. I was forced to face my
own internalized homophobia and anti-Semitism, as being with Jay
seemed to threaten my ability to "pass" as straight and gentile. Even
though I was doing a lot of public speaking as a gay Jew, I felt vulnerable about not necessarily having a choice of when and whether to
"pass" in other situations. Recognizing what was going on helped me
and my relationship with Jay.

Another Jewish man I dated raised similar issues in a different way.
I met Mark in a leather bar in New York and was instantly attracted.
Our similarities—coming from comparable religious backgrounds,
discovering that we had been college classmates, enjoying dark
bearded men like ourselves—seemed to be key to our mutual attraction. When we went out together, people often asked if we were
brothers, and in fact, we often sparred and bantered as I do with my
actual brother. Being with Mark made me feel very gay and very Jewish, but in this case, I thoroughly enjoyed it.

The Joys of Being Gay and Jewish

Despite the problems and pain, I find a great deal of pleasure and
happiness in realizing my identities as a gay man and a Jew. I feel satisfaction and comfort in attending services at a gay shul. I delight in
the laughter and feelings of shared experience while watching self-
affirming gay and lesbian Jewish entertainers. I feel special strength
in naming myself publicly as a gay Jew.

Perhaps what is most satisfying to me, is to find friends—other gay
and lesbian Jews—with whom I feel fully at home. I do not feel this
way with all gay and lesbian Jews, and there are gay gentiles and heterosexual Jews, as well as heterosexual gentiles, with whom I feel a
similar meeting of the minds. But there is something about being with
my gay and lesbian Jewish friends that makes me feel special, complete, and fully at peace. Spending an afternoon in a Jewish neighborhood, eating at a local deli with gay and lesbian friends, feels as if all
of who I am has a place in the world.

PART 5

....

Reaching Out:
Lesbian and Gay Jews in the
Jewish Community

INTRODUCTION

....

LESBIAN AND GAY JEWS HAVE ALWAYS BEEN INTEGRALLY INVOLVED in Jewish communal life, but almost always invisibly. The phenomenon of openly gay Jews participating in the religious, political, and social life of the community is a new one. Where we have been visible, others have had an opportunity to learn about who we are much more profoundly and rapidly. The essays in this section deal with these issues of visibility and learning, as well as social change. They also make clear that all of us—lesbian, gay, bisexual, and heterosexual—pay a high price for invisibility.

Janet Marder discusses her own growth as a rabbi of a gay and lesbian congregation. Her story is especially important, as she candidly admits the questions and discomfort still experienced by most heterosexual Jews, and she is equally forthright in describing what she has learned during her five years in that pulpit. Marder makes a strong argument for full acknowledgment of the dignity and humanity of lesbians and gay men, ending with her expression of gratitude that her two young daughters will grow up with many loving lesbian "aunts" and gay "uncles," and they will not have to rid themselves of the burden of homophobia when they reach adulthood.

In contrast, "La Escondida" is a lesbian rabbi unable to write under her own name. Her powerful Jewish commitment and call to the rabbinate are moving in themselves, but made more so in that she must hide part of herself in the community which she so enriches. She compares her situation to that of the *Marranos*, the Spanish Jews who were forced to pretend they had converted to Christianity, only able to practice Judaism covertly and fearfully.

Sue Levi Elwell describes how various Jewish institutions have responded to gay and lesbian issues during the past twenty years of the modern gay and lesbian liberation movement. She discusses three basic stances: condemnation, liberal tolerance, and commitment to full inclusion. She outlines the uneven yet encouraging trend toward the inclusion of lesbian and gay Jews, examining how, over time, an increasing number of people identify gay and lesbian Jews as "us" rather than as "them."

Following Elwell's essay, Andy Rose continues the "us and them" theme in describing some of the Jewish community efforts thus far to respond to the challenge of AIDS, which tragically has spurred more acknowledgment of the existence of gay and lesbian Jews than anything else to date. AIDS continues to offer opportunities for responsiveness and reconciliation, bringing out the best and the worst in our communal institutions, as in the rest of society.

Getting to Know the Gay and Lesbian Shul:
A Rabbi Moves from Tolerance
to Acceptance

....

Janet R. Marder

MAX AND ERNEST RECENTLY CELEBRATED THEIR TWENTIETH ANNI-versary. They have much in common: both are courtly gentlemen in their early sixties, Holocaust survivors, and agnostics with a strong commitment to Jewish culture. Max's mother has Alzheimer's disease. Max visits her faithfully, though it breaks his heart each time he sees her. Ernest suffers from high blood pressure and has undergone major surgery. "Our lives are intertwined," Max told me recently. "We give each other friendship, comfort, and joy."

Sandy and Elinor, a warm-hearted couple in their mid-thirties, met in a temple adult education class. Sandy is a Jew by choice. She converted through the Conservative movement, lived in Israel for a year, and now speaks and reads fluent Hebrew. Elinor grew up in an obser-vant Jewish home in the Midwest, spent time among the Orthodox in Jerusalem, and now identifies with the Reform movement. Sandy is a carpenter and amateur naturalist; Elinor a technical writer. Both study *Tanakh* in Hebrew each week with the rabbi and attend classes in Talmud and in Israeli folk dancing. They are very much in love and are thinking of becoming parents.

George is a genial, easygoing man in his early thirties. He is a suc-cessful salesman and is highly valued by his employer, who harbors fond hopes of marrying George off to "a nice girl." When he mentions this to George, he receives only a pleasant but noncommittal smile. A devoutly observant Jew, George davens regularly on Shabbat morning at his local Orthodox shul; his fellow worshipers wonder where he davens on Friday nights.

These names are not real, but the people are. They are all members of Beth Chayim Chadashim (BCC)—the House of New Life—the world's first gay and lesbian synagogue, located in Los Angeles. I have served as their rabbi for five years. I begin to write by describing them, and not with generalizations, for my work with BCC has taught me the dangers of generalizing. As I write about gay and lesbian Jews, I picture real people, as unique in their individuality as heterosexual Jews are.

Initial Prejudices and Doubts

In April of 1983, when I faced my first interview with BCC's rabbinic search committee, I knew only generalizations and abstractions. My mind was filled with images—some frightening, some repellent—of "the gay community" and "the gay life-style." I had almost no personal knowledge of gay people. My information came from newspapers and popular magazines that assured me that homosexuals were sinful and/or sick, promiscuous and hedonistic, and lived wretched, lonely lives—hanging out in bars and bathhouses, engaging in unspeakably sordid acts.

I had also been told by interested acquaintances (including some rabbinic colleagues) that gay men were "bitchy" and "difficult," while lesbians "hated men" and would probably hate me, too, since I am a straight woman. Some expressed vague concern about the influences to which I would be subjecting my (as yet unborn) children. Others warned me that I would place my career in jeopardy by accepting a job at the "gay temple"; forever after I would be suspected of being a lesbian, and no "normal" synagogue would ever hire me.

Why, given these discouraging words, did I apply for the position at BCC? Part of it was simply feeling that any congregation of Jews deserved responsible rabbinic leadership. But more important was the advice of my husband, Shelly, also a rabbi. He had professional contact with a group of BCC members who conduct monthly Shabbat service at a local nursing home. Shelly told me that the BCC volunteers led a service that was warmer and more spirited than any he had ever seen in a nursing facility. There was clearly something special about these men and women who took such pleasure in giving. Being the rabbi of such a group, Shelly thought, would have rewards far beyond the norm. "Go for it," he urged.

I have to give that search committee a lot of credit. They saw a rabbi who was naive, with thoughts that were very much in flux. Fortunately, however, they also saw that I was willing to learn, so they took a chance on me. They told me frankly that some members of the congregation clearly would have preferred a gay or lesbian rabbi, but that the committee felt it would be wrong to subject others to discrimination analogous to what they themselves encountered. Thus, their prime considerations had been to find someone to serve as a good Jewish teacher and an understanding pastoral counselor.

I felt considerable anxiety about both expectations. First of all, how could I teach Judaism honestly to a group I believed to be Jewishly illicit? How could I tell my congregants the truth—that our religious tradition clearly and vehemently rejects their way of life—and still inspire them to be devoted to that tradition? How could I ask gay men to love a Torah that condemns them to death for their sexual behavior? Moreover, how did I really feel about that tradition—its overpowering emphasis on marriage, the imperative to have children, the primacy of the family as the vehicle for transmitting Judaism? Could I still affirm those values while ministering to a congregation whose existence seemed to subvert them?

In addition, I was filled with doubts about my ability to counsel men and women who lived, I thought, so differently from me and everyone I knew. How would I ever understand their problems and help them? In fact, I was rather embarrassed by the concept of public "displays" of homosexuality; the thought of two men embracing or dancing together made me quite uneasy. Worse yet, I fully expected to hear details about my congregants' lives that would make me feel morally queasy. In other words, I wanted them to be honest with me, but deep inside I was afraid of what they might say.

Today, after many trials and many more errors, I hardly recognize myself. My beliefs have changed slowly, but in profound ways that affect my entire outlook on life. My thinking has shifted most significantly in three areas: the nature of homosexuality, the role of halakhah in liberal Judaism, and the place of lesbian and gay Jews in our community.

The Nature of Homosexuality

As soon as I was hired by BCC, I set out to learn whatever I could about homosexuality. I read works of psychologists, psychiatrists, sociologists, and physicians. (See the Bibliography in the appendix of this book.) I also read the accounts of "insiders," such as Howard Brown's *Familiar Faces Hidden Lives: The Story of Homosexual Men in America Today*[1] and Evelyn Torton Beck's *Nice Jewish Girls: A Lesbian Anthology*,[2] which began to give me a picture of whole lives lived by whole people.

Even these limited forays into the subject of homosexuality showed me that scientific studies were far from conclusive. Some regarded homosexuality as physiologically based, others traced it to environmental factors; some viewed it as "curable," others saw it as predetermined and immutable.

I began to see that the main division in studies of homosexuality is between those who classify it as undesirable "deviant" behavior, regardless of etiology, and those who accept it as natural, legitimate behavior in no way inferior to heterosexuality. I continued to read and learn, but I gradually found myself less interested in what the experts said, paying more attention to my own observations of the several hundred gay men and lesbians I came to know over the next couple of years. The more I came to know my congregants, the less capable I was of seeing their ways of life as undesirable, unhealthy, and unnatural.

Yale University professor John Boswell's landmark work, *Christianity, Social Tolerance, and Homosexuality*, helped me see the fundamental confusion in the use of the term "unnatural." Boswell distinguishes between those who use the term "natural" in a "realistic" sense (that is, to describe what exists in the observable universe) and those who use it in an "ideal" sense (identifying "nature" with "the good"). Clearly, says Boswell, homosexuality is "natural" in the first sense; it is widespread among human beings, and it has been observed among many animal species in the wild as well as in captivity. Use of the term "natural" in an "ideal" sense, Boswell points out, is obviously determined largely by cultural values; employed thus, the term "unnatural" becomes "a vehement circumlocution for 'bad' or 'unacceptable.'"[3]

Some would argue, for instance, that homosexuality is "unnatural" in an evolutionary sense because it is nonreproductive behavior. Boswell replies that few would condemn masturbation as "unnatural," although it has the same reproductive consequences as homosexuality. I began to realize how selective and arbitrary we are in our determinations of which actions are "natural" and "unnatural" for human beings. After all, medieval Christians viewed Jews as "abnormal" and "unnatural" creatures, a small and despised segment of the population who refused to accept Jesus as the messiah.

Boswell's words helped me to become conscious of how my own cultural biases shaped my perceptions. As a result, I began to see nothing inherently "unnatural" about my congregants' behavior. Rather, I saw differences to which I quickly became accustomed. Soon I was no longer struck by the novelty of two men holding hands or dancing together; I saw, instead, their very "natural" need for affection and companionship.

Similarly, as I came to know my congregants as individuals, I could no longer tolerate generalizations about homosexuality as pathological or sinful. Certainly I met some gay people whose lives were wretchedly unhappy. But most of the misery in their lives seemed to be the result of family rejection, social bigotry, or internalized self-hate—not due to any misery endemic to homosexuality itself. There are gay people I meet who act in ways that strike me as sick or immoral. But this is no less true of straight people I meet, and few would condemn heterosexuality as immoral—despite the high incidence of rape, incest, child abuse, adultery, family violence, promiscuity, and venereal disease among heterosexuals. The sad, the sick, and the sinful are a minority in the gay community, as they are in the straight population. My congregants are men and women who are as healthy, loving, and morally responsible as any I have known in my life.

My attitude toward homosexuality has moved from uncertain tolerance to full acceptance. I see it now as a sexual orientation offering the same opportunities for love, fulfillment, spiritual growth, and ethical action as heterosexuality. I still do not know what "causes" homosexuality, but I must confess that at this point I do not much care—any more than I care about what "causes" some people to have a special aptitude for music and others for baseball. I simply accept with pleasure the diversity of our species.

Halakhah in Liberal Judaism

My changing perceptions of homosexuality forced me to confront the role that halakhah plays in my life as a rabbi and liberal Jew. Part of my study of homosexuality naturally focused on halakhic discussions of the issue, and it did not take long to see that in our religious tradition, homosexuality is rejected unequivocally. Jewish legal opinions ranged from Asher Bar-Zev's view that homosexuality is a "physiologically determined behavioral disorder"[4] to Rabbi Hershel Matt's 1976 view that homosexual acts are performed "under constraint" (*me'ones*) and hence must be judged somewhat more leniently,[5] to Rabbi Solomon Freehof's Reform responsum, which deems homosexuality "a grave sin."[6] Some rabbis (notably Matt, who continued to grapple with these issues with a great deal of sensitivity until his death in 1987) urged tolerance, kindness, and compassion for *homosexuals*, but I could find no published rabbinic statements declaring *homosexuality* an acceptable Jewish way of life. And so I had to decide: how much did it matter to me that the voice of my tradition, without exception, ran counter to the evidence of my experience and the deepest promptings of my conscience?

For me the choice was clear. I could not be guided by laws that seem profoundly unjust and immoral. I believe and I teach my congregants that Jewish law condemns their way of life. But I teach also that I cannot accept that law as authoritative. It is part of my history—it belongs to me—but it has no binding claim on me. In my view, the Jewish condemnation of homosexuality is the work of human beings—limited, imperfect, fearful of what is different, and, above all, concerned with ensuring tribal survival. In short, I think our ancestors were wrong about a number of things, and homosexuality is one of them.

I am also a fallible human being, and it may be that my judgments will someday be proven wrong. But for now, I have no choice but to decide for myself which parts of our tradition I hold sacred. In fact, the Jewish values and principles I regard as eternal, transcendent, and divinely ordained do *not* condemn homosexuality. The Judaism I cherish and affirm teaches love of humanity, respect for the spark of divinity in every person, and the human right to live with dignity. The God I worship endorses loving, responsible, and committed human relationships, regardless of the sex of the persons involved. There is no Jewish *legal* basis for this belief; my personal faith simply tells me that the duty to love my neighbor as myself is a compelling *mitzvah*, while the duty to condemn and to kill homosexuals for committing "abominations" most certainly is not.

This attempt to grapple with a law I find abhorrent in a tradition to which I am utterly committed has taught me a lesson: liberal Jews can rationalize or equivocate only so long. There comes a time when our deepest convictions demand that we break with halakhah—and do so without apology, without attempts to unearth a minority legal opinion somewhere that supports our position. Reverence for tradition is no virtue when it promotes injustice and human suffering.

Lesbians and Gays in the Jewish Community

I once thought that, at least in the liberal Jewish community, gay people were accorded as much respect and recognition as could reasonably be expected. After all, hadn't the (Reform) Central Conference of American Rabbis in 1977 adopted a strong resolution supporting civil rights for homosexuals? Hadn't the Union of American Hebrew Congregations (UAHC) accepted a gay/lesbian congregation as a full member? (Now, in fact, there are four such congregations in the UAHC.) Today, however, I realize what our community denies gay and lesbian Jews: for instance, the right to marry.

Rabbi Solomon Freehof wrote in 1973 that "to officiate at a so-called 'marriage' of two homosexuals and to describe their mode of life as kiddushin (sacred) is a contravention of all that is respected in Jewish life."[7] Once I could agree with Rabbi Freehof. Now, I think of Max and Ernest, of Sandy and Elinor, and of so many others—and I know that their lives together certainly exemplify the qualities of kiddushin: love, respect, faithfulness, ultimate commitment, a tender consideration for each other's welfare, a desire to establish a Jewish home that is a *mikdash me'at*, a small sanctuary. Such a relationship is to my mind no less holy than a heterosexual marriage. And it never ceases to amaze me that so many homosexual couples, in the absence of any social or religious expectation that their relationship will embody holiness, nevertheless create such relationships.

A marriage between persons of the same sex would almost certainly never be accepted by halakhic Jews. Even so, it seems only right that rabbis who share my beliefs make an effort to respond to the needs of those gay and lesbian Jews who feel that their religion ignores or denigrates their loving commitments and the families they establish.

Just as liberal Judaism has thus far shied away from according homosexual couples any public acknowledgment or approbation, so also have we been almost entirely unwilling to allow *openly* gay and lesbian Jews to assume positions of leadership in our community. (There are, of course, many who are not open.) The Reconstructionist Rabbinical College is the only seminary whose faculty has voted that openly gay men and lesbians may be admitted as rabbinical students. I know of no institutions prepared to invest openly gay people as cantors or train them as religious school teachers. The message conveyed to my congregants by the community to which they belong is clear: you are welcome as long as you are invisible. We will tolerate your homosexuality, but we will certainly not hold you up as role models to be admired and emulated.

There was a time when this line of reasoning made sense to me. Why shouldn't one's sexual orientation be a private matter? Wouldn't a "known homosexual" be a dangerous model, especially for impressionable young people? Now I see that the reasoning makes sense only as long as we believe homosexuality is a shameful, abhorrent disease we fear will infect our children. If there is nothing wrong with being gay, there is no reason for gay people to hide their identities— any more than I hide my wedding ring and other public symbols of my heterosexuality.

Good Jewish leaders are always in short supply. It is foolish and destructive for us to reject persons who are ready, willing, and eminently able to serve our people. I can offer no "proof" that a lesbian or gay man can be a mensch, except that I know many who are.

My years with BCC have left me at times bewildered and frustrated. I have tried to understand why liberal Jews, who say they are not bound by ethically repellent statements in the halakhah, and who say they are devoted to justice and equality, still balk at granting justice and equality to gay and lesbian Jews. I have tried to understand why they cling so tenaciously to denigrating stereotypes about "the homosexual life-style" and its alleged threats to the purity of Jewish life.

I can find no rational basis for this behavior. It seems to me, instead, that prejudice, fear, and ignorance are keeping many liberal

Jews from doing what is logical and right. It is prejudice that keeps them from seeing sanctity in a loving commitment between persons of the same sex; prejudice that assures them that gay or lesbian Jews, no matter how learned and ethical, can never be role models for the Jewish community; prejudice that prevents them from recognizing that heterosexuality is not the only path to healthy, joyous, and committed Jewish life.

As long as these prejudices persist, there will be a need for congregations like BCC. And I would suggest that when those prejudices are eradicated, and gay and lesbian Jews are fully respected and loved as our brothers and sisters, the issue of separate gay/lesbian synagogues will become moot. Because openly lesbian and gay Jews will be welcome in any synagogue they choose, the mainstream Jewish community will no longer feel threatened if some of them choose to worship together in their own synagogues—simply because they share many values and enjoy being together. I look forward to the day when BCC exists not primarily as a refuge from homophobia, but simply as a vibrant Jewish congregation with a character and spirit all its own.

I know that prejudice against lesbians and gays is deeply rooted, but I also know from my own experience that it is possible to become educated and to change profoundly. In doing so, for any of us, there is simply no substitute for an open mind and direct contact with gay people. Any heterosexual who is serious about getting an education will find plenty of opportunities to get to know homosexuals either in person or through first-person writings. Lesbians and gay men are all around, and all it usually takes to bring them out is a friendly, sensitive, and respectful manner.

Above and beyond my moments of frustration, I feel profoundly blessed to have devoted five years of my life to working with Beth Chayim Chadashim. Apart from the intrinsic joy of working with an active, questing, and spirited community, I feel grateful for the education I've been given—a chance to see with my own eyes and make up my own mind rather than swallowing the judgments and slogans of others.

I'm grateful also that my daughters are spending the crucial years of their early childhood in the presence of hundreds of loving gay "uncles" and lesbian "aunts"; they, thank God, will grow up without the ugly myths and stereotypes that afflicted me. Perhaps that is the greatest gift my congregants have given me.

Journey toward Wholeness:
Reflections of a Lesbian Rabbi

....

La Escondida

RECENTLY, I HEARD A REPORT ON NATIONAL PUBLIC RADIO ABOUT "the secret Jews of New Mexico," remnants of the *Marranos*, the crypto-Jews of late medieval Spain who hid their Jewish identities in order to escape persecution at the hands of the Spanish Inquisition. These New Mexican Jews, outwardly Catholics, call themselves "los escondidos" (the hidden ones). They still live in secret, quietly teaching their children ancient Jewish rituals, quietly observing as much of Jewish practice as they know after centuries of separation from mainstream Judaism. Even now, in 1988, they hide, fearful that revealing their true identities will bring them harm, fearful that someone, somewhere, will persecute them for being who they really are.

As I listened to the report, my emotions were stirred. As a student of Jewish history, I was fascinated by the tenacity of these people and their success in surviving through centuries of clandestine life, without validation and support from the larger Jewish world. As a Jew who lives much of her own life in secret, fearful of revealing all of who I am, fearful of the harm that may come to me if I do, I felt the pain and sadness of my co-religionists in New Mexico.

Because it is risky for me to reveal my true identity at this point in my career, I write this essay under a pseudonym. Like the Jews of New Mexico, I too am an "escondida," a hidden one. I am a Jew. I am a woman. I am a rabbi. I am a lesbian.

Being a Jew has always been the axis around which my life has rotated. I grew up in a deeply committed Jewish home, with ardently

218

Zionist parents who were dedicated to the birth and growth of a Jewish homeland in which the highest ideals of social justice would be
realized. My home was filled with love for the Hebrew language, a
fascination with Jewish history and culture, and a deeply ingrained
commitment to the survival of the Jewish people. Though not "religious" in the traditional sense, my parents were profoundly Jewish in
a cultural, historical, and emotional sense. I can imagine no other way
of being in the world than being a Jew who is actively and passionately connected to my people.

As an adult I spent several years in Israel, where I saw my Jewishness in cultural, historical, and national terms. I took great pride in
my people's growth, in the country we were building, in Israel's artis-
tic flowering, in the intellectual achievements of this small nation.
I thought that being a Jew and an Israeli were synonymous—and that
my life was whole.

After completing my B.A. in Israel, I returned to the United States
to pursue graduate studies in Jewish history. Back in America, I soon
came to realize that my life as a Jew was incomplete—it had always
focused on the historical and cultural evolution of my people, but I
knew little about the spiritual and religious aspects of Judaism. I felt
the need to connect with God, with my own soul, and with my
people's faith and belief system. I realized that there was a whole
world within Judaism that I hadn't yet explored and that I needed
in my life. While my intellect was being nourished, my soul, too,
needed to find its home within Judaism.

Simultaneous with this realization came another powerful discovery about myself: I am a lesbian. I had fallen in love with a woman.
After fighting society's frightening and confusing stereotypes, I acknowledged that I had felt most comfortable and most whole throughout my life in close relationships with other girls and women. My
deepest emotional attachments had always been with women, my
most profound feelings of love, affection, intimate connection, and
physical attraction had always been for women. With this acknowledgment, I was able to shake off the oppressive stereotypes and begin
a long-term relationship with the woman whom I loved deeply.

For several years I lived a bifurcated existence. My academic and
professional life as a scholar of Jewish history was entirely separate
from my personal life, and my spiritual quest was done alone. Typical
to the intellectual that I am, I read books about Jewish spirituality and

faith, but I was not actively engaged in seeking my *own* life within the spiritual context of Judaism. Wholeness for me as a Jew was still an elusive goal.

I know now that part of the reason I didn't venture forth into a living community of Jews was that I feared being rejected as a lesbian. Soon, to my great relief, I discovered there was a lesbian and gay outreach synagogue where I lived. I remember how I felt as my partner and I walked through the synagogue doors for the first time. The conflicts within me began to abate, as I sensed the possibility of integrating the different aspects of my being. In this modest building, I began to feel that I could be a Jew and a lesbian. I could pray as a Jew, learn as a Jew, rejoice in my loving relationship with a woman, and have others celebrate with me.

This synagogue, Beth Ameinu ("House of Our People"; the synagogue's name is fictitious), indeed offered to me possibilities of an enriching new connection with my people. I became actively involved in the congregation, serving on the synagogue's board, as head of its ritual committee and as a frequent leader of Shabbat services. Soon, I found that this piece of Judaism that had been missing for me, its spiritual and religious dimension, was coming alive. I no longer needed to sit alone and read books—I could pray and sing with a community as a *whole* human being: Jewish and lesbian.

Over time, I began to feel that my professional life, though intellectually challenging, was also incomplete. As Judaism's horizons expanded for me, I felt that teaching it from a purely intellectual perspective was not enough. As a professor of Jewish history, I did not experience wholeness. In this capacity, my task was to teach Judaism in a consciously clinical and objective manner. I often felt like a disembodied mind, imparting knowledge about Judaism without also sharing its *ruach*, its spirit. It became increasingly difficult for me to offer my students a dispassionate Judaism. It simply meant too much to me to do that.

A new awareness pushed me forward on my journey. I came to realize that I wanted my professional life to reflect my deepest personal commitments: I knew that I wanted to be a rabbi. After several years of thinking seriously about the direction my life should take, and considering the life changes my decision might require, I applied to a rabbinical seminary. In my application I explained my motivations for becoming a rabbi:

What I really want to do is help people reach the more profound spiritual dimension connected with their Judaism. I want to be able to work with other Jews to create meaningful rituals, to find their way toward their own religious/spiritual evolution . . . I want to teach within a Jewish context (not exclusively in a secular university) where I am not constrained by the obligation to be objective and coldly intellectual.

I want to help provide that food for the soul as well as the mind. I find that as a woman, as a feminist, there are worlds to be found within Judaism, worlds to explore, principles to be studied and challenged, a history of Jewish women to be reclaimed and a life of ritual for women to be developed. I want to be a part of that process . . .

Now, in the final stages of my rabbinical studies, and after working for two years as a rabbi of a small congregation, these are still ideals that energize me.

In my congregational work, I have seen my ideals come alive in a community of real people. I have developed an excellent relationship with my congregants. We have grown from a tiny group of individuals to a larger congregation that seeks to infuse meaning into our lives as Jews. In my congregation we pray and sing together, we sometimes have long and impassioned discussions about Judaism and its meaning for our lives, we study Torah, we have classes in which I teach about the Jewish prayerbook, about the holidays, about Jewish history. In my congregation, we celebrate *simkhes* together, and we mourn and console one another when sadness enters the life of a member of our community. I have grown to love many of my congregants, and they have grown to love me. And yet, *I do not feel whole within this community.* Though there is a deep affection between my congregants and me, there is not deep honesty: I have hidden a crucial part of my identity from them. They know me as their rabbi; they assume I am heterosexual; they have no idea that I am a lesbian.

Along with my idealism about becoming a rabbi have come some terribly disturbing realizations about how I must live my life as a congregational rabbi. Sadly, even as I pursue wholeness in my professional life, I have found that some of the personal integration I felt at Beth Ameinu has left me. Again I live a bifurcated life. Though I have a wonderful support system of good friends with whom I can be fully myself, the fact that I cannot be wholly honest about who I am to my congregants is painful to me. Nevertheless, despite the pain that I feel, I know that it would be professionally foolish to reveal to them who I am in my totality. If I were to come out to my congregants, in all probability I would lose my job as their rabbi. I do not believe that these warm and lovely people are ready to know that their rabbi is a lesbian.

Item.—Two years ago, I gave an impassioned sermon about AIDS to my congregation on the High Holy Days. In the context of the emotional self-evaluation that Jews engage in at this time of year, I spoke about empathy and compassion, acceptance and marginalization— and I suggested that our congregation become involved, even in a small way, in the struggle against AIDS. I suggested that we collect food for people with AIDS who are no longer able to shop for themselves and who may be financially impoverished by the astronomical costs of medical care. My suggestion was received well by my congregants and we engaged in a fairly successful food collection. Every few weeks, I delivered the collected cans of food to the local AIDS project.

A few months after the High Holy Days, in reporting the gratitude that the AIDS project had expressed to our congregation, I suggested that we might wish to let the project know that if there were Jewish people with AIDS who wished to worship in a community, the doors of our synagogue would be open to them. I was immediately confronted by a storm of reaction from my congregants, who are usually fairly receptive to my suggestions. I was told not to extend such an invitation to people with AIDS, that my congregation did not wish to be known as "the gay synagogue," and that they did not wish to be "ostracized" or "marginalized" within the larger Jewish community. I felt the pain of this incident deep within me: "If they only knew that their rabbi was a lesbian," I thought. I remained silent and accepted my congregants' instructions. I felt hurt and deeply ashamed at my inability to reveal myself to them, and to force them to confront their own prejudices. I also understood that I needed to protect myself professionally.

Item.—Recently, I met with two congregants, a young couple who were soon to be blessed with a baby. I have a particularly close relationship with this couple, since only eighteen months earlier I officiated at their wedding. Together we created a very special marriage

ceremony and spent many, many hours together (in my home), discussing their relationship, their common future, their hopes and
dreams and the ways in which they wanted to express their feelings
of love and commitment to one another within a Jewish ceremonial
context. We were now repeating the same process and creating a
baby-naming ceremony. At one of our meetings, I pulled out a thick
file of ceremonies I have collected over time, and began to show them
different pieces that might be meaningful to them. Since they are both
musically inclined, I suggested a song by Fred Small, which expresses
wonderfully a parent's blessing to a child:

> You can be anybody you want to be
> You can love whomever you will
> You can travel any country where your heart leads,
> And know I will love you still.
> You can live by yourself, you can gather friends around,
> You can choose one special one.
> And the only measure of your words and your deeds
> Will be the love you leave behind when you're done.

As I sang this chorus to the song, the couple beamed, loving each
line. As I continued, however, to the line: "some women love women,
some men love men," the couple immediately gasped and together
said, "Oh no! We don't want that! *Who* wrote that song?" Trying to
keep my voice as even as possible, I mentioned Fred Small's name and
said that I thought the blessing of the song was that it guaranteed love
to one's child in whatever way the child might grow—and that was
the greatest blessing I believed parents could give their children. In a
subsequent meeting, they told me that they didn't want "that gay
song" included in their baby-naming ceremony. Again, I remained silent, accepting their comments without protest, fearful that I might
lose my calm or "objective" front with them, fearful that if I became
too impassioned, they might discover who *I* really was. At that moment, I again realized that I was "escondida"—in hiding.

Item.—I have been considering interviewing for a job as rabbi of another congregation that might be better able to afford my salary after
my ordination. When the prospective congregants called to invite me
to spend Shabbat with them, they very kindly invited me for dinner
before services. One of the committee members asked me, "Will you
be coming alone? Of course, you know you are welcome to bring your

boyfriend or husband. Are you married?" "No, I am not married," I replied. This woman then asked me, "So you will be coming alone?" "Yes," I replied. "Will you always be coming alone?" she continued, clearly curious about the status of my love life, but not wishing to appear too instrusive.

At that moment, the temptation to lie washed over me. Perhaps I could tell them that my boyfriend was unable to join me that Friday, but he would be visiting at another time. I did not lie. *I could not lie.* I simply replied, "I will be coming alone on Friday," never really answering her question about my relationship status.

That same day, a heterosexual friend and classmate at the rabbinical seminary commented to me: "I know that it makes things a lot easier when I tell them that my wife will be joining me for services. They all think, 'How nice, the rabbi is married.'"

After this conversation, I was again reminded of how invisible my emotional life is to so many people. Because I cannot speak of my love relationship to others whom I serve in a professional capacity, because I cannot say *the woman* I love might come with me to services, I appear an emotionally stunted individual to these congregants. I am in my late thirties, and as far as they are concerned I am single and unattached. It appears that I simply have no love life. In some very significant way, I become different from them: the Jewish version of a nun. I cannot communicate with them on an emotional level, because I cannot be honest with them about my own emotional life. I am impoverished and the people with whom I work are impoverished.

Item.—November 1987: In my congregation, I have noticed a woman and two men who attend services regularly whom I think are gay. Though they don't seem to be unfriendly people, they socialize only on a superficial level with other congregants, revealing little about themselves. While other community members stay around to chat, drink coffee, and enjoy each other's company, they usually leave fairly quickly after the service is over. I suspect that their aloofness stems from a fear of self-disclosure and its possible consequences— people in the congregation might not be as friendly to them.

I would like to reach out to these three, to let them know they are really welcome here, that to be Jewish and gay *is* possible, and that it can even be a rewarding experience if one is able to integrate the different parts of oneself. I chat with them as I do with all my congregants. I do not come out to them, nor they to me. I feel duplicitous.

These have been the sad moments of my life as a rabbi who is also a lesbian. Other moments have been better, providing me with a sense of wholeness that is precious to me.

Item.—January 1988: One of the young men whom I think is gay seeks me out after services and asks if we can speak privately. He reveals to me that he is gay, that he is going through a very painful separation with his lover with whom he has had a relationship for four years—and that he needs my help. He needs to talk, he needs to know that as a rabbi, I don't disapprove of him and that he will be welcome in the synagogue. He needs to know that within a Jewish context, he will have support. He needs to know that "God does not condemn him," as he puts it, because he is gay.

The young man also tells me he feels he cannot come out to other congregants. "They won't understand," he says. As I listen to him, my head is spinning. Do I tell him that I am a lesbian? Do I say, "Of course, I understand the pain that you are feeling. I have been through this kind of separation"? Do I simply tell him that as a rabbi I don't disapprove of him and that he will always find support and understanding from me? Do I talk to him about God? Can I remain professionally aloof, revealing nothing of myself as this young man sits before me, pain distorting his handsome face?

I make a split-second decision. I cannot be an "escondida," a hidden one, especially to another gay person. I give him a hug, I tell him about myself, I tell him that I understand, I talk to him about God, I talk to him about being a Jew. I offer him comfort and support and I listen to him. I urge him to keep coming to our congregation, though I understand that he may not feel he can reveal himself to his fellow congregants. To my great pleasure, he does return—and each Shabbat he prays and sings with a community that accepts him as a Jew, but is not yet ready to accept him as a gay man. Nevertheless, there is a bond between him and me. I am his rabbi, and I am his friend. We are no longer invisible to one another. His life is enriched, as is mine.

Item.—In the High Holy Day sermon I mentioned earlier, I spoke about a young Jewish woman with AIDS who lives in the same city where my congregation is located. Having learned about her from an article in a national magazine, I wondered out loud "if she is in a synagogue praying with a community." I wondered whether she had a community of Jews "who will nurture her and give her the loving, the caring, the respect, and the support she needs."

I had thought seriously about *not* delivering my sermon on AIDS for fear of appearing too "outspoken," for fear of appearing too involved in an issue that was still mistakenly thought of by many as "a gay men's issue." I wondered whether I should steer clear of anything even remotely connected to gay concerns because someone might make a connection between gay issues and me. But after worrying about it for a while, I concluded that there are limits to how much one should worry about such things. I decided that as a member of an often invisible minority, I could not make myself even more invisible by remaining silent about an issue of great concern to me and to our society in general. There were limits even to my own "hiddenness." I made a conscious decision, *which stems from my identity as a lesbian,* that however controversial my sermon might be, I could not remain silent.

I will always be grateful that I gave that sermon. After services were over, a thin woman stood apart from the crowd and waited to speak with me. After almost everyone else had left, she approached me and asked to speak with me alone. Once we had gone into another room, the woman told me that *she* was the person about whom I had just spoken. Of course, I did not know that she would be in my synagogue that Yom Kippur day. But the fact is that *she* had heard me. Taking my hands in hers, she said to me: "I haven't been in a synagogue in years. When I got AIDS, I was sure that God had abandoned me. But now that my life may be over soon, I felt the need to come back to my Jewish roots. I have never heard a rabbi speak the way you did today. Thank you. I want you to know that it means a great deal to me. I think you've helped me come home." We embraced and we cried together—and I offered what help I could; a listening ear, compassion, a connection with her Jewishness by a connection to me as her rabbi.

This young woman does not attend services regularly. She is now too ill to do so, but I have visited her, and we have talked. I believe that my being available to her as a rabbi is helping. In all likelihood, I will officiate at her funeral, and I hope that I can provide some solace to her family. There is deep sadness here at the loss of a fine human being. But I feel that my decisions *based on the entirety of who I am* and my work as a rabbi have been redeemed by my encounter with this woman.

There are other positive and valuable aspects to my identity as a lesbian and my work as a rabbi. I believe that I am more sensitive to "the stranger who walks in our land," those Jews who sit at the edges of our communities, somewhat marginalized, somewhat outside of the mainstream. I believe that I may be more attuned to them because I, too, often feel like an outsider, unable to reveal my full self to my community. I believe that because many people judge me and my lesbian identity harshly, I may be more sensitive to judgmentalism in general. I have learned that there are many, many ways of living one's life as a decent human being—and that my responsibility is not to judge but to establish human connection. I believe, as Abraham Joshua Heschel once wrote, that "my first task in every encounter is to comprehend the personhood of every human being I face, to sense the kinship of being human, the solidarity of being."[1]

My experience as a rabbi in a mainstream (rather than exclusively gay or lesbian) congregation has brought me great satisfaction, but it has also brought me doubts. When I dream of my work as a rabbi, I envision working with *Jews*—not exclusively young Jews, not exclusively old Jews, not exclusively gay and lesbian Jews, not exclusively heterosexual Jews. I simply want to work with *Jews*.

I often fear that I will not be given a chance (by a mainstream community that so often rejects gay people) to simply work with Jews if I come out. I fear that I will become marginal, ostracized from the general community of Jews and confined to working only with lesbian and gay Jews. While my experience at Beth Ameinu was precious to me, and I would not have traded my life in that congregation for anything, I dream of a time when there will be no need for a separate gay and lesbian congregation. As I seek wholeness for myself, an integration of all aspects of myself, I pray for such wholeness for my people as well.

I began this essay by writing about the hidden Jews of New Mexico, "los escondidos." It is my deepest hope that there will come a time when they and I will come out into the light of day and feel unthreatened, able to reveal the *totality* of our identities, able to be safe and valued in a world they know will fully accept us. May this day come speedily and in our time.

The Lesbian and Gay Movement:
Jewish Community Responses

Sue Levi Elwell

IN OCTOBER 1988, THE OFFICERS OF A LARGE, WELL-ESTABLISHED Reform synagogue on the West Coast sat in executive session discussing the necessity of changing the definition of family as it appeared in the temple constitution.[1] The catalyst for this discussion was the application for membership from a family consisting of a Jewish woman and her female partner. During the discussion, it was acknowledged that these would not be the first gay members of this congregation, but that they would be the first openly gay members. "It's about time," commented the senior rabbi of the congregation.

Reflecting on this incident, one might say that we've come a long way. Or have we? Have we in the Jewish community "come a long way" in our recognition that our community includes men and women whose lives exemplify a wide range of choices, experiences, and commitments? Is the example cited above simply one of many such acknowledgments of the rich diversity of our community, or is this an isolated instance reflecting only the liberal politics of a single institution? Are lesbian and gay Jews now free to "come out of the closet"?

The metaphor of the closet is often employed to describe the lives of secrecy and self-denial that many gays and lesbians feel forced to lead. The dark, closed world of a closet aptly describes the isolation of many gay men and lesbians who are shut away from the bright worlds in which they wish to live as whole people. When one is finally ready to claim one's homosexuality, and to thereby take an important step toward wholeness, one "comes out of the closet" and becomes more visible.

Because of the negative attitudes toward homosexuality articulated in traditional Jewish texts, as well as the universal Jewish imperative of heterosexual union that results in the creation and nurturance of each new generation, "coming out" into the Jewish community has required enormous courage. Nevertheless, many of our brothers and sisters, sons and daughters, mothers and fathers, uncles and aunts, have bravely opened the doors and now stand in the light of our houses of study, of gathering, and of prayer.

Over the past twenty years, the American Jewish community has exhibited a broad range of responses to gay and lesbian issues. This complex conglomeration of synagogues, charitable and service organizatons, educational institutions, and political groups rarely speaks with only one voice on any issue. As to the opening of closet doors, Jewish community responses have fallen into three major categories.

First, there are some who are deeply regretful that the closets have swung open. Faithful to halakhah, the tradition of Jewish law, they beg, "Go back. The closet is where your homosexuality belongs. The Torah condemns not you, but your behavior. Homosexual behavior sets you apart; by such behavior you become *other*. By such behavior, you become not *you* but *them*. You may sit with us, pray with us, study with us, raise money with us. Be a Jew with us, but leave your homosexuality at home, in the closet."

A second group realizes that the gaping door is not so easily refastened. Supporting the civil rights of gay men and lesbians is consonant with the commitment of the members of this group to the Jewish imperative for social justice. But when gay men and lesbians want to become full members of our communities, participating openly in all aspects of synagogue and organizational life, members of this second group have difficulty behaving in accordance with their liberal rhetoric and political sympathies. They are unwilling to fully open their hearts and their homes, their synagogues and pulpits and schoolrooms. Once they have granted civil rights to gay and lesbian Jews, and perhaps acknowledged their right to a synagogue of their own, they want to push their new "friends" back into the closet. They may say, "Haven't we given you what you want? You have your rights, you have your synagogues. Be a whole person in the world at large, but we're not quite ready for you to be a whole Jew, at least not in the community where we live with our children."

Finally, a third group advocates full inclusion of gays and lesbians in every aspect of Jewish life. Both their religious and their political convictions lead them to embrace the gay and lesbian Jews in their midst as full members of a complex and varied Jewish community. For these Jews, gay and lesbian Jews are "we," not "they," and not "you." Rather than denying or ignoring the challenges of bringing gays and lesbians into all aspects of synagogue, organizational, and institutional life, members of this third group celebrate the opportunity to strengthen the Jewish community. They believe that Jews do not belong in closets. Rather, members of this third group are using closets for storing *siddurim* (prayerbooks), *taleysim* (prayer shawls), placards, and pamphlets.

For the most part, the first group has included most representatives of the Orthodox community, as well as others. Citing biblical texts that call the male homosexual act an "abomination," writers like Rabbi Norman Lamm argue that homosexual behavior is *essentially* objectionable and counter to any understanding of Jewish law or practice.[2] The repeated use of the third-person pronoun symbolizes their position: gay and lesbian Jews are "other," those whose experience is not "ours."

The second response has been that of many mainstream organizations, liberal Jewish institutions, and some individual Jews: supporting the civil rights of gays and lesbians, but still hesitant about the implications of their complete integration as open participants into so-called normative or mainstream Jewish institutions and organizations. For example, in 1975, at their biennial convention, the Union of American Hebrew Congregations (the congregational arm of the Reform movement) passed a resolution calling for full civil rights for homosexuals in the civic sphere. At the 1977 biennial, however, the resolution was recast, deleting an explicit "call for non-discrimination within Jewish communal and Reform organizations."[3] Nevertheless, and despite two *responsa* upholding the traditional position,[4] congregations with special outreach to lesbian and gay Jews were welcomed into the organization. These resolutions, however, signified the discomfort and ambivalence that have coexisted with good intentions and progressive pronouncements. Other organizations have exhibited their discomfort with this issue by failing to address it altogether. To date, neither the Rabbinical Assembly nor United Synagogue of America (the rabbinic and congregational arms of the Conservative movement) have issued any resolutions on the civil rights of gay men and lesbians.

From the late 1970s through the 1980s, many prominent Jewish organizations took public stands opposing discrimination based on sexual orientation. Such resolutions were passed by the American Jewish Congress in 1980 and by the National Board of Governors of the American Jewish Committee in 1986. In several communities, Jewish organizations have come together to support the civil rights of gay men and lesbians. For example, in the fall of 1986, several Jewish organizations in Los Angeles banded together to oppose a California proposition sponsored by Lyndon LaRouche that proposed quarantine of all persons suspected of carrying the AIDS virus. That same year, several Jewish organizations in New York City came together to support a gay civil rights bill, as a few had in years past.

In addition to spurring political involvement, a few local groups have forged ahead to publicly address the difficult personal and communal issues of homophobia and consciousness raising, of exclusion and inclusion. In April 1986, Stephen Wise Free Synagogue, a Reform temple in New York City, hosted a daylong conference entitled "Lesbian and Gay Jews in the Jewish Community." This pioneering effort, initiated by Rabbi Helene Ferris and the congregation's Social Action Committee, was cosponsored by eighteen local Jewish institutions and organizations. The conference brought together nearly five hundred participants—lesbian and gay Jews, their families, friends, rabbis, lay leaders, and Jewish communal professionals—"to address both the issues of alienation and oppression confronting lesbian and gay Jews and their families and the fears and concerns of the larger Jewish community." [5]

The Stephen Wise conference was a crucial first step, for it enabled many who suffered alone to share their pain. When it was over, one participant asked whether we are ready to acknowledge the pain and risk that were shared as a "source of power for making the Jewish community whole." [6] For those who attended a subsequent symposium, "Single and Jewish: Communal and Personal Perspectives," held in November 1986 and sponsored by the American Jewish Committee, the answer to this question was a resounding *no*. In their prepared remarks on Jewish singles, none of the presenters acknowledged the existence of gay men and lesbians.

A very different local response came several years ago in San Francisco, when local Hadassah women, upon recognizing that they had neglected to consider lesbians as potential members, took steps to deliberately seek them out. After some preliminary conversations, Jewish lesbian activists received membership information in the mail, including a query printed on lavender paper asking, "Why aren't more Jewish lesbians members of Hadassah?"

Some national organizations have been moved to act as a result of the positions taken by their local affiliate organizations, while other national organizations have asserted more leadership, sometimes bringing reluctant constituents along with them. In 1987, a full ten years after welcoming synagogues with outreach to the gay and lesbian community into its membership, the Union of American Hebrew Congregations passed a resolution urging its congregations and affiliates to "encourage lesbian and gay Jews to share and participate in the worship, leadership, and general congregational life of all synagogues." The resolution went on to urge the employment of synagogue personnel "without regard to sexual orientation."[7] However, the specific issue of ordaining gay and lesbian rabbis was referred to a special committee of the Central Conference of American Rabbis, which has not yet voted on this critical issue.

The question of whether or not to ordain openly identified gay men and lesbians as rabbis has been a difficult and painful question for all concerned. In 1985, the faculty of the Reconstructionist Rabbinical College quietly decided that sexual preference would *not* be an issue in deciding the appropriateness of any candidate's application for admission to the college. The issue has not, however, been raised before the lay membership of the Reconstructionist movement, the Federation of Reconstructionist Congregations and Havurot, meaning that openly gay and lesbian seminary graduates may not be readily employable. The Reform movement, as noted above, has been struggling for some years with the issue of ordination of gay and lesbian rabbis. While a number of gay and lesbian rabbis have been ordained at the various campuses of the Hebrew Union College–Jewish Institute of Religion, very few of these rabbis are openly identified as gay or lesbian in the congregations and communities they serve. And the Conservative movement has not dealt with the issue at all, although some Conservative leaders readily acknowledge that there are gay men and lesbians among those ordained by the Jewish Theological Seminary.

The third group is made up of those who have struggled toward using the first-person "we" when speaking of gay and lesbian Jews. New Jewish Agenda was the first national Jewish organization to include a full range of gay and lesbian concerns in its national platform. Agenda leadership has included openly gay men and lesbians as national officers, and its regional and national conventions have consistently included sessions on gay and lesbian issues. Of course, even an organization that articulates such a commitment includes individuals who vary in their degree of accepting lesbian and gay issues as their own.

Saying "we" remains the most difficult position for most mainstream Jewish organizations and institutions to take when thinking about including gay and lesbian Jews. As increasing numbers of Jews "come out" to their families and communities, more and more individuals are ready to accept and perhaps even publicly acknowledge the diversity of our community. And, for some, AIDS has increased the urgency of confronting our own homophobia.

In March 1989, at a Los Angeles community service in support of persons with AIDS and their loved ones, Rabbi Alexander Schindler, president of the Union of American Hebrew Congregations, suggested that we reconsider the meaning of the *Magen David*, which the Nazis "irrevocably rendered the . . . preeminent Jewish sign."

> Today as we meet to remember those who have died of AIDS, to speak of their suffering and our own, there is another meaning that we can attach to the Magen David. It is an interpretation that any Jewish child with a crayon can tell you: that the Star of David contains, within it, the triangle.
>
> For those of us here who would, a generation ago, have been wearing the pink triangle as a badge of shame and a mark of death; for those of us here who today wear it as a badge of honor and resistance and identity: it is time to complete the outline of your Jewish star.
>
> For those of us who have been willingly blind to the geometry of Jewish life, who would keep invisible the presence of the triangle within the Shield of David: it is time to complete the outline of our Jewish star.[8]

By embracing the pink triangle, the sign that the Nazis compelled those branded as homosexual to wear, as an integral part of the six-pointed star, Rabbi Schindler places himself squarely among those who not only stand *for* but who also stand *with* gay and lesbian Jews:

I declare myself the compassionate ally of every person heterosexual and homosexual, Jew and non-Jew, who is wrestling with
the shame, the confusion, the fear, the endless torment involved
in the inner struggle for sexual identity. It is a struggle that includes, but also goes beyond, civil liberties. It is, when all is said
and done, a struggle for the integrity of selfhood.[9]

Of course, Schindler cannot speak for all Reform Jews. But his remarks are heard in Reform communities across the continent, firmly
placing the issue of inclusion and recognition of gay and lesbian Jews
on the Reform agenda.

For some lesbian and gay Jews, the most powerful sense of inclusion has come not through pronouncements, resolutions, or invitations to join a community, but through ceremonies that welcome gay
and lesbian Jews into Jewish religious life. At the 1985 B'nai Or Kallah,
a small group of lesbians and gay men created a "coming out" ritual
as part of a Shabbat morning Torah service. Despite the evanescence
of the community that gathered together in prayer, song, and affirmation on that Shabbat morning, the ritual of celebration changed lives.
Those who created the ceremony felt affirmed as Jews as they never
had before, and the others in attendance felt, for the first time, the
richness of a community that celebrates its own diversity.[10]

Because so few prominent individuals and "mainstream" groups fit
into this third category, some gay men and lesbians have had to look
beyond the organized Jewish community for support, and have created organizations of their own. In late 1986, a small group of gay and
lesbian Jewish professionals—educators, social workers, administra-
tors, cantors, and rabbis—created a network called Ameinu, "Our
People." Ameinu has reached out to others who work within the Jewish community, many of whom remain invisible to their congregants
or co-workers. After three years of existence, Ameinu has members in
fifteen states and in Canada. For some, its annual meeting has become the most important professional meeting they attend each year,
offering a unique opportunity to feel integrated and whole.

As we look toward the 1990s, it seems that the civil and religious
rights of gay and lesbian Jews are *not* on the agenda of most organizations and institutions that make up the American Jewish community.
This will change only as an increasing number of Jewish leaders recognize that perpetuating a notion of "we" and "they" echoes the sul-

len, misguided query of the wicked child of the Haggadah. Perhaps the tragedy of AIDS will move some to reconsider their position. Others may recognize the faces of their own sons and daughters among those who remain trapped in, or have recently emerged from, the closet. Still others may see that as long as we separate ourselves from one another, we deny our common Source and frustrate the messianic hope of deliverance.

How far have we in the Jewish community come? A long way, perhaps, from the time when the idea of a "synagogue for homosexuals" seemed oxymoronic. We have come a long way from the time when the only opportunity for religious expression for Jewish lesbians and gay men was through liberal churches or marginal spiritual communities.

But we in the Jewish community still have a long way to go toward becoming the *am kadosh* we are challenged to become. We cannot become holy until we are whole. We cannot become holy until we embrace all those who wish to study and to learn, to practice and to teach, to build and to serve. We cannot become holy until we remove the hinges from the closet doors and walk together, praising all our choices, into the light of our shared future.[11]

"They" Are Us:
Responding to the Challenge of AIDS

....

Andy Rose

NOTHING IN RECENT MEMORY HAS SO THOROUGHLY TESTED SOCIAL institutions as has the emergence of the AIDS crisis. Growing nightmarishly through the 1980s, this viral epidemic has brought out the best and the worst in many of us. And since it has been framed from early on as a moral issue in addition to (or even instead of) a public health issue, religious communities have been particularly pushed, often unwillingly, to take "moral stands" on the epidemic. Jewish agencies and congregations, among others, have been forced to ask, "What are we about?" as this crisis has broadened and worsened.

AIDS is surely not a "gay disease." But just as surely, the *response* (or lack thereof) to AIDS in this country has had everything to do with people's beliefs and feelings about homosexuality. AIDS has forced many people for the first time to deal with gay men as human beings who live and die, often with undeniable courage and dignity. And it has begun to challenge well-worn assumptions that gay people and their families are Them, not Us.

In the Jewish community, as elsewhere, responses to AIDS must be examined not only in the context of responses to homosexuality, but also in the broader context of responses to any stigmatized issue. AIDS brings together some of the most difficult issues in our culture: sexuality, drug abuse, illness, disability, and death. In addition to the general aversion to tackling any of these issues, many in the Jewish community have a particularly hard time admitting that stigmatized problems ever happen to Us (bad things happen only to Them). Whether it is alcoholism or domestic violence or AIDS, the main response is denial: "not in my family . . . not in my synagogue . . . not in my community." Of course that is not true, and denial only serves to make people feel more isolated, and their problems more intractable.

In the past ten years, a small yet significant countertrend has emerged, directing us to bring such issues out into the open. To whatever degree a community has been able to bring other difficult issues out of the closet, the response to AIDS has been made easier. AIDS has become a litmus issue, a measure of how we confront our own myths. This has revealed remarkable openness and compassion in many places, as well as denial and mean-spirited judgments in others.

It is worth noting that in spite of much denial and distancing, Jews as a group are quite highly attuned to medical issues. Intellectual curiosity about the phenomenon of AIDS runs high in the Jewish community. Identification and compassion tend to follow later.

The first Jewish institutions to respond to AIDS were, of course, lesbian and gay congregations and organizations. Despite the denial and terror that gripped the gay community during the early years of the epidemic, we had to do something when our friends began to get sick. We faced deep, difficult questions: how do we deal with our thirty-five-year-old peers being hospitalized repeatedly, becoming impoverished, and needing to contend with a bewildering array of medical and social services? What about the uncertainty of the future, and the stated and unstated questions of "who's next?" How do we educate ourselves, our sexual partners, and anyone who will listen about changing behavior in order to save lives? And most difficult, how do we relate to all those people who don't seem to understand that our world has been turned upside down, changed forever?

At Sha'ar Zahav, a predominantly gay and lesbian congregation in San Francisco, a well-loved board member "came out" as a person with AIDS at the conclusion of services one Shabbat in 1982. The congregation was stunned, yet quickly mobilized itself to establish an AIDS fund, expand its *Bikkur Cholim* Committee, and sponsor an annual Women's Havurah blood drive.[1] Sha'ar Zahav members were instrumental in introducing an AIDS resolution at the 1985 UAHC Biennial Conference in Los Angeles, breaking ground for other major national Jewish organizations to follow.

In Los Angeles in 1986, members of Beth Chayim Chadashim developed a proposal to start Project Nechama, a program of AIDS educational outreach for the entire Jewish community.[2] This project received its initial funding from a special Jewish Federation Council program to support innovative synagogue-based activities. That level of Federation acknowledgment and support was a first for a gay and lesbian congregation, symbolic of how AIDS has, ironically and tragically, brought gay-related issues into Jewish mainstream settings.

Meanwhile in Washington, D.C., a Bet Mishpacha congregant tried to pull together a National Jewish AIDS Project with the support of the Reconstructionist movement and other organizations. The attempt was largely unsuccessful because of a number of factors, including the fact that the issue was simply not yet regarded as a "Jewish issue," by many people at that time (as late as 1986).

Despite denial and disbelief, situations inevitably began to emerge in congregations and agencies throughout the country. A distraught family would work up enough nerve, in the midst of despair and desperation, to talk with the rabbi about their sick son. A man with AIDS would call a Jewish family service agency for help with a rent or health insurance emergency. A Jewish Community Center health club director would begin to get concerned questions about swimming in the pool or using gym equipment that others had sweat upon.

In many cases, concerns were first expressed in terms of children. After all, if this virus really could not discriminate, wouldn't our own young people possibly be at risk? For this reason, among the first organizations to develop meaningful responses to AIDS were two youth groups, B'nai Brith Youth Organization (BBYO)[3] and National Federation of Temple Youth (NFTY),[4] whose leadership realized the importance of taking a stand. This necessarily involved talking about sex, acknowledging the possibility of sexual activity, and, further, understanding that our youth are not exclusively heterosexual, nor are they destined to be. The challenge was—and still is—to sufficiently raise our young people's level of concern so that they will actually modify their behavior, while not raising a generation of young people who feel bleak, powerless, and fearful of expressing their sexuality as an integral part of their humanity.

Communal response to AIDS began to escalate more significantly in 1987. Many major conferences, including the Conference of Jewish Communal Service, the UAHC Biennial (at which Surgeon General Koop addressed the plenary), the Hillel staff conference, and the Council of Jewish Federations' General Assembly all included AIDS on their agendas. The American Jewish Congress, American Jewish

Committee, and other organizations began to develop resolutions which addressed issues of education, discrimination, and health and social services.

As with any "new" issue, action tends to lag behind conference workshops and organizational resolutions. This is understandable, yet has been highly frustrating in the midst of a crisis that is steadily worsening and where community response is already lagging behind where it should be. In the absence of vigorous and visible action to the contrary, most people with AIDS, along with their families, friends, and caregivers have continued to assume that religious institutions are more judgmental than helpful, and therefore to be avoided.

Yet some responses did become more visible. The UAHC AIDS Committee distributed educational materials to all Reform movement leaders and has vigorously pressed to get AIDS onto more individual and congregational agendas.[5] *Keeping Posted,* the UAHC's magazine for youth and educators, devoted a special 1987 issue to AIDS.[6] In 1988, the United Synagogue of America began to distribute its own AIDS packet as well,[7] following several AIDS resolutions passed by Conservative movement bodies in 1987. Other Jewish organizations, notably B'nai Brith, have also developed packets of materials.[8]

Perhaps the most important development has been the emergence of local community responses to AIDS. In San Francisco in 1986, a full-time AIDS project coordinator was hired by a consortium of congregations and Jewish agencies dedicated to assisting Jews with AIDS and their families and also to reaching Jewish youth and adults with educational programs.[9] Project Nechama in Los Angeles has continued to educate many Jews, and New York Jewish agencies have developed an array of services that include volunteer and public policy components.[10] Jewish organizational coalitions in Philadelphia, St. Louis, Boston, Denver, and Chicago have organized AIDS conferences, and there is activity in many other cities, some of which are integrating AIDS services into existing agency programs.

Rabbis have played an increasingly central role in addressing AIDS in a serious and thoughtful manner. Some have written sermons and articles that have been circulated widely during the past few years, providing a theological and ethical context for addressing AIDS as a Jewish issue. One article of particular significance was written by

Rabbi Daniel Freelander of New Jersey, who has spoken publicly of his brother's death from AIDS, making it possible for other family members to come forward more openly.[11]

Rabbis and other leaders from all branches of Judaism, including Orthodoxy,[12] have addressed themselves to AIDS. There tends to be broad agreement on upholding the mitzvah of bikkur cholim and treating anyone who is sick with unqualified compassion. Opinions diverge, however, regarding the appropriate content of AIDS education (how explicit, and with which assumptions regarding homosexuality and premarital sex), who is to be regarded as "family" of a person with AIDS, and sometimes even the issue of "God's retribution."

Some of these issues also tend to arise in AIDS interfaith work, in which Jews have participated both locally and nationally. These interreligious efforts have been especially important, given the destructive actions of religious fundamentalists, who grabbed the spotlight early in the epidemic with vicious condemnations of those who were sick and dying. Gradually, others in the religious communities have developed their own pastoral, educational, direct service, and public policy responses. Among Jewish organizations, the American Jewish Committee has played a particularly strong role in fostering positive interfaith responses to AIDS at a national level.[13]

The Jewish press has played a helpful yet limited role in reporting on AIDS issues and Jewish community responses. The *B'nai Brith International Jewish Monthly* published an article in 1987 that challenged the community to wake up to the issue.[14] *Reform Judaism* has printed several articles,[15] as has the *Journal of Jewish Communal Service*,[16] and the *United Synagogue Review* published a compassionate essay in 1988.[17] The Jewish Telegraphic Agency has consistently sent AIDS news out on its wires, and a few local Jewish newspapers have published their own articles on "bringing the epidemic home" with profiles of local Jewish individuals and families touched directly by AIDS. On the whole, however, there has been a dearth of reporting, due in part to excessively narrow definitions of what constitutes "a Jewish issue" and exacerbated by Jewish community denial regarding AIDS.

As is usually true, scattered individuals and groups from Boston, Dallas, and many other communities have quietly undertaken efforts that can only be described as heroic. Some are people who were touched very personally by AIDS and knew they must do something. Others have simply opened their hearts to those who might appear "different," or they have recognized the political importance of taking a visible stand against any kind of scapegoating. Whatever their initial motivation for involvement, all agree that their lives will never be the same.

Despite the trend toward greater involvement, the financial and staff resources committed by Jewish communal organizations to deal with AIDS still remain very small, certainly not befitting the major public health crisis of our time. We are still far behind and not running nearly fast enough to catch up.

Progress is, of course, uneven. On the one hand, an increasing number of people have moved from just wanting to know how to keep this virus away from them and their children, to now wanting to do something concrete for people with AIDS. On the other hand, there are *chevra kadisha* members unwilling to perform the mitzvah of *tahara* when a person dies of AIDS, or people who privately or even publicly assert that gays are basically getting what we deserve for "flaunting the laws of nature." Such attitudes will unfortunately persist, but will not deter us from moving ahead on the issue.

The future of the AIDS epidemic is uncertain for all of us, but there are a few things we can count on. It will continue to hit close to home for an increasing number of people, some of whom never dreamed that it would. It will continue to spread among those who can afford it the least, in terms of financial resources and social supports. It will continue to test all of us in how we choose to respond.

AIDS continues to challenge Jews, along with all others. We are forced to look at our theology: do we see God as a willful punisher or a compassionate presence? We are challenged to deal openly with sexuality in general and homosexuality in particular. We are challenged to accept the reality of how families are constructed: that they may include lovers, partners, and intimate friends as well as parents, sisters, brothers, and children. Finally, we are moved to draw from our own basic precepts and historical experiences: *Bikkur Cholim*, directing us to ensure that no one who is sick gets isolated from community when they need it the most; *Pikuach Nefesh*, mandating us to educate about AIDS prevention in order to protect life, even at the risk of our discomfort in dealing with sexual behavior; and our own history of being scapegoated, especially during epidemics, which must move us to stand up when it happens to others. For They could be Us. And they are.

EPILOGUE

Transforming Our Visions into Action

······························

Christie Balka and Andy Rose

THE AUTHORS IN THIS VOLUME HAVE WRITTEN TO REVEAL, TO CLAR-
ify, to instruct, and to inspire. They challenge us to expand our visions and synthesize new ones, and to move resolutely forward.

Clearly, we in the Jewish community are moving beyond the old
debates about whether gay and lesbian Jews really exist, and whether
we who constitute ten percent of the adult population are entitled to
basic rights. It is time to move beyond those questions of "existence"
and "rights" to the issues of full acknowledgment, acceptance, and
inclusion. And inclusion, by implication, moves us toward a broader
and deeper sense of transformation. Any organism—individual, community, nation—is transformed as it opens itself to more fully include: that is how we stay alive.

In that spirit of transformation and renewal we offer our visions for
our future Jewish community. We are confident that these images will
spur all of us toward bold and creative actions.

—Jewish youth will grow up knowing that heterosexuality is not assumed for them; that they will be supported by parents, educators,
   and others in growing to know their individual sexual orientations;
   and that their realizations and choices will be affirmed and celebrated. They will have access to lesbian and gay Jewish adults as
   role models—as rabbis, as teachers, as camp counselors, as friends
   woven into the fabric of the lives of their own families.
—Jewish curricula for both youth and adults will address issues of
   sexuality, diversity as a positive value, our own Jewish history regarding "otherness" and scapegoating, and the full spectrum of

types of discrimination that exist in our world. They will also include specific mention of lesbians and gay men throughout Jewish history.

—"Jewish family" will be understood to include the full range of Jewish families that actually exist. This new understanding will not be considered as a social problem or as a sign of the demise of the family, but rather as a sign of the diversity and vitality of Jewish family life.

—Gay and lesbian Jews who choose to parent, or are engaged in parenting children from former heterosexual relationships, will be acknowledged and encouraged by Jewish communal institutions. In recognition of the fact that there are many ways to nurture future generations, support will be extended as well to those who choose not to parent, but contribute to children's lives in other ways.

—Jewish agencies and congregations will have strong, unambiguous policies of nondiscrimination and inclusion with regard to membership, provision of services, and employment practices. Employment policies will apply to rabbis, cantors, educators, and youth leaders, among others.

—Communal acknowledgment and support will exist for the large number of ways lesbian and gay Jews will choose to consecrate and celebrate their relationships. These options will include synagogue ceremonies with family members and congregants comfortably participating. At heterosexual weddings, those attending will be reminded that the privileges accorded to married couples are not accorded to all, and will take the opportunity to contribute to efforts to legally acknowledge domestic partnerships.

—All Jews will warmly welcome the unique perspectives of lesbian and gay Jews and will proudly acknowledge our past and current contributions to Jewish cultural, spiritual, educational, and political life.

—Inclusive language, reflecting an awareness of the historical exclusion of women, lesbians, and gay men and a commitment to redressing it, will become standard practice in Jewish liturgy and communal rituals.

—Jewish communities will evolve new traditions of observance and celebration of gay and lesbian experience. As Rebecca Alpert suggests in her essay in this volume, the two weeks in the spring during which *Parshat Ahare Mot* and *Parshat Kedoshim* are read from the

Torah will become focal times of the year to raise awareness regarding gay and lesbian issues and to renew commitments to the kinds of visions enumerated here. "Shabbat Pride," as described by Yoel Kahn in his essay here, will be celebrated by all.

—Jewish community relations and political entities will vigorously support efforts to institute or strengthen nondiscrimination laws and policies with regard to lesbians and gay men. They will also support domestic partnership legislation, efforts to stem the rising tide of antigay violence, and the many proposals needed to respond adequately and compassionately to the AIDS crisis, for however long that crisis remains with us.

—For the foreseeable future, lesbian and gay Jews will need a broad range of options for Jewish involvement. These will include predominantly lesbian and gay congregations, *chavurot*, and organizations, in addition to opportunities for "mainstreaming" into all other congregations and Jewish organizations. Homophobia will unfortunately be with us for a long time to come, and we will continue to need separate institutions as "havens" in which lesbians and gay men can heal wounds, affirm ourselves, and build community. These separate institutions will be understood and warmly welcomed by the Jewish community as a whole.

—Jewish communities and individuals will be willing to undertake a thorough, honest, and ongoing examination of the many ways that homophobia and sexism have affected our perceptions and behavior. This will necessarily involve a deep willingness to listen and to learn, beyond comfort, embarrassment, and defensiveness. Also necessarily, this will lead to even stronger commitments to act.

Our visions extend not only to our Jewish community, but also to our lesbian and gay communities. Drawing from the wisdom and richness of our historical and contemporary experience as Jews, we offer our hopes for the future:

—That the lesbian and gay community embrace our full religious, cultural, racial, and ethnic diversity; that our cultural events in particular strive to reflect who we are as a whole; and that community events be scheduled and conducted with sensitivity to Jewish concerns and the Jewish calendar.

—That we learn from the long and remarkably successful experience of the Jews from in building networks of communal institutions to meet educational, social service, cultural, recreational, financial, and political needs.

—That we learn from Jewish experience about the crucial importance of preserving and transmitting history. Perhaps we need to set up "Coming Out Schools" and other educational opportunities parallel to Hebrew schools and other Jewish educational institutions.

—That we nurture and respect the process of evolving individual and communal rituals—to celebrate new life and new beginnings, to remember and to grieve our losses, to affirm our relationships, to mark historic events. That in doing so, we draw from the wisdom of Jewish and other traditions.

—That we grow to understand even more deeply the power of being determined to survive against all odds, and the necessity to continue at all times to affirm and celebrate life.

For Jewish Educators:
Teaching about Homosexuality

······························

Denise L. Eger and Lesley M. Silverstone

HOMOSEXUALITY IS A TOPIC THAT GENERALLY RECEIVES LITTLE DIS-
cussion in the Jewish classroom. Few educators feel prepared to address this issue—or any aspect of human sexuality—relegating it to
the inadequate realm of public school gym class anatomy lessons. In
doing so, we do our young people a disservice, failing to address such
issues as moral context, self-esteem, or homophobia. In this article,
we suggest several concrete approaches to teaching about homosexuality in Jewish educational settings.

Homosexuality is part of the variety of human experience. Our students, teachers, children, rabbis, and cantors may be lesbian or gay,
each with his or her own dignity and personhood. If we ground ourselves in the knowledge that all of us are created in the divine image,
then there must be room for gay and lesbian people in the spectrum
of humanness. While our traditional texts either ignore or contradict
this point,[1] we believe that our contemporary experience must also inform our Jewish worldview. Given that lesbians and gay men are created in God's image, we must find ways to communicate this understanding in our religious school classrooms.

First we must address a frequently stated concern: do we teach
about homosexuality, or do we teach homosexuality? Given the many
myths that abound about homosexuals and homosexuality, it is necessary to clarify at the outset that no one can teach another person to
be gay or lesbian. It is a process of self-discovery, not unlike discovering anything else about one's personality and make-up. Thus when
we explore issues surrounding this topic, we as educators must be

clear about our tasks. We are here to help our students frame questions for themselves and open avenues of exploration about all people.

Text-Centered Approach

Of the many possible approaches to teaching about homosexuality in the Jewish classroom, the one most often used is the text-centered approach. Utilizing biblical references along with talmudic discussion, the classic arguments against homosexuality are presented. This approach may or may not include more recent expositions of these classic arguments, including responsa of Solomon Freehof, Norman Lamm, and others. Unfortunately, utilizing only these texts will leave students with an extremely limited and, of course, negative concept of homosexuality.

The text-centered approach can easily be expanded to include additional articles and opinions, including those of Rabbi Hershel Matt and Rabbi Robert Kirschner, as well as material from this anthology. Our students can then trace the changing perceptions and opinions of Jewish individuals and movements, and may also consider parallel changes among experts in psychology, medicine, and other fields. This text-centered method is best used with high school students or adults who are already adept at text analysis and able to consider subjects critically.

The text-centered approach requires an explanation of other issues. Among them might be a discussion of the various theories of whether homosexuality occurs naturally and inevitably in any culture, or if it is somehow "caused" by environmental factors. It would also be helpful to discuss the gay liberation movement and the concerns of lesbian and gay Jews, drawing on articles from this book, among others (see Bibliography). One particularly good source for Jewish educators is a special issue on homosexuality of *Keeping Posted* (vol. 32, no. 2), a magazine for high school students and adults published by the Union of American Hebrew Congregations. This issue presents sensitive and useful information in a very readable manner.

In-Class Speakers

We strongly recommend that Jewish curricula about homosexuality include hearing directly from lesbian and gay Jews, especially when also using the text-centered approach. High school students and others may tend to view texts in isolation, drawing conclusions without understanding the human impact. They will learn much from hearing a speaker discuss her or his own issues of coming out, working out relationships with parents, facing discrimination, and integrating gay and Jewish identities. It is particularly important for our students who are silently struggling with their own sexual identities to know that there are positive, healthy role models of lesbian and gay Jewish adults.

Finding appropriate speakers may initially be challenging; hopefully it will be part of your own learning process. Contacting the nearest gay congregation or *chavurah* is a good place to start. Other gay community service organizations often have speakers bureaus and will probably be glad to help. If you think you do not know any gay or lesbian people and you have none of these resources available to you, you might use first-hand accounts from this book, *Keeping Posted,* or other sources as a basis for discussion.

In both the aforementioned approaches, it will be helpful to have a good list of discussion-sparking questions, such as the following:

1. What do traditional Jewish texts say about homosexuality? What was the historical context of these writings?

2. What are some of the new interpretations of these texts? Can you think of some of your own?

3. Read the biblical story of Jonathan and David. Some have suggested that their relationship was more than just a close friendship. What do you think?

4. Many historians now say that in every culture, in every historical era, some percentage of people have been homosexual. If this is true, what is the effect of prohibiting homosexuality?

5. How are lesbians and gay men discriminated against? Are there parallels between this kind of discrimination and anti-Semitism?

6. Are there other groups of Jews who tend to be hidden in the Jewish community? Who? Why do you think that happens?

7. Do you hear people make comments or jokes about lesbians and gay men? If so, how do you feel about it?

8. How do you think you would feel if your best friend told you that she or he were gay?

These questions span a wide range of academic and personal concerns; please feel free to add your own.

Jewish Family

Strengthening Jewish family life is central to most curricular goals in Jewish education. We customarily teach about life-cycle observances and core Jewish values in the context of the Jewish family unit. But as we well know, the make-up of the Jewish family is changing. We are presented with single-parent families, blended families, and so many other variations. However, one area that is usually neglected is the family constellation that includes one or more gay or lesbian member. Homosexuality is rarely addressed in the context of learning about the family. We know, though, that gay people do have families and form loving and committed relationships that extend over the years.

We suggest emphasizing to our students of all ages that there are many different kinds of Jewish families, without valuing one as the "right" kind. This is probably familiar to most children, either through personal experience or through television, which has shown a variety of family situations on programs such as "Kate and Allie," "Full House," and "My Two Dads." Each of these shows feature parental role models who are not birth parents. Although none of these characters are portrayed as gay or lesbian, they help to introduce the concept of "difference" in families, which can be made specific to gay or lesbian parents, when appropriate. Educators can also use one of the small but growing number of children's books that show families with gay parents.[2]

In order to spark discussion, we suggest asking the questions: "What makes a family? What do family members do for each other?" Answers are likely to include: people who are related to one another, people who love each other, people who take care of each other. This can lead into a broader discussion of how different kinds of families love and care for each other in many ways. Further, we can present this diversity as a positive value, rather than a social problem that somehow threatens our lives.

Of course, it can be mentioned that now gay and lesbian couples are having ceremonies that affirm their commitment to one another within a Jewish context.[3] This conveys that lesbians and gay men form family units and consecrate that commitment in a specifically Jewish manner.

With young children we need to generally discuss the issue of "difference." We talk about Jews and Gentiles, Diaspora and Israeli Jews, people of all races. By presenting the breadth of human experience to children in a positive manner, they begin to learn that "different" is okay, and even desirable. Hopefully, they will learn more easily to accept differences in others.

Identity and Self-Esteem

Building and strengthening positive Jewish identity is a core concern of all Jewish educators. We grapple to identify the best methods for accomplishing this key task. Some say that we teach "identity" by teaching the meaning and ritual of Jewish holidays. Others say we teach it by involving our students in community events. We also teach about positive Jewish identity by discussing Jewish values and morals. Whatever curricular path we emphasize, we must find ways to allow our students to explore all aspects of their identities as Jews and as human beings.

In order to feel good about one's identity, one must feel good about oneself in general. We find in Leviticus 19:18 the commandment: "Love your neighbor as yourself." Self-worth is not a given, but something that we must practice and internalize. As teachers of Torah, it is our responsibility to help our students discover who they are and reinforce their feelings of self-worth and self-esteem. If they are secure with themselves, our students will also be more accepting of others, including those who are lesbian or gay.

Too often we teachers assume that all our students are heterosexual. But chances are, there are students in our classrooms who have already begun wondering whether they are or not. For these students, stressing self-esteem may be especially important. These young people often feel confused and scared, and frequently do not know where they can turn. They are constantly bombarded by heterosexual models of behavior and have few, if any, positive gay or lesbian role models. It is therefore imperative that we address this issue in the religious school classroom in a sensitive and supportive manner. We can achieve this by assuming diversity rather than exclusive heterosexuality, by the way we address or avoid issues, by the way we handle homophobic comments or "jokes" in the classroom, and by generally being approachable and supportive of our students. There are also several books on the market that address the issue of teens who discover they are lesbian or gay. As educators it is helpful for us to be familiar with them and perhaps utilize all or parts of them in the contexts of our classrooms.[4]

Although helping students develop good feelings about themselves is important for teachers of all grades, we must be particularly sensitive to our junior high school students. At a time when there are many changes in their lives, these students are often struggling to discover who they are and what they believe in. Many issues can be explored in the classroom if the teacher is comfortable handling such serious topics as identity, self-esteem, relationships, sexuality in general, and homosexuality in particular. Among the excellent resources available for teaching self-esteem to this age group are Ellen Mack's curriculum on youth self-esteem and suicide prevention[5] and Shirley Barish's *Six Kallot*,[6] which includes a weekend entitled "Courage to Be." We also recommend the Billy Joel video, "You're Only Human (Second Wind)," which looks at how we deal with mistakes as we go through life. This is available from the UAHC Task Force on Youth Suicide with an accompanying lesson plan on self-esteem.[7]

Sexuality

The topic of sexuality is certainly complex and potentially intimidating for educators. We are fortunate to have some excellent books to use, such as Sol Gordon's *Raising a Child Conservatively in a Sexually Permissive World*.[8] But we still must confront how to discuss sexuality within a Jewish context. We suggest that a good starting point is communicating that in Judaism, sexuality is regarded as a gift from God. One implication of this is that whatever one's sexual orientation, it is divinely sanctioned. Whether we are heterosexual or homosexual, we strive to value our relationships through the concept of *kadosh*, or holiness. When we regard committed, loving relationships as holy, we move toward treating all people with the dignity that is their right. By conveying positive attitudes about sexuality to our students, we can provide them with a safe haven—a place where they can feel secure discussing the issues and sorting out where they stand.

Although the subject of sexuality is difficult for many people to discuss, it is even harder for someone who is gay and fears the reactions of others. Most gay men and lesbians are afraid that if their friends and family find out, they won't be accepted by them. These fears, unfortunately, are not unfounded: lesbians and gay men experience discrimination in employment, housing, child custody, and in many other ways. The incidence of violence against gay people is alarmingly high. It is incumbent on us to convey to our students that, as Jews, we regard this as unacceptable. Given our people's experiences of oppression and discrimination, we are mandated to be particularly sensitive to the irrational fear and hatred of any group of people. We must explain to our students the meaning of homophobia, and the ways in which it is no different than racism, sexism, or anti-Semitism. We are responsible for teaching our students that all human beings, created in the divine image, must be treated with common courtesy, respect, and dignity.

We have tried to show how the Jewish educator can be more sensitive to the issue of homosexuality. Clearly, there are many possible approaches. We have suggested ideas for a text-centered approach, the in-class speaker, integration into family and life-cycle units, addressing issues of identity and self-esteem, and facing concerns related to sexuality and homophobia. The issue of homosexuality intersects with so many of our curricular concerns that we must be prepared to explore it as it arises within a variety of contexts. Perhaps the best lesson we can learn as Jewish educators is that we cannot be silent on any challenging issue.

Resources

  I. Biblical references to homosexuality include Leviticus 18:22 and 20:13, Genesis 19 (the story of Sodom and Gemorrah), and 1 Samuel 20:1–24 (the story of David and Jonathan). [Editors' note: Please see Alpert, Rogow, and Hirsh essays in this book.]

 II. Talmudic references include the following: Kiddushin 82a, Sanhedrin 53a, Yevamot 83b, Keritut 2a, Yevamot 76a, Shabbat 65a, Jerusalem Talmud, Gittin 49c.

III. Mishneh Torah references include Hilchot Issurei Biah I.5 and Hilchot Issurei Biah XXI.8.

IV. Curricular references include the following:

1. Baumblatt, Lori B. *Human Sexuality: A Jewish Response.* Available from the Tartak Resource Center of Hebrew Union College—Jewish Institute of Religion, 3077 University Ave., Los Angeles, CA 90007.
2. Mack, Ellen. "Youth Self-Esteem and Anti-Suicide Curriculum." Available c/o Beth-El Congregation, PO Box 2232, Fort Worth, TX 76113.
3. "To See the World through Jewish Eyes," the UAHC William and Francis Schuster Curriculum. Guidelines for the High School Years. New York: UAHC, 1985.

V. Articles for classroom use include the following:

1. Eger, Denise. "Gay, Jewish and the Reform Movement." *Compass* (Fall 1988): 15–16. This article explores the Reform movement's response to homosexuality and also focuses on the presentation of homosexuality in the UAHC's Schuster curriculum.
2. Kirschner, Robert. "Halakhah and Homosexuality." *Judaism* (Fall 1988): 450–58. This article is an excellent resource for any text analysis lesson on this subject. It also provides a review of medical and psychological research on the subject.

Additional resources are found in this book's overall Bibliography section.

APPENDIX 2

Homophobia Workshop Model

·······························

Tom Rawson

WHEN A SYNAGOGUE, JEWISH ORGANIZATION, OR AGENCY DECIDES to tackle homophobia, a workshop on the topic can play a significant role. In the context of a supportive group, a workshop enables participants to examine their personal issues related to homophobia, their relationships with people of different sexual orientations, their own sexual identities, and the ways in which attitudes about lesbians and gay men are perpetuated in society-at-large and in the Jewish community in particular. Workshops often help groups plan strategies for including lesbians and gay men among their ranks.

We call these "Unlearning Homophobia" workshops[1] to emphasize that homophobia is an attitude that everyone in our culture learns, which can be "unlearned" through exposure to sound information, by listening to others, and by reflecting on our own experiences.

In Unlearning Homophobia workshops, participants are asked to share their perceptions in an atmosphere free of judgment. In doing so, participants come to see how their own attitudes are no different from those of friends and colleagues—how, in fact, all of us have been shaped by the homophobic attitudes of our society, and how we can challenge these attitudes. The goal of Unlearning Homophobia workshops is to empower participants to challenge homophobia on a personal, institutional, and societal level.

To help participants make connections between their personal attitudes and prevalent cultural attitudes about lesbians and gay men, it is important to create an atmosphere conducive to personal sharing. To build trust among participants, certain ground rules are recommended for these workshops. First, participants are asked to adhere to strict confidentiality once they leave the workshop. Second, they are asked not to judge or criticize one another in the workshop. Third, small group exercises are structured to enable participants to take timed turns speaking, rather than carrying on freewheeling discussions that may be full of interruption or dominated by those who have an easier time speaking in groups. (This approach encourages better listening.) Finally, after each small group exercise, a few volunteers are asked to share perceptions from their small groups. This helps participants make connections, and it provides the leaders with an opportunity to underscore key points as they arise during the course of the workshop.

In each workshop we explore the considerable parallels between gay and Jewish experience. The information provided about lesbian and gay life often resonates with participants' understanding of anti-Semitism, resistance, and community. In fact, participants are encouraged to make these connections: the workshop is partially based on the premise that Jewish experience provides a basis for empathy with the concerns of lesbians and gay men.

The following pages describe what occurs in Unlearning Homophobia workshops, what they can and can't accomplish, and when they might be appropriate. To set up a workshop, you should contact a trained group leader.

Goals

The first thing to consider when planning an Unlearning Homophobia workshop is, *what are you trying to accomplish?* Workshops can be used to help a group of staff or lay leaders of varying sexual preferences improve their work together. They can be used to help predominantly or entirely heterosexual organizations figure out how to welcome lesbians and gay men. Or they can assist a coalition of Jewish groups work better in relation to the lesbian and gay community.

One thing a workshop *isn't* good for is outreach. We've heard a number of requests for workshops that sound something like this: "Our membership is all straight. We think there are a lot of Jewish lesbians and gay men who'd be interested in what we do, so we'd like to do a workshop and invite them so they can join." The underlying motivation ("get them to join") will tend to make it tough for the lesbians and gay men to participate on an equal footing or feel comfortable in the workshop. In this kind of situation it will work better to do a workshop for the all-straight group on their homophobia. Once this happens, the group will be in a better position to understand the needs of lesbians and gay men and truly to welcome them.

Time

To allow enough time for significant issues to emerge and be adequately addressed, you will need, ideally, four to six hours. A two-hour session may succeed in introducing a small number of participants to the subject matter.

Participants

When planning a workshop, you'll need to make careful decisions about who should participate. You might have to choose between an open workshop for your membership, or a smaller one specifically for the organization's leaders. Your coalition might require a closed workshop for its steering committee, or possibly a more open one with a limited number of representatives from each organization. This depends on the size and structure of your organization, as well as its goals for the workshop. (A workshop leader will be able to help you make these choices.)

Probably the biggest question about participants relates to the workshop being open to people of all sexual orientations. We've found that, in most situations, the most effective initial workshops are those specifically for heterosexuals. In discussing homophobia, many heterosexuals need to talk about feelings of discomfort, as well as the stereotypes and misinformation we've acquired about lesbians and gay men. This may be made more difficult by the presence of lesbians and gay men.

In addition, many heterosexuals haven't had an opportunity even to notice that they're heterosexual. Because the dominant culture in our society is heterosexual, being heterosexual is taken as a "given." As a result, issues of sexuality and sexual preference that are all too obvious to lesbians and gay men go unnoticed by those of us who are heterosexual. Separate work on these issues helps provide a common base of understanding before discussing them in a mixed group.

Because homophobia isolates lesbians and gay men from heterosexuals in a variety of ways, many people don't like the idea of separating off one group for the workshop—especially in an organization where people already know each other and work together. This can make the idea of a separate workshop a bit hard to sell, but we feel it's worthwhile. Depending on the size and nature of your group, another option is to separate lesbians and gay men and heterosexuals into two groups after introductions, and to reconvene at the end of the workshop.

One question we've dealt with repeatedly is how to make workshops work for people who identify as bisexual. Our usual approach is to ask people to make a choice on the basis of their best evaluation of their present situation. That is, a bisexual man presently involved in a heterosexual relationship would consider himself in the heterosexual group for the purpose of the workshop. Although this solution does not represent a complete analysis of the complex issue of bisexuality, it works well for the purposes of this workshop.

Content

Every workshop we've done has been unique, designed for the group that requested it. Therefore, the approaches listed below should be read as a general picture of content, rather than as a strict agenda.

Large group introductions usually involve each participant briefly stating who they are and why they're participating in the workshop. Even if people already know each other, this helps build a sense of common purpose. Ground rules can be introduced at this point.

Small group introductions usually follow. In groups of two or three, each person takes a turn to talk about how she or he feels about the workshop in general, or to answer a specific question (e.g., "What do you like and what do you find difficult about being heterosexual?"). Many participants find it easier to explore their feelings in a small group.

Recounting early memories often helps participants understand how homophobia affects everyone from an early age. In small groups, participants might be asked to think about times when they were told as a child that it "wasn't right" to be affectionate with someone of the same gender. Later, the leader may ask a few volunteers to share their experiences with the large group.

Exploring similarities between society's treatment of lesbians and gay men and Jews usually occurs in a large group discussion followed by small group exercises. This part of the workshop can be particularly powerful for those who are sensitive to the existence of anti-Semitism and are committed to Jewish life, but who may not see that lesbians and gay men face similar issues. It can also help participants understand what lesbian and gay Jews bring to the Jewish community, and in turn how they can be better served by the community.

A brief *informational presentation*, usually by a workshop leader, helps familiarize participants with the particular dynamics of homophobia and heterosexism.

Listening to lesbians and gay men in speakouts and fishbowl exercises enables participants to gain a more in-depth picture of lesbian and gay experience. In a fishbowl exercise, a volunteer group of lesbians and gay men (if this is a mixed workshop) sit in the center of a circle and engage in dialogue with one another, while heterosexual participants, (positioned around the outside of the circle or "fishbowl") listen. The goal is for participants to gain a better understanding of what it's like to be gay or lesbian. After a predetermined amount of time, the groups switch positions: heterosexual participants move into the center of the circle and discuss what its like to be heterosexual, while lesbian and gay participants listen. This format can also work as a way for heterosexuals to talk about being heterosexual.

Similar exercises on *confronting homophobia* give participants a chance to role play and practice ways to respond to homophobic jokes, remarks, and actions. This part of the workshop gives participants the practical experience and confidence to address homophobia they encounter in their everyday lives. Again, these exercises can take place either in small or large groups.

Problem solving exercises provide an opportunity to explore a hypothetical scenario in which homophobia is present, and discuss constructive solutions. For example, one scenario might look something like this:

An openly lesbian candidate applies for a position as rabbi of your congregation. She has somewhat less rabbinic experience than her competition, but considerably more experience running a school, which will be a major part of her job. Some vocal members with children in the school have threatened to leave the congregation if a lesbian is hired. What do you do?

This exercise can take place either in small or large groups, depending on the amount of time available for the workshop.

Separate groups of lesbians and gay men, and heterosexuals can be used to build trust and discuss common concerns in a mixed workshop. Many people feel most comfortable in these groups and find them to be the best part of the workshop. To use this formula effectively a long (five- to six-hour) workshop is recommended.

An *evaluation and closing* are important parts of the workshop, giving the leaders valuable feedback and the participants a chance to review what they've learned.

Leadership

It's best for these workshops to be conducted by experienced leaders. Most people find it difficult to talk openly about sexual identity, and leaders will know how to put participants at ease, elicit responses to discussion questions, and handle difficult issues that arise in the course of the workshop. The resource section in the back of the book will tell you where such leaders can be found.

It often works best for the workshops to be led by teams of two: a gay man and a heterosexual woman, or a lesbian and a heterosexual man. The mixture of gender and sexual identity provides different perspectives on the issues, and offers a model of cooperation and common work that spans the rigid boundaries that the workshop seeks to change.

Resources

································

Ameinu
P.O. Box 1423
Cooper Station
New York, NY 10276
(*network of lesbians and gay men
working professionally in the Jewish
community*)

Lesbian and Gay Rights Project
American Civil Liberties Union
132 W. 43rd Street
New York, NY 10036

Equity Institute
Tucker-Taft Building
48 N. Pleasant Street
Amherst, MA 01002
(*provides workshops on homophobia*)

DiversityWorks, Inc.: social change
educators and consultants
201 N. Valley Road
Pelham, MA 01022
(*provides workshops on homophobia*)

Fund for Human Dignity
666 Broadway, Suite 410
New York, NY 10012
(*national lesbian and gay resource center
and crisis line*)

Hetrick-Martin Institute for the
Protection of Lesbian and Gay Youth
401 West Street
New York, NY 10014
(*social services and advocacy for lesbian
and gay youth*)

Lambda Legal Defense and
Education Fund
132 W. 43rd Street
New York, NY 10036
(*public interest law firm*)

Parents and Friends of Lesbians and
Gays (PFLAG)
P.O. Box 20308
Denver, CO 80220
(*nationwide network provides support
and advocacy*)

New Jewish Agenda
64 Fulton Street
New York, NY 10038
(*provides workshops on homophobia,
educational resources*)

National Gay Rights Advocates
540 Castro Street
San Francisco, CA 94114
(*public interest law firm*)

National Gay and Lesbian
Task Force
1517 U Street, N.W.
Washington, D.C. 20009

Senior Action in a Gay Environment
(SAGE)
208 W. 13th Street
New York, NY 10011
(*social service and advocacy*)

Jewish Lesbian Daughters of
Holocaust Survivors
P.O. Box 6194
Boston, MA 02114

Union of American Hebrew
Congregations
838 Fifth Avenue
New York, NY 10021
(*has commission on AIDS, publishes*
Keeping Posted)

World Congress of Gay and Lesbian
Jewish Organizations
1901 Wyoming Ave., N.W.
Washington, D.C. 20009

NOTES

....

Introduction

1. *Conversos* are also commonly known as *Marranos*, a term which has its origins in the Spanish word for "pig."

2. Many Jewish lesbians experience ourselves as "triply other," due to the invisibility of our gender, in addition to our sexual orientation and Jewish identity. In addition, lesbian and gay Jews who are disabled, Sephardic, working class, or have other identities which differ from the mainstream feel "triply" or "quadruply" other.

3. For National Lesbian and Gay Task Force 1988 study on antigay violence, write to: NLGTF, 1517 U Street, N.W., Washington, D.C., 20009.

4. Just as the terms of Jewish assimilation have changed over time, the terms of "passing" have changed depending on the mores of the particular era. In the first half of this century, for example, lesbians often dressed as men in order to avoid harassment on the street.

5. See *The Coming Out Stories*, ed. Julia Penelope and Susan Wolf (Persephone Press, 1981); *Testimonies: A Collection of Lesbian Coming Out Stories*, ed. Sarah Holmes (Alyson, 1988); *Revelations: A Collection of Gay Male Coming Out Stories*, ed. Wayne Curtis (Alyson, 1988); and *Like Coming Home: Coming Out Letters*, ed. Meg Umans (Banned Books, 1988).

Empowered by the experience of coming out, lesbians have been among the first to come out about other taboo issues, in society at large and in the Jewish community in particular. These issues include domestic violence, incest, and substance abuse.

6. One example is Harvey Milk, an openly gay member of San Francisco's Board of Supervisors. Reportedly, Milk was profoundly influenced by a story of the Warsaw Ghetto Uprising which he heard as a child. See Randy Shilts, *The Mayor of Castro Street: The Life and Times of Harvey Milk* (St. Martin, 1982).

7. While each contributor to this anthology might not use the same vo-

cabulary to describe his or her experience, each writes from a commitment to feminism, to lesbian and gay liberation, and to reshaping Jewish life.

8. See Arthur Waskow, *These Holy Sparks: The Rebirth of the Jewish People* (Harper and Row, 1983).

9. This did not occur without serious strains between lesbians and heterosexual feminists, perhaps best symbolized by Betty Friedan's expulsion of lesbians from the National Organization for Women.

10. John D'Emilio, *Sexual Politics, Sexual Communities: The Making of a Homosexual Minority in the United States, 1940–1970* (University of Chicago Press, 1983).

11. Daughters of Bilitis still maintains chapters in several cities in the United States.

12. At the same time, lesbians and gay men often clashed on issues of sexism. For example, many of us found ourselves on opposite sides of the barricades in disputes over pornography laws in the 1970s. Then, as now, our class interests (influenced by our gender differences) diverged widely, leading us to support opposing policies and candidates for office.

13. Members of other racial and ethnic minorities have been engaged in a similar enterprise. In recent years a number of anthologies exploring the connections between race, ethnicity, gender and sexual orientation, and in some cases religious identity have appeared. These include *Home Girls: A Black Feminist Anthology*, ed. Barbara Smith (Kitchen Table/Women of Color Press, 1983); *In the Life: A Black Gay Anthology*, ed. Joseph Beam (Alyson, 1986); *A Gathering of Spirit: Writing and Art by North American Indian Women*, ed. Beth Brant (Sinister Wisdom Books, 1984); *This Bridge Called My Back: Writings by Radical Women of Color*, ed. Cherrie Moraga and Gloria Anzaldua (Kitchen Table/Women of Color Press); and *Breaking Silence: Lesbian Nuns* (Naiad Press, 1985).

14. This was the largest civil rights march in United States history, with an estimated 750,000 people converging on the capital to demand civil rights for lesbians and gay men.

15. Marcia Falk, "Notes on Composing New Blessings: Toward a Feminist-Jewish Reconstruction of Prayer," *Journal of Feminist Studies in Religion* 3, no. 1 (Spring 1987): 53.

Confessions of a "Feygele-Boichik"/Burt E. Schuman

1. On Sunday afternoons in Brooklyn, it was common for ultra-Orthodox and Hasidic men to make the rounds of Jewish homes, collecting for local yeshivot or for charitable programs, such as hospital visitation societies.

Different like Moses/Alan D. Zamochnick

1. These demonstrations were organized by the Mattachine Society during the early and mid 1960s each Fourth of July. They were the forerunners of the modern gay rights movement, which began with the Stonewall riot of 1969.

2. Jerome D. Schein and Lester J. Waldman, eds., *The Deaf Jew in the Modern World* (New York: Ktav, 1986). This category was also used for women in some cases.

You Didn't Talk about These Things/Felice Yeskel

1. Rita Mae Brown, *Rubyfruit Jungle* (New York: Bantam, 1973). This novel, which appeared in the early years of the second wave of feminism, centers around lesbian Molly Bolt.

2. A children's game played on the sidewalk with bottle caps.

3. A cross between tackle football and capture the flag.

Hiding Is Unhealthy for the Soul/Rachel Wahba

1. *Shaddai* represents the name of God and is often engraved on Jewish religious symbols.

2. When the pro-Nazi government of Rashid Ali collapsed in June 1941, riots followed. One hundred seventy-five Jews were killed, many were tortured, and approximately one thousand injured. Jewish homes and businesses were looted, with nine hundred of the homes destroyed.

3. In 1955–56, those Jews who had remained in Egypt were stripped of all material possessions and expelled. Those of us already out were stripped of any citizenship claims, becoming stateless.

4. In *The Other Jews: The Sephardim Today* (New York: Basic Books, 1989), Daniel J. Elazar argues that distinguishing Sephardim as "Eastern" versus Ashkenazim as "Western" serves to reinforce the view of the former as backward and the latter as progressive, given the common assumption that the West is more culturally advanced. He suggests "Northern" and "Southern" as being more geographically accurate and less automatically biased.

5. Memmi's books include *The Pillar of Salt* (Chicago: J. Phillip O'Hara, 1955), *The Colonizer and the Colonized* (Boston: Beacon, 1972), *The Liberation of the Jew* (New York: Viking, 1973) and *Jews and Arabs* (Chicago: J. Phillip O'Hara, 1975).

In God's Image/Rebecca T. Alpert

1. Although the Leviticus text specifically refers to relationships between men, lesbians experience the power of this prohibition in reference to themselves as well.

2. I am indebted to Norman Lamm's essay, "Judaism and the Modern Attitude towards Homosexuality," *Encyclopedia Judaica Yearbook* (1974), pp. 194–205, for the citations of these interpretations.

3. Ibid. Lamm gives an extensive presentation of all traditional discussion of the subject of homosexuality, not only that which pertains to Leviticus.

4. Ibid., p. 198.

5. "Judaism and Homosexuality: A Response," *Central Conference of American Rabbis Journal* (Summer 1973), p. 31.

6. I am indebted to the writings of Rabbi Hershel Matt (of blessed memory) for this interpretation.

7. Waskow suggested this interpretation in a private conversation.

Speaking the Unspeakable/Faith Rogow

1. Adrienne Rich, *On Lies, Secrets, and Silence* (New York: Norton, 1979), p. 199.

2. Michael Meyer, ed., *Ideas of Jewish History* (New York: Behrman House, 1974), p. xi.

3. For the sake of brevity, this essay will use the term "gay" to refer to both gay men and lesbians. This usage in no way implies that lesbian experience is secondary to or identical to gay male experience.

4. For example, Nathaniel Lehrman, "Homosexuality and Judaism: Are They Compatible?" *Judaism* 32 (Fall 1983): 392–404; Abraham B. Hecht, quoted in Enrique Rueda, *The Homosexual Network* (Old Greenwich, Conn.: Devin Adair, 1982), p. 372; Robert Gordis, *Love and Sex: A Modern Jewish Perspective* (New York: Farrar, Straus, and Giroux, 1978); Louis M. Epstein, *Sex Laws and Customs in Judaism* (New York: KTAV, 1948).

5. For example, Robert Gordis, "Homosexuality and Traditional Religion," *Judaism* 32 (Fall 1983): 390.

6. For a summary of textual references, see Ellen M. Umansky, "Jewish Attitudes toward Homosexuality: A Review of Contemporary Sources," *Reconstructionist* 51, no. 2 (1985): 9–15.

7. We also must be careful not to overgeneralize from rabbinical records, which recount opinions of community leaders, but do not always reflect the sentiment or practice of the community at large. It would be a historical rarity to find that the entire community agreed with its leaders on all questions.

Some instances of disagreement have been documented by Jacob Katz in *Tradition and Crisis* (New York: Schocken, 1961).

8. For example, Lawrence Stone, "Sex in the West," *New Republic* 193, no. 2 (July 8, 1985): 25–37; Estelle B. Freedman et al., eds., *The Lesbian Issue: Essays from "Signs"* (Chicago: University of Chicago Press, 1985).

9. John Boswell, *Christianity, Social Tolerance, and Homosexuality* (Chicago: University of Chicago Press, 1980), p. 94.

10. Ibid., p. 95.

11. Ibid., p. 100. Other texts include Isaiah 44:19; Ezekiel 7:20, 16:36; and Jeremiah 16:18.

12. They also must be reconciled with passages that occur frequently, in places like *Pirke Avot,* that call for loving others and judging others cautiously.

13. Other stories might include Isaac and Ishmael, Ruth and Naomi, R. Yohanan and Resh Lakish, and so on.

14. Boswell, *Christianity, Social Tolerance, and Homosexuality,* p. 17.

15. For a summary of the varying arguments in gay historiography, see the introduction of Jonathan Ned Katz, *Gay/Lesbian Almanac* (New York: Harper and Row, 1983); also Estelle Freedman, "Sexuality in Nineteenth Century America," *Reviews in American History* 10, no. 4 (1982): 200–201.

16. Judy Grahn, *Another Mother Tongue: Gay Words, Gay Worlds* (Boston: Beacon, 1984).

17. See Katz, *Gay/Lesbian Almanac;* Carol Smith Rosenberg, "The Female World of Love and Ritual: Relations between Women in Nineteenth-Century America," *Signs: Journal of Women in Culture and Society* 1, no. 1 (Fall 1975): 1–29; Lillian Faderman, *Surpassing the Love of Men* (New York: Morrow, 1981); Martha Vicinius, "Distance and Desire: English Boarding School Friendships," *The Lesbian Issue: Essays from "Signs,"* pp. 43–65.

18. Jeffrey Weeks, *Coming Out: Homosexual Politics in Britain from the Nineteenth Century to the Present* (London: Quartet Books, 1977).

19. Boswell, *Christianity, Social Tolerance, and Homosexuality,* p. 92.

20. Katz, *Gay/Lesbian Almanac,* p. 1.

21. Ibid., p. 16.

22. For example, Sol Gordon in *Judaism* 32 (Fall 1983): 406 ff; also Lehrman, "Homosexuality and Judaism," in same issue.

23. Quoted in John D'Emilio, *Sexual Politics, Sexual Communities: The Making of a Homosexual Minority in the United States, 1940–1970* (Chicago: University of Chicago Press, 1983), p. 153.

24. Boswell, *Christianity, Social Tolerance, and Homosexuality,* p. 14; also see Richard Plant's *The Pink Triangle.*

25. In other instances of works by or about Jews, the gay experience is ignored or denied, as in the original film version of Lillian Hellman's *The Children's Hour,* or more recently *Julia* and *Yentl.*

26. See Richard Plant, *The Pink Triangle* (New York: Henry Holt, 1986), and Heinz Heger, *The Men with the Pink Triangle* (Boston: Alyson, 1980).

27. Hecht in Rueda, *The Homosexual Network*, p. 372.

28. Lehrman, "Homosexuality and Judaism," pp. 394 ff.

29. Particularly good research has been done on Native American culture. For example, see Will Roscoe's *Living the Spirit* (New York: St. Martin's, 1988). Also see Boswell, *Christianity, Social Tolerance, and Homosexuality*, on ancient Greece and Rome, and the sources cited in note 8 above.

30. For example, Harriet Alpert, ed., *We Are Everywhere: Writings by and about Lesbian Parents;* Sandra Pollack and Jeanne Vaughn, eds., *Politics of the Heart: A Lesbian Parenting Anthology;* Loralee MacPike, ed., *There's Something I've Been Meaning to Tell You* (forthcoming from Naiad Press); *Rocking the Cradle—Lesbian Mothers: A Challenge in Family Living* (Boston: Alyson).

31. Umansky, "Jewish Attitudes toward Homosexuality," p. 13.

32. Marie Syrkin, "Feminist Overkill," *Midstream* 24, no. 1 (January 1978): 54–57; also Samuel McCracken, "Are Homosexuals Gay?" *Commentary* 67, no. 1 (January 1976): 19–29.

33. Free Forum Books has printed the text of the *Bowers* v. *Hardwick* decision. Sodomy is currently illegal in twenty states and bills to outlaw homosexuality or restrict gay rights are pending in several other states. For current information and statistics on gay bashing, consult the National Gay and Lesbian Task Force, 1517 U Street, N.W., Washington, D.C. 20009.

34. Other examples include Alice Bloch's *The Law of Return* (Boston: Alyson, 1983); Leslea Newman's *A Letter to Harvey Milk* (Ithaca, N.Y.: Firebrand Books) 1988; Kaier Curtin's "Yiddish Lesbian Play Rocks Broadway," *Lillith* 19 (Spring 1988) 13–14; David Leavitt's *The Lost Language of Cranes* (New York: Knopf, 1986).

35. *Pirke Avot*, 3.11.

In Search of Role Models/Jody Hirsh

1. Robert Gordis, *Love and Sex: A Modern Jewish Perspective* (New York: Farrar, Straus, and Giroux, 1978), p. 150.

2. The word "gay" is a problematic one when used in a historical context. Certainly we can find no "gays" in history who correspond to the contemporary sense of the word as far as its implication of a "gay" life-style, or self-identification as being exclusively homosexual. I use the word, however, to connote homosexual acts. Since I am attempting to discuss the possibility of reading history in a way that includes lesbians and gay men, I usually will employ the term "gay" to refer to women as well as men.

3. 1 Samuel 20:40–41.

4. Francis Brown, S. R. Driver, and Charles A. Briggs, *A Hebrew and English Lexicon of the Old Testament* (Oxford: Clarendon Press, 1907, 1955), p. 152.

5. 2 Samuel 1:26–27.

6. Ruth 1:16–17.

7. Genesis 45:1–3.

8. 2 Samuel 13:18.

9. Arthur Evans, *Witchcraft and the Gay Counterculture* (Boston: Fag Rag Books, 1978), p. 17.

10. Genesis 39:1–6.

11. The term *saris* comes from the Hebrew root meaning "to castrate." In this context, however, it has usually been translated as "officer."

12. Genesis Rabba 86.3.

13. Genesis 39:10–12.

14. Waskow discussed this idea in an informal group conversation.

15. Norman Roth, "'Deal Gently with the Young Man': Love of Boys in Medieval Poetry of Spain," *Speculum* 57, no. 1 (1982): 23.

16. Chaim Shirman, *ha-Shirah ha-Ivrit beSfarad uv'Provence* (Hebrew poetry of Spain and Provence) (Jerusalem: The Bialik Institute, 1959), 2:445.

17. Ibid., 2:367.

18. I am indebted to David Biale for pointing out to me the history of Betula of Ludomir.

Gerry's Story/Jeffrey Shandler

1. SAGE (Senior Action in a Gay Environment) is a social service agency for gay senior citizens in New York City, and was founded in 1978. The oldest such organization in the United States, SAGE provides at-home support for individual clients, runs a drop-in center in Greenwich Village, and sponsors other social and cultural events for the elderly gay community. The agency engages in public education on the needs and strengths of gay seniors.

Redefining Family/Martha A. Ackelsberg

1. See Martha A. Ackelsberg, "Families and the Jewish Community: A Feminist Perspective," *Response* 48 (Spring 1985): 5.

2. I am using the term "liberal Jews" to refer to a group that includes liberal or Left Conservatives, Reform, and Reconstructionist—that is, those groups of Jews who do not feel themselves bound by halakha in the strict sense. Those who do live more strictly halakhic lives (i.e., Right Conservatives and Orthodox) have tended to rule out full acceptance of gay and lesbian Jews on halakhic grounds.

3. For further elaboration of arguments developed in this section, see my "Families and the Jewish Community" and "Sisters or Comrades? The Politics of Friends and Families," in *Families, Politics, and Public Policies*, ed. Irene Diamond (New York: Longman, 1983), pp. 339–56.

4. This essay builds on previous work of mine. In addition to "Families and the Jewish Community," see "Family or Community? A Response to Susan Handelman," *Sh'ma* 17 (20 March 1987), and "Toward a More Inclusive Community," *New Menorah*, 2d ser., no. 9, pp. 4, 16.

5. See, for example, Susan Handelman, "Family: A Religiously Mandated Ideal," *Sh'ma* 17 (20 March 1987).

6. Statistics on the changing composition of families in the society generally are readily available in census data. For a nonhysterical summary of these data, see Sar Levitan and Richard S. Belous, *What's Happening to the American Family?* (Baltimore: Johns Hopkins University Press, 1981). Studies indicate, for example, that one in every seven families is headed by a woman; and only about 14 percent of families are "traditional," that is to say, with father in the workforce, mother at home, and two children. Similar statistics about the composition of families in the Jewish community do not seem to exist. The trends are summarized in Steven M. Cohen, *American Modernity and Jewish Identity* (New York: Tavistock, 1983), especially chapter 6. Data on the construction of households and on the marital status of households among Jewish families in the New York City region can be found in Steven M. Cohen and Paul Ritterband, "The Social Characteristics of the New York Area Jewish Community, 1981," *American Jewish Yearbook, 1984*, vol. 84 (New York and Philadelphia: American Jewish Committee and Jewish Publication Society, 1983), pp. 128–161. On differences between Jewish and non-Jewish families, see Andrew Cherlin and Carin Celebuski, "Are Jewish Families Different?" *Journal of Marriage and the Family* (November 1983): 903–10.

7. Mark Zborowsky and Elizabeth Hertzog's evocative and romanticized vision of life in Eastern European shtetl communities (New York: Schocken, 1952).

8. See, for example, Rayna Rapp, "Family and Class in Contemporary America: Notes toward an Understanding of Ideology," in *Rethinking the Family: Some Feminist Questions*, ed. Barrie Thorne with Marilyn Yalom (New York: Longman, 1982): pp. 168–87. On abuse and lack of mutuality within Jewish families, see Faith Solela, "Family Violence: Silence Isn't Golden Anymore," *Response* 48 (Spring 1985): 101–6.

9. For a fuller discussion of this issue, see Martha A. Ackelsberg, "Sisters or Comrades? The Politics of Friends and Families," in *Families, Politics, and Public Policies*, ed. Irene Diamond (New York: Longman, 1983), pp. 339–56.

10. Andrew Cherlin, "Changing Family and Household: Contemporary Lessons from Historical Research," *Annual Review of Sociology*, 9 (1983), espe-

cially pp. 63–64. On changes in Jewish families, see Steven M. Cohen and Paula Hyman, *The Evolving Jewish Family* (New York: Holmes and Meier, 1986).

11. *Chevrei kadisha* were community-sponsored voluntary charitable organizations that prepared the dead for burial, and supported the burial costs of those who were unable to pay on their own; *hachnasat kallah* groups provided dowries and wedding necessaries for indigent brides in the community. These were only two of a variety of similarly organized groups, designed to meet the needs of indigent Jews in a community.

12. The alternatives of adoption or foster parenting, of course, are often much more limited for gays and lesbians than they are for heterosexual couples; and, in most states, more limited for gays and lesbians than for heterosexual singles.

13. Handelman, "Family, A Religiously Mandated Ideal," *Sh'ma* 17 (20 March 1987).

Toward a New Theology of Sexuality/Judith Plaskow

1. Samuel Glasner, "Judaism and Sex," *Encyclopedia of Sexual Behavior*, ed. Albert Ellis and Albert Abarbanel (New York: Hawthorn, 1967), 2:575–84. Cited in Joan Scherer Brewer, *Sex and the Modern Jewish Woman: An Annotated Bibliography* (Fresh Meadows, N.Y.: Biblio Press, 1986), B-10.

2. Martha Vicinus, "Sexuality and Power: A Review of Current Work in the History of Sexuality," *Feminist Studies* 8, no. 1 (Spring 1982): 136.

3. Seymour Siegel, "Some Aspects of the Jewish Tradition's View of Sex," *Jews and Divorce*, ed. Jacob Freid (New York: KTAV, 1968), pp. 168–69.

4. Jacob Neusner, *A History of the Mishnaic Law of Women*, 5 vols. (Leiden: E. J. Brill, 1980), 5:271–72.

5. Audre Lorde, "Uses of the Erotic: The Erotic as Power," *Sister Outsider* (Trumansburg, N.Y.: Crossing Press, 1984), pp. 53–59. Compare Vicinus, "Sexuality and Power," p. 136.

6. Lorde, "Uses of the Erotic," p. 57.

7. Beverly Wildung Harrison, "The Power of Anger in the Work of Love: Christian Ethics for Women and Other Strangers," "Sexuality and Social Policy," and "Misogyny and Homophobia: The Unexplored Connections," all in *Making the Connections: Essays in Feminist Social Ethics* (Boston: Beacon, 1985), pp. 13, 87, 149.

8. Harrison, "The Power of Anger," p. 14.

9. James Nelson, *Between Two Gardens: Reflections on Sexuality and Religious Experience* (New York: Pilgrim Press, 1983), p. 6; Harrison, "Misogyny and Homophobia," p. 149.

10. For this insight, and for all I will say in the rest of this essay, I am pro-

foundly indebted to four years of discussion of sexuality and spirituality with my sisters in B'not Esh. See Martha Ackelsberg, "Spirituality, Community, and Politics: B'not Esh and the Feminist Reconstruction of Judaism," *Journal of Feminist Studies in Religion* 2, no. 2 (Fall 1986): 115.

11. Arthur Green, "A Contemporary Approach to Jewish Sexuality," *The Second Jewish Catalog*, ed. Sharon Strassfeld and Michael Strassfeld (Philadelphia: Jewish Publication Society, 1976), p. 98.

12. Nelson, *Between Two Gardens*, p. 7.

13. Adrienne Rich, *Of Woman Born: Motherhood as Experience and Institution* (New York: Norton, 1976), p. 285.

14. Lorde, "Uses of the Erotic," p. 57.

15. Ibid., p. 55.

16. Ibid., p. 57.

17. Louis M. Epstein, *Sex Laws and Customs in Judaism* (New York: KTAV, 1967), p. 14.

18. Robert Gordis, *Love and Sex: A Modern Jewish Perspective* (New York: Farrar, Straus, and Giroux, 1978), p. 106.

19. Harrison, "The Power of Anger," pp. 13–14.

20. Lorde, "Uses of the Erotic," p. 59.

21. I am grateful to Denni Liebowitz for putting the issue in this way. Conversation, fall 1983.

22. Martha Ackelsberg, "Families and the Jewish Community: A Feminist Perspective," *Response* 14, no. 4 (Spring 1985): 15–16.

23. David M. Feldman, *Marital Relations, Birth Control, and Abortion in Jewish Law* (New York: Schocken Books, 1974), chaps. 2, 4, 5; Martha Ackelsberg, "Family or Community?" *Sh'ma* 17 (March 20, 1987): 76–78.

24. Green, "A Contemporary Approach," p. 98.

Joining Together/Aliza Maggid

1. I am grateful to Aaron Cooper for sharing material he prepared for an article to be published in the *Journal of Homosexuality*. I am also grateful to Lorry Sorgman for providing extensive historical information and editorial suggestions.

Naming Is Not a Simple Act/Evelyn Torton Beck

1. Evelyn Torton Beck, ed., *Nice Jewish Girls: A Lesbian Anthology* (Persephone Press, 1982; reprint, Trumansburg, N.Y.: Crossing Press, 1984, revised and expanded edition Beacon Press, 1989). This was the first book to break

the silence surrounding the existence of Jewish lesbian lives; it includes fiction, poetry, autobiographic and analytical essays, as well as photographs by Ashkenazi, Sephardic, and Afro-American Jews.

2. See *Washington Jewish Week*, "Study Page," Rabbi Joshua O. Haberman (July 14, 1988), p. 22. This quotation appears in the *Pirke Avot*, chapter 2, verse 5, and is also repeated verbatim in 4:7 by Rabbi Zadok.

3. This study was undertaken by Mark Zborowski and Elizabeth Herzog (New York: Schocken Books, 1962). *Shtetl* is the name given to the small-town Jewish communities in Eastern Europe where Yiddish culture flourished. These were obliterated by the end of World War II and most of their inhabitants murdered or deported to the Nazi concentration camps.

4. Grahn writes, "Tens of thousands of Gay men formed a separate category of concentration camp victims. They were forced to wear pink triangles, as the Jews wore yellow, and were mistreated and murdered in a similar manner, especially in the work camps." Judy Grahn, *Another Mother Tongue: Gay Words, Gay Worlds* (Boston: Beacon, 1984), p. 279. See also Heinz Heger, *The Men with the Pink Triangle* (Boston: Alyson, 1980).

5. "JAP" is the acronym for "Jewish American Princess." In recent years anti-Semitism has combined with racism and misogyny to create a form of violence against Jewish women that is known as "JAP baiting." For analysis of this phenomenon, see *Sojourner* (Sept. 1988) and *Lilith* (Fall 1987).

6. Grahn is the only historian of lesbian feminist culture who documents Jewish lesbian contributions to that culture and attempts to formulate a heroic topology of the Jewish Lesbian Feminist. See "Judith the Hebrew and Others," pp. 185–91.

7. Grahn, *Another Mother Tongue*, p. xvi.

8. Deuteronomy 6:4.

9. Marranos were Jews who were forced to convert to Christianity during the Inquisition in Spain and Portugal but kept up Jewish practices. While some remained Jewish, others really became Christian over time, but retained vestiges of Jewish ritual.

10. Grahn, *Another Mother Tongue*, p. xvi.

11. This is the title of an important book written by Jill Johnston in 1975 in which she declared the peoplehood of lesbians.

12. To bring these three colors together, the cover of *Nice Jewish Girls* was to have been purple, white, and blue; white had to be omitted because the small lesbian-feminist press that produced it could not afford a third color.

13. I thank Lee not only for this formulation, but for many stimulating discussions of these matters, as well as superb editing.

14. I wish to thank Michael Ragussis for helping me to sharpen some of these insights. The complexities of "unnaming," "renaming," and "misnaming" can be found in his book, *Acts of Naming: The Family Plot in Fiction*

(New York: Oxford University Press, 1986). While the specific focus of this book is on nineteenth-century British fiction, the theoretical discussion is very provocative and useful.

15. In the lesbian feminist community this has played itself out in numerous ways. In the early 1970s (the first wave of "lesbian-feminist" politicization), only those who had never been married and had never had children were considered "authentic" lesbians; "butch" and "fem" lesbians were not viewed as real feminists. Today, lesbians who become sexually involved with men are considered to have "reverted" to heterosexuality, are "stripped" of their lesbian credentials, and are usually not welcomed in community activities.

16. "Bother the world. . . . Paint the space you are in with your principles and your views. Many of us complain about the lack of leadership and a lack of organization. If you are missing something, it is the sound of your own voice." Bernice Johnson Reagon, quoted in an advertisement for *off our backs* (1986).

17. Polanyi develops the concept of "tacit knowledge" in *Personal Knowledge: Towards a Postcritical Philosophy* (Chicago: University of Chicago Press, 1958).

18. For example, author Ruth Baetz lived with another woman in a committed sexual relationship for five years, but did not name herself "lesbian" until that relationship broke up. See *Lesbian Crossroads: Personal Stories of Lesbian Struggles and Triumphs* (New York: Morrow, 1980), p. 5.

19. The experimental and evolving ceremonies developed by the group known as B'not Esh (Daughters of Fire), an ongoing Jewish feminist community to which I belong (and which meets annually for four days at a retreat center), are the most spiritually satisfying for me. (For a more complete description of the practices of *B'not Esh*, see the essay by Martha Ackelsberg in *Journal of Feminist Studies in Religion* 2, no. 2 [Winter 1986]: 105–6.) That group uses, among other sources, the transformed blessings created by Marcia Falk, which are gender-free in both the Hebrew and the English, and convey a reconceptualized sense of what a blessing can be. The most satisfying "mixed" group ritual I ever attended was a Shabbat service led by Marcia Falk at the 1987 New Jewish Agenda conference, which included the full spectrum of Jews who attended that conference, including children. Sometimes the most spiritually rewarding moments come in small holiday ceremonies held in my own home, in the company of other lesbians.

20. Leonard Fein, *Where Are We? The Inner Life of America's Jews* (New York: Harper and Row, 1988), p. xvi. Unfortunately, this book is seriously marred by the author's failure to discuss the feminist challenge (let alone the lesbianfeminist challenge) to normative Judaism or to include any discussion of lesbian and gay Jews. The book's scholarship is also faulty in that the author

failed to include in his lengthy bibliography any of the significant Jewish feminist texts that have been published in the last two decades. His ignorance is especially revealed when he inaccurately states that hardly any of the leading intellectuals who helped launch the feminist movement were Jewish! (p. 227).

21. While this movement was extremely informal, the Jewish lesbian-feminist groups meeting in people's living rooms in cities like Boston, Seattle, Minneapolis, San Francisco, Oakland, Los Angeles, Manhattan, Brooklyn, Washington, D.C., Chicago, Philadelphia, Madison, Austin, Detroit, Portland, Santa Fe, London, and Haifa did resemble each other in many ways. To my knowledge, no one has made a systematic study of these groups, nor, because of their informal nature, is it likely that a reliable record could be found. A well thought-out oral history project (to be undertaken *soon*) seems the only way to document this unique form of Jewish community.

22. This speech was delivered at a national meeting of the American Association of Higher Education in Washington, D.C., and is entitled, "Faculty and Student Development in the 80's: Renewing the Community of Scholars," and appears in *Current Issues in Higher Education* (1980).

23. I am thinking particularly of the Jewish Lesbian Group in Washington, D.C., which continues to meet regularly though its membership has shrunk to five from the original thirteen. I myself am no longer a member, though I still attend the group's holiday events. The Madison, Wisconsin, group to which I belonged as a founding member while I lived in Madison, officially disbanded in 1988, though it had atrophied considerably since 1984. It had been in existence since 1978. One of the problems that plagued Jewish lesbian-feminist groups was the tension between the desire to organize a community, which would mean opening the groups to whoever wanted to join, and the need for continuity and the kind of intimacy that only a small and stable group provides.

24. See for example, Letty Pogrebin, "Anti-Semitism in the Women's Movement," *Ms* (June 1982), pp. 45–49, 62–72), and Letty Pogrebin, "Coming Out as a Jew," *Ms.* (August 1987); Selma Miriam, "Anti-Semitism in the Women's Community," *Sinister Wisdom* 19 (1982); Melanie Kaye/Kantrowitz "Anti-Semitism, Homophobia, and The Good White Knight," *off our backs* 12 (May 1982): 30–31; and Evelyn Torton Beck, *Nice Jewish Girls* (1982) and "The Politics of Jewish Invisibility" *NWSA Journal* (Fall 1988).

25. This meeting occurred at the first Wisconsin convention of the National Lesbian Feminist Organization (NLFO), which was held on November 10–12, 1978, in Milwaukee, Wisconsin. Although Jewish issues had not been among the many topics listed in the publicity, a large number of participants and conference planners were Jews.

26. Major cultural events, which included readings from *Nice Jewish Girls* and other works by Jewish lesbians, took place in, among other cities, Boston,

Washington, D.C., New York City, Minneapolis, Madison, San Francisco, Los Angeles; these events drew audiences of up to five hundred.

27. The Washington, D.C. lesbian feminist group I described in note 23 above held a public teaching seder in 1983 as a means of educating the larger women's community specifically about the Passover holiday. It was enormously successful and drew over a hundred women.

28. See, for example, *The Freedom Seder* by Arthur Waskow (1969), which has gone through five editions, the most recent included in *The Shalom Seders: Three Haggadahs,* compiled by New Jewish Agenda (New York: Adama Press, 1984), p. 8.

29. Most of the lesbian-feminist seders are neither copyrighted nor published in book form, but are circulated widely as photocopied material—thus quite literally "handed down" and modified from year to year. One exception is Judith Stein's *A New Hagaddah: A Jewish Lesbian Seder* (April 1984; Nisan 5744), published by Bobbeh Meisehs Press, 137 Tremont Street, Cambridge, MA 02139, and available for $4.

30. This term was coined by Georg Simmel, *Conflict and the Web of Group Affiliations,* trans. Kurt Wolff and Reinhard Bendix (New York: Free Press, 1964), and is used effectively in describing the networks created by immigrant Jews in the United States by Gerald Sorin in *The Prophetic Minority: American Jewish Immigrant Radicals, 1880–1920* (Bloomington: Indiana University Press, 1985), p. 5. I found this book extremely useful in thinking about contemporary Jewish radical (i.e., lesbian-feminist) groups.

31. A particularly thoughtful essay on lesbian parenting is provided by Jewish lesbian-feminist activist Nancy Polikoff in *Politics of the Heart: Lesbian Parenting* (Ithaca, N.Y.: Firebrand Press, 1987).

32. Though many who have converted to Judaism prefer to call themselves "Jews by choice," others find the term offensive. Because I believe every Jew "chooses" whether to own Jewish identity or to assimilate, I prefer to retain the term "convert."

33. From a conversation with Lee Knefelkamp on July 22, 1988. For a more complete discussion of this theme, see her essay, "Living in the In-Between," in the new edition of *Nice Jewish Girls* (Beacon Press, 1989).

34. Because of recent developments in Israel that threaten to make the "Law of Return" apply only to those who have had an Orthodox conversion, this issue is likely to become even more sensitive and widely discussed in the United States.

35. They are also soliciting material for an anthology of writings by JLDHS, tentatively entitled *The Hour of the Rooster, The Hour of the Owl,* from a prose-poem by that name. For further information contact JLDHS, PO Box 6194, Boston, MA 02114.

36. The beginnings of such discussions erupted (because of lesbian in-

visibility) at the conference on "Women Surviving the Holocaust," which took place in 1983 and was documented in the *Proceedings of the Conference*, edited by Esther Katz and Joan Miriam Ringleheim, and which can be obtained from The Institute for Research in History, 432 Park Avenue South, New York, N.Y. 10016. See also Vera Laska, *Women in the Resistance and the Holocaust: The Voices of Eyewitnesses* (Westport, Conn.: Greenwood Press, 1983), and as yet unpublished work by Susan E. Cernyak-Spatz (University of North Carolina, Charlotte) and Ruth Angress (University of California, Irvine).

37. See Sorin, *The Prophetic Minority.*

38. Ibid., p. 3, emphasis mine.

39. As defined by Irving Howe and Eliezer Greenberg in their introduction to *A Treasury of Yiddish Stories* (New York: Schocken Books, 1973), p. 29.

The Liturgy of Gay and Lesbian Jews/Yoel H. Kahn

1. Published, identifiably gay liturgy has emerged from the lesbian and gay synagogue movement. While other lesbian and gay Jews, as individuals and in groups, have developed their own special liturgies, they are beyond the scope of this article. On the liturgy of Congregation Sha'ar Zahav, see R. M. Rankin and G. Koenigsburg, "Let the Day Come Which is All Shabbat: The Liturgy of the Gay Outreach Synagogue," *Journal of Reform Judaism* 33, no. 1 (Spring 1986), and "With David and Jonathan, With Ruth and Naomi We Remember You," *New Menorah* 2d series, no. 2 (1986).

2. While many otherwise "out of the closet" lesbian and gay Jews worship regularly in mainstream congregations, they are almost always invisible *as gay people* in those synagogues.

3. See L. A. Hoffman, *Beyond the Text: A Holistic Approach to Liturgy* (Bloomington: Indiana University Press, 1987).

4. Conservative features are (1) more Hebrew than found in the Reform liturgy (at least pre-*Gates of Prayer*) and (2) passages that had been removed from the liturgy by the Reform movement were included (e.g., the second and third paragraphs of the *Sh'ma*). This is the style of the prayerbooks written at Congregation Beth Simchat Torah in New York. An exception to this pattern is Beth Chayim Chadashim in Los Angeles, which has been associated with the Reform movement since its founding.

5. This kind of thinking is obviously not limited to gay and lesbian Jews; Jewish feminists, for example, have had to go through a parallel process.

6. This section is based on a workshop first presented at the 10th International Conference of the World Congress of Gay and Lesbian Jews, Amsterdam, Holland, July 1987.

7. An authorized Reform prayerbook would never use the expression "the coming of the Messiah." At Sha'ar Zahav, we have recently changed this phrase to "make creation whole."

8. In some early versions, this passage includes the sentence, "It can be hard to keep a straight face in a straight world." According to Daniel Chesir, this reading was composed by Alan Roth while he was a member of Congregation Or Chadash in Chicago.

9. Lesbian and gay Jews have compared themselves to Marranos, the medieval Jews who were forced to convert and practice their Judaism in secret. See "Sarah's children are no strangers to hiding . . ." *Machzor U'becharta Chaim* (Yom Kippur) (Congregation Sha'ar Zahav, 1984), p. 18.

10. Earlier versions included the phrase "remember those *who wasted their lives* by suppressing their true natures." This was criticized as judgmental and inappropriate and therefore removed. The reference to those "struck down in our own city" once referred to antigay violence. For many, it now recalls those who have died from AIDS. The closing sentence of the most recent version places greater emphasis on human responsibility than earlier versions, which ended: "Call an end to the hate and oppression that we have known for so long."

11. More commonly: "Glad songs of victory in the tents of the righteous" [RSV, Psalm 118:15] or "The tents of the victorious [or: righteous] resound with joyous shouts of liberation." [New JPS].

12. The concept of new haftarot and criteria for selection were first suggested to me by Rabbi Margaret Wenig.

13. The opening lines of the traditional *Aleinu* prayer are: "We must priase the Lord of all, the Maker of heaven and earth, who has set us apart from the other families of earth, giving us a destiny unique among the nations . . ."

14. Some have criticized this text because it does not include the words "gay and lesbian." A revised, more inclusive version of the older text discussed above has now been added to our prayerbook: "Sometimes we seem forced to hide the qualities that distinguish us from others. We feel cast out because we are Jewish, Lesbian or Gay, old or young; and we conceal the unique attributes with which we, in God's image, are created." Also see the alternative *Aleinu* in *B'chol Levavcha*, p. 201.

15. This is one of two texts used at Congregation Sha'ar Zahav.

16. For example, "*Avinu Malkaynu, Imeinu Malkataynu*" [Our Father, our King, our Mother, our Queen] in the High Holy Day liturgy of Congregation Sha'ar Zahav, San Francisco.

17. See Marcia Falk, "Notes on Composing New Blessings: Toward a Feminist-Jewish Reconstruction of Prayer," *Journal of Feminist Studies in Religion* 3, no. 1 (Spring 1987): 39–53. Falk dissolves the tradition's dualism between sacred and profane, Sabbath and weekday in her new blessing for the conclusion of the Sabbath:

> Let us distinguish parts within the whole
> and bless their differences.
> Like Sabbath and the six days of creation,
> may our lives be made whole through relation.
> As rest makes the Sabbath holy,
> may our work make holy the week.
> Let us separate Sabbath from week
> and hallow them both.

18. Several selections are included in T. Carmi, ed., *Penguin Book of Hebrew Poetry* (New York: Viking, 1981).

19. Any number of Whitman's poems are appropriate for liturgical use. The *yotzeir* prayer, on the theme of God's presence in nature, or the Morning Blessings are wonderfully interpreted by the passage "The smoke of my own breath . . . my respiration and inspiration . . ." (*Song of Myself*, sec. 2.)

20. Adrienne Rich, *The Fact of a Doorframe* (New York: Norton, 1984), p. 264.

21. This also protects the officiant from officiating at a marriage without a license.

22. Other names used for such a ceremony include *Brit Ahava* ("Covenant of Love"), Ceremony of Loving Dedication, Holy Union, and Commitment Ceremony.

23. Some celebrants feel that the *sheva berachot* are too closely identified with the symbolism of heterosexual marriage and therefore do not use them as a model.

24. In fact, we reject the sexism and patriarchal categories of the halakhic system. This liturgical formula text is appropriate for use at any kiddushin ceremony, whether heterosexual or homosexual.

25. For example, Marge Piercy's new *Nishmat* and other writing from the P'nai Or liturgy project.

26. This litany, taken from Judy Chicago, *Dinner Party* (New York: Anchor, 1979), can be used for the *Aleinu* section of the service. This passage combines the *Aleinu*'s call for making the world whole (*tikkun olam*) with the ideals of our community. The repeated phrase, "And then" points to the biblical verse that concludes the traditional *Aleinu*: "*On that day* God's Name shall be one." Its liturgical use was suggested to me by Rabbi Sue Levi Elwell.

Getting to Know the Gay and Lesbian Shul/Janet R. Marder

1. Howard Brown, *Familiar Faces Hidden Lives: The Story of Homosexual Men in America Today* (Harcourt Brace Jovanovich, 1976).

2. Evelyn Torton Beck, *Nice Jewish Girls: A Lesbian Anthology* (Watertown, Mass.: Persephone Press, 1982).

3. John Boswell, *Christianity, Social Tolerance, and Homosexuality: Gay People from the Beginning of the Christian Era to the Fourteenth Century* (Chicago: University of Chicago Press, 1980), pp. 11–13.

4. Asher Bar-Zev, "Homosexuality and the Jewish Tradition," *Reconstructionist* 42 (May 1976): 20–24.

5. Hershel Matt, "Sin, Crime, Sickness or Alternative Life Style?: A Jewish Approach to Homosexuality," *Judaism* 27, no. 1 (1976): 13–24.

6. Solomon Freehof, *American Reform Responsa: Jewish Questions, Rabbinic Answers,* Collected Responsa of the Central Conference of American Rabbis 1889–1983 (Central Conference of American Rabbis, 1983), pp. 49–52.

7. Ibid., pp. 51–52.

Journey toward Wholeness/La Escondida

1. Abraham Joshua Heschel, "No Religion Is an Island," *Disputation and Dialogue: Readings in the Jewish-Christian Encounter,* ed. Frank Ephraim Talmage (New York: Ktav, 1975), p. 347.

The Lesbian and Gay Movement/Sue Levi Elwell

1. I would like to thank Rabbi Clifford Librach for his critique of an earlier draft of this essay.

2. See Yoel Kahn's extensive discussion of the traditional Jewish response to homosexuality in "Judaism and Homosexuality: The Traditional/Progressive Debate," *Journal of Homosexuality* 3, no. 19 (Winter 1989).

3. Ibid.

4. See essays by Dr. Eugene Mihaly and Rabbi Solomon Freehof in *CCAR Journal* 20, no. 3 (Summer 1973).

5. Brochure describing the conference held on 20 April 1986, Stephen Wise Free Synagogue, 30 West 68th Street, New York, N.Y., 10023.

6. Christie Balka, "Beginning to See the Light," *Genesis* 2 (June–July 1986): 10. See also "The Courage to Welcome Differences," an excerpt from a sermon delivered by Rabbi Helene Ferris in the same issue of *Genesis* 2 (p. 11).

7. Resolutions adopted by the Fifty-ninth General Assembly of the Union of American Hebrew Congregations, Chicago, 29 October–3 November 1987.

8. Address at the Jewish community service in support of People with AIDS, Leo Baeck Temple, Los Angeles, California, 12 March 1989, p. 3.

9. Ibid., p. 5.

10. See "The Torah and the Truth: Coming Out of the Closet," *New Menorah,* 2d ser. 5 (1986).

11. The notion of "praising all our choices" is proclaimed in Marge Piercy's poem "The sabbath of mutual respect," in *Circles on the Water* (New York: Knopf, 1982), pp. 270–72.

"They" Are Us/Andy Rose

1. See Mike Rankin, "Reaching In: The Synagogue That Lives with AIDS," *Moment* 11, no. 1 (December 1985).

2. Nechama's educational materials are available at 6505 Wilshire Boulevard, Suite 510, Los Angeles, CA, 90048.

3. BBYO program materials are available at 1640 Rhode Island Avenue N.W., Washington, D.C., 20036.

4. NFTY program materials are available at 838 Fifth Avenue, New York, N.Y., 10021.

5. "Confronting the AIDS Crisis" and other written materials are available from the UAHC at 838 Fifth Avenue, New York, N.Y., 10021.

6. *Keeping Posted* 33, no. 2 (November 1987).

7. "AIDS: A Jewish Response" is available from the United Synagogue of America at 155 Fifth Avenue, New York, N.Y., 10010.

8. "AIDS: We Care" is published by the B'nai Brith Commission on Community Volunteer Services at 1640 Rhode Island Avenue N.W., Washington, D.C., 20036.

9. See Andy Rose, "Jewish Agency Services to People with AIDS and Their Families," *Journal of Jewish Communal Service* 64, no. 1 (Fall 1987). For further information contact Jewish Family and Children's Services, 1600 Scott Street, San Francisco, CA, 94115.

10. The AIDS Project of the Jewish Board of Family and Children's Services can be contacted at 26 Court Street, Suite 800, Brooklyn, N.Y., 11201.

11. Daniel H. Freelander, "AIDS: A Personal Plea," *Reform Judaism* 16, no. 2 (Winter 1987–88).

12. See Rabbi Barry Freundel, "AIDS: A Traditional Response," *Jewish Action* (Winter 1986–87).

13. The American Jewish Committee as well as the UAHC participated in founding the AIDS National Interfaith Network, the leading interreligious effort to respond to AIDS pastoral, educational, and public policy issues. That organization can be contacted at 132 W. 31st Street, 17th floor, New York, N.Y., 10117.

14. Andrea Jolles, "AIDS and the Silent Jewish Majority," *B'nai Brith International Jewish Monthly* (April 1987).

15. See *Reform Judaism* 14, no. 2 and 15, no. 1 for examples.

16. See Jeffrey R. Solomon, "AIDS: A Jewish Communal Challenge for the

'90s," *Journal of Jewish Communal Service* 65, no. 1 (Fall 1988) in addition to the Rose article previously cited.

17. Rabbi Gerald C. Skolnik, "AIDS and Synagogue Life," *United Synagogue Review* (Fall 1988).

Appendix 1/Denise L. Eger and Lesley M. Silverstein

1. Biblical texts, specifically Leviticus 18:22 and 20:13, forbid male homosexual relations. Further, Maimonides Mishneh Torah codifies the prohibitions and also discusses lesbianism.

2. For example, Susanne Bosche's *Jenny Lives with Eric and Martin* (London: Gay Men's Press, 1983).

3. See "A Ceremony of Commitment" by Paul Horowitz and Scott Klein in this volume.

4. Among some of the better books are *Reflections of a Rock Lobster* by Aaron Fricke (Boston: Alyson, 1983), *One Teenager in Ten: Writings by Gay and Lesbian Youth*, ed. Ann Heron (Boston: Alyson, 1983), and *Annie on My Mind* by Nancy Garden (New York: Farrar, Straus and Giroux, 1982).

5. "Youth Self-Esteem and Anti-Suicide Curriculum" is available from Ellen Mack, c/o Beth-El Congregation, P.O. Box 2232, Fort Worth, TX, 76113.

6. Shirley Barish, *Six Kallot* (Denver: Alternatives in Religious Education, 1978).

7. UAHC Task Force on Youth Suicide, 838 Fifth Avenue, New York, N.Y., 10021.

8. Sol Gordon and Judith Gordon, *Raising a Child Conservatively in a Sexually Permissive World* (New York: Simon and Schuster, 1983).

Appendix 2/Tom Rawson

1. "We" refers to the feminist task force of New Jewish Agenda, which developed this workshop for Jewish groups based, in part, on the pioneering work of the late Ricky Sherover Marcuse and others on "Unlearning Racism," and the work on homophobia done by Suzanne Pharr of the National Coalition against Domestic Violence.

GLOSSARY

....

The following non-English words and English colloquial terms appear in the pages of this anthology. H connotes Hebrew; Y connotes Yiddish; E connotes English; L connotes Ladino; Lt connotes Latin and G connotes Greek. [Editors' note: Special thanks to Rebecca T. Alpert for help with this glossary.]

Aleinu (H) Ancient prayer of praise for God normally recited at the end of the prayer service.

aliyah (H, pl. *aliyot*) Literally, ascent. An honor bestowed on a person who says the blessing before and after the public Torah reading.

Amidah (H) The central prayer of the worship service, normally composed of eighteen benedictions.

am kadosh (H) Holy people.

apikoros (G) One who flagrantly refuses to observe Jewish law and custom.

Ashkenazi (H, pl. *Ashkenazim*) Jews of Northern European origin.

bar/bat mitzvah (H, pl. *b'nai mitzvah*) Literally, son/daughter of the commandments. Indicates the age of majority in Jewish tradition (for girls at twelve, for boys at thirteen).

beracha (H, pl. *berachot*) blessing.

Bereshit (H) The biblical book of Genesis, called in Hebrew by its first word, "In the beginning."

bialy (Y) A roll, similar to a bagel, but without a hole in the center.

bikkur cholim (H) Visiting the sick, considered an important commandment.

bima (H) Raised section of the synagogue where the leader stands and the Torah is read.

butch (E) Term for lesbians who assume a stereotypically male role.

brit milah (H), *bris* (Y) Ritual circumcision of eight-day-old boys, which, according to biblical commandment, symbolizes entrance into the covenant of the Jewish people. In the last decade, feminists have developed naming ceremonies to welcome children of both sexes into the community.

cantor (E) Person who sings and chants during the worship service.

challah (H) Twisted loaf of sweet bread

eaten by Jews on the Sabbath and holidays.

cavurah (H, pl. *cavurot*) Friendship circle. Refers to a small group of Jews who gather together for prayer, study, and holiday and other celebrations.

chevra kadisha (A) Holy society. Commonly refers to a group of people who wash and dress a dead body to prepare it for burial.

chevra tefila (H) Prayer community.

chuppah (H) The canopy under which the couple stands at a Jewish wedding.

the closet (E) Term used to refer to the situation of gay men and lesbians who keep their sexual identities hidden.

coming out (E) The experience of revealing one's gay or lesbian identity to oneself and others. Refers to "the closet" (q.v.).

daven (Y) To pray in a traditional Jewish mode, including sing-song intonation, body movements, and soulful intention.

d'var torah (H, pl. *d'vrei torah*) Commentary on the Jewish text, often delivered in the course of a prayer service or other official gathering.

dyke (E) Term for lesbian. Although it originated as a derogatory term, some lesbians have reclaimed the term in the last two decades and use it when referring to themselves.

Eretz Yisrael (H) Literally, the land of Israel.

fairy (E) Term for gay men. Although the original meaning was derogatory, some gay men have since reclaimed this term and use it, when referring to each other, with pride.

fem(me) (E) Term for a lesbian who assumes a stereotypically female role.

feygele (Y) Little bird. Slang term for gay men, often used derogatorily.

frume (f.), *frum* (m.) (Y) Scrupulously observant.

gmilut chassidim (H) Acts of loving kindness.

hachnasat kallah (H) Welcoming the bride.

haftarah (H) A selection from the Prophetic books of the Bible selected for reading on the Sabbath. The portion selected is thematically tied to the parsha.

Haggadah (H) Literally, story. The text that is used at the Passover seder to explain the rituals.

halacha, halakha (H) Literally, path. Jewish law.

hamentaschen (Y) Literally, Haman's hat. A triangular cake filled with seeds or fruit, eaten during the festial of Purim.

Havdalah (H) The ceremony that marks the end of the Sabbath.

heterosexism (G,E) Discrimination against lesbians and gay men.

High Holy Days (E) Ten days observed as the beginning of the Jewish New Year, beginning with Rosh Hashanah, the new year and concluding with Yom Kippur, a day of fasting and atonement.

homophobia (G) Fear of lesbians and gay men.

hora (H) Israeli folk dance.

ima (H) Mother.

kabbalah (H) Medieval Jewish body of mysticism.

Kaddish (H) Literally, sanctification. A prayer of praise for God, used as a memorial prayer to remember the dead.

kashruth (H) The system of laws (keeping kosher) that regulates the dietary and kitchen habits of observant Jews.

kiddush (H) Sanctification. The term usually refers to the blessing said with wine on the Sabbath and holidays.

kiddushin (H) Jewish wedding ceremony.

kike (E) Derogatory term for Eastern European Jews.

kitl (Y) White garment worn by men on special occasions and in which one is buried.

Kol Nidre (H) Literally, all vows. Text that precedes the Yom Kippur service. The words refer to a legal annulment of vows. The text is chanted to a haunting melody.

kvel (Y) To exclaim with pride.

kvetch (Y) To complain, a complainer.

Lesbian and Gay Pride, Freedom Day (E) Annual celebration of lesbian and gay pride held on the anniversary of the Stonewall Rebellion in cities throughout North America. Usually marked by a parade and other cultural and political events.

Magen David (H) The six-pointed star associated with Jews and the State of Israel.

Marranos (L) Jews who were forced to hide their identity in Spain after the Inquisition. Outwardly, Marranos adopted all the customs and practices of Catholics, while privately they maintained a level of Jewish ritual observance.

mazal tov (H), *mazel tov* (Y) Congratulations.

mechitzah (H) The physical barrier used to separate men and women in a traditional prayer service.

menorah (H) Candelabrum lit during the festival of Hanukkah.

mentsh (Y) A good person.

mentshlikhkayt (Y) The art of kind behavior.

meshugeneh (Y) A little crazy.

midrash (H) Stories explaining the meanings of Jewish texts.

minyan (H) A prayer quorum consisting of ten. Although in the past, only men counted as part of a minyan, women have come to be included in the minyan in all but the most traditional circles.

mishpacha (H) Family.

mitzrayim (H) Egypt.

mohel (H) The person who performs the ritual circumcision.

negiyah (H) The prohibition concerning touching a person of another gender.

nelly (E) Derogatory term used to describe an effeminate gay man.

parsha (H, pl. parshiot) The section of the Torah to be read on a given week. The Torah is read in an annual cycle, one section per week.

Pentateuch (E) The five books of Moses, the first five books in the Bible.

Pesach (H) Passover, the springtime

festival which marks the Jewish people's liberation from Egypt.

piyyutim (H) Prayers written by poets in the Middle Ages that have been incorporated into the liturgy of the Jews.

Purim (H) The Jewish festival that commemorates the liberation of the Jews under Persian rule as described in the biblical book of Esther.

responsum (Lt) Rabbinic response to a legal question.

Rosh Hashanah (H) The Jewish New Year.

ruach (H) Literally, wind. Spirit or enthusiasm.

schlemiel (Y) Jerk.

schvartses (Y) Derogatory reference to African Americans.

seder (H) Literally, order. The seder is the ceremony conducted by Jews in our homes on the first (and in some cases the second) night of Passover. It consists of recitation and discussion of the symbols and story of the Exodus from Egypt.

Shabbat (H), *shabbos* (Y) (pl. *Shabbatot*) The Jewish sabbath, observed from sundown Friday to sundown Saturday.

Sephardi (H, pl. *Sephardim*) Jews from Southern Europe, North Africa, and the Middle East.

sheygets (Y) A man who is not Jewish. Often used derogatorily.

shidekh (Y) A match.

shiva (H) Seven-day period of mourning following a death.

shofar (H) A ram's horn, used as a sacred musical instrument at various occasions in the beginning of the Jewish year and most notably during synagogue services on Rosh Hashanah.

shul (Y) Synagogue.

shtibl (Y) A small village.

shtetl (Y) A small village.

siddur (H, pl. *siddurim*) Prayerbook.

simkhes (Y, pl.) Joyous occasions.

Stonewall Rebellion (E) A riot that took place in June 1969, when gay patrons of the Stonewall Inn, a New York gay bar, spontaneously fought back against a routine police raid. This event marks the commonly accepted beginning of the modern gay liberation movement.

sukkah (H, pl. *sukkot*) A temporary dwelling erected by Jews during the fall holiday of Sukkot. The festival commemorates the wanderings of the Jews in the desert and is also a harvest festival.

Talmud (H) The many volume compendium of Jewish laws and lore consisting of the Mishnah (second-century law code) and Gemara (commentary on the Mishnah) compiled during the fifth century C.E.

tallit (H), *talis* (Y, pl. *taleysim*) Fringed prayer shawl, with tzitzit on the four corners.

Tanakh (H) Hebrew acronym for the three major sections of the Hebrew Bible. T = Torah (the five books of Moses); N = Neviim (the prophets); and KH = ketuvim (writings).

tefillin (H) Phylacteries. Leather amulets placed on the head and arm during weekday morning prayers in fulfillment of the biblical command,

"You shall bind them for a sign upon your hand, and they shall be frontlets between your eyes" (Deut. 6:4). Only adult males are commanded to wear them, but recently women have begun to observe this commandment as well.

tikkun olam (H) Literally, to repair the world.

to'evah (H) Abomination, anathema.

Torah (H) The five books of Moses. Also refers generally to Jewish teaching.

tsimmes (Y) A sweet stew of meat, potatoes, and fruits, usually served on holidays and festive occasions.

tzaddik (H) Literally, righteousness. Acts of giving, considered obligatory under Jewish law.

tzitzit (H) Knotted cords worn on garments in fulfillment of the biblical command to wear a tangible reminder to observe the commandments.

yarmulke (Y) Skullcap traditionally worn by Jewish men and now worn by Jewish women as a religious obligation.

yeshiva (H, pl. *yeshivot*) A house of study. Name used for Jewish day school.

yetzer hara (H) In Jewish thought, people are believed to be influenced by good and evil forces, expressed as yetzer tov (the good inclination) and yetzer hara (the evil inclination).

yidishkayt (Y) The quality of Jewishness. Being well-versed in all things Jewish.

Yizkor (H) The rite that memorializes the dead. Yizkor is recited four times annually on significant Jewish Holy Days.

Yom HaShoah (H) The day set aside annually in the spring to commemorate the Holocaust.

Yom Kippur (H) The final day of the High Holy Days, observed through fasting, prayer, self-examination and redirection.

Yom Tov (H) Holiday.

zaddik (H) A righteous individual.

ANNOTATED
BIBLIOGRAPHY

....

This bibliography strives to list a representative sample of background sources on gay and lesbian issues in general, and Judaism and homosexuality in particular. Though containing much valuable material, it is by no means exhaustive.

This list is derived in part from two more extensive bibliographies: "Lesbian and Gay Liberation: A Bibliography for the Jewish Community" published by New Jewish Agenda, 64 Fulton St. #1100, New York, NY 10038; and "Jewish Sources on Homosexuality" compiled by Rabbi Yoel Kahn, Congregation Sha'ar Zahav, 220 Danvers St., San Francisco, CA 94114.

Gay and Lesbian History

Boswell, John. *Christianity, Social Tolerance, and Homosexuality: Gay People in Western Europe from the Beginning of the Christian Era to the Fourteenth Century.* Chicago: University of Chicago Press, 1980. This widely acclaimed book written by a Yale scholar brings a wealth of new historical material to light in its examination of religious and societal attitudes toward homosexuality. Among its many landmark contributions, the book documents early historical parallels between the scapegoating of homosexuals and the scapegoating of Jews.

D'Emilio, John. *Sexual Politics, Sexual Communities: The Making of a Homosexual Minority in the United States, 1940–1970.* Chicago: University of Chicago Press, 1983. This book documents the oppression experienced by lesbians and gay men in the not-so-distant past and explores the early history of the modern gay liberation movement. It brings to life the individual heroism and organizational efforts that preceded the Stonewall Riot of 1969.

Grahn, Judy. *Another Mother Tongue: Gay Words, Gay Worlds*. Boston: Beacon Press, 1984. This ground-breaking book presents a panorama of lesbian and gay cultural history. It offers particularly striking insights about mythology and language.

Heger, Heinz. *The Men with the Pink Triangle*. Boston: Alyson Publications, 1980. Heger, a gay Holocaust survivor, tells his own story of imprisonment under the Third Reich. An introduction gives an overview of this terrible chapter of gay history, which has only recently been coming to light.

Katz, Jonathan. *Gay American History: Lesbians and Gay Men in the USA: A Documentary Anthology*. New York: Harper and Row, 1986. This sourcebook, the first of its kind, offers a wealth of material on lesbian and gay experience in the United States from colonial times through the mid-1970s.

Katz, Jonathan. *Gay/Lesbian Almanac: A New Documentary*. San Francisco: Harper and Row, 1983. This volume includes additional archival research focusing on the early colonial period and the modern "invention of the homosexual."

Plant, Richard, *The Pink Triangle: The Nazi War against Homosexuals*. New York: Henry Holt and Company, 1986. This books offers the first in-depth investigation of the persecution of homosexuals under the Third Reich. It is written by a gay Jewish refugee from Nazi Germany who emigrated to the United States in 1938.

Shilts, Randy. *The Mayor of Castro Street*. New York: St. Martin's Press, 1982. This book is a moving biography of Jewish gay political leader, Harvey Milk, who was elected to the San Francisco Board of Supervisors and then assassinated in 1978. The book paints a picture of the political, social, and cultural life of the burgeoning gay and lesbian community in 1970s San Francisco.

Life Cycle and Family Issues

Adelman, Marcy, ed. *Long Time Passing: Lives of Older Lesbians*. Boston: Alyson Publications, 1986. These stories of older women describe their lives before the emergence of feminism and gay liberation; their age-related concerns; and issues of relationships, sexuality, loneliness and community.

Bridges of Respect: Creating Support for Lesbian and Gay Youth. American Friends Service Committee, 1988. Directed toward parents, religious leaders, and all adults who work with youth, this resource guide provides valuable information and program models.

Curtis, Wayne, ed. *Revelations: A Collection of Gay Male Coming Out Stories.* Boston: Alyson Publications, 1988. Twenty-two men from their teens to their seventies reveal the struggles and the liberation of coming out. Some writers use pseudonyms, a sign of the danger and oppression that still exists.

Fairchild, Betty, and Nancy Hayward. *Now That You Know: What Every Parent Should Know about Homosexuality.* San Diego: Harcourt Brace Jovanovich, 1979. This book is written by and for parents who have discovered that they have gay or lesbian children. It includes basic information and personal narratives, and features a particularly good section on gays and religion.

Gay Fathers: Some of Their Stories, Experiences, and Advice. Gay Fathers of Toronto, 1981. Gay fathers discuss issues of coming out and staying involved in their children's lives. This book was published before the 1980s trend toward some gay men choosing to parent through adoption, insemination, or other means.

Heron, Ann, ed. *One Teenager in Ten: Writings by Gay and Lesbian Youth.* Boston: Alyson Publications, 1983. Twenty-six young women and men write about coming to terms with being "different," deciding whether and how to come out, and moving ahead with their lives.

Holmes, Sarah, ed. *Testimonies: A Collection of Lesbian Coming Out Stories.* Boston: Alyson Publications, 1988. Women tell their stories of discovery, coming out, finding the lesbian community, and developing political awareness.

Pies, Cheri. *Considering Parenthood.* San Francisco: Spinsters/Aunt Lute, 1988. This book serves as a comprehensive guide for lesbians making choices about parenting, including workbook-style exercises and important considerations.

Pollack, Sandra, and Jeanne Vaughan, eds. *Politics of the Heart: A Lesbian Parenting Anthology.* Ithaca, N.Y.: Firebrand Press, 1988. This compilation of prose and poetry covers a broad range of lesbian parenting experiences: biological, adoptive, co-parenting, and others. The book includes parents of all ages.

Silverstein, Charles. *A Family Matter: A Parent's Guide to Homosexuality.* New York: McGraw-Hill, 1977. This book was the first to address this issue in an informative, sympathetic and respectful manner. Dr. Silverstein discusses such concerns as how to bring up the subject, the importance of listening, and dealing with feelings of blame or guilt.

Vacha, Keith. *Quiet Fire: Memoirs of Older Gay Men.* Trumansburg, N.Y.: Crossing Press, 1985. Seventeen older gay men talk about their lives.

Lesbian and Gay Jewish Literature

Beck, Evelyn Torton, ed. *Nice Jewish Girls: A Lesbian Anthology.* Watertown, Mass.: Persephone Press, 1982; reprint, Beacon Press, 1989. This pioneering book, edited by a contributor to this volume, was the first to affirm the uniqueness and variety of Jewish lesbian experience. It succeeded in raising consciousness in the lesbian community as a whole. The book includes personal stories, scholarly essays, poetry, and photographs.

Bloch, Alice. *The Law of Return.* Boston: Alyson Publications, 1983. This novel describes an American woman living in Israel, exploring her Jewishness while also claiming her voice as a woman and a lesbian.

Coming Out, Coming Home: Lesbian and Gay Jews and the Jewish Community. New York: New Jewish Agenda, 1987. This short booklet covers a lot of important ground, addressing the full inclusion of lesbians and gay men in Jewish communal life.

Fierstein, Harvey. *Torch Song Trilogy.* New York: New American Library, 1988. Originally published in 1981, *Torch Song* has become a modern classic, first as a Broadway play and now as a movie. It chronicles the triumphs and tragedies of a gay Jewish drag queen, including his relationships with his mother, his lovers, and his adopted son.

Geller, Ruth. *Triangles.* Trumansburg, N.Y.: Crossing Press, 1984. Geller, a Jewish lesbian, wrote this novel based on the life of her grandmother.

Glickman, Gary. *Years from Now.* New York: New American Library, 1987. This novel describes three generations of a Jewish family, seen in part through the eyes of the gay grandson.

Kaye/Kantrowitz, Melanie, and Irena Klepfisz, eds. *The Tribe of Dina: Jewish Women's Anthology.* Updated edition. Boston: Beacon Press, 1989. This special double issue of a lesbian-feminist journal features the experiences of lesbian and heterosexual Jewish women in the United States and in Israel. It includes fiction, poetry, essays, and artwork.

Newman, Leslea. *A Letter to Harvey Milk*. Ithaca, N.Y.: Firebrand Books, 1988. This anthology of nine short stories written by a Jewish lesbian chronicles the lives of her circle of friends, their relationships, and their families.

Out of Our Kitchen Closets: San Francisco Gay Jewish Cooking. Congregation Sha'ar Zahav. San Francisco, 1987. This lively and well-designed cookbook is written in the best tradition of synagogue cookbooks. It includes a history of this gay and lesbian congregation, as well as warm and wonderful stories of family recipes.

Rich, Adrienne. *Blood, Bread and Poetry*. New York: Norton, 1986. This compilation of selected prose includes "Split at the Root: An Essay on Jewish Identity." Rich has published many other works that illuminate her artistry and her unique Jewish lesbian-feminist perspective. These include *On Lies, Secrets, and Silence* (1979), *The Fact of a Doorframe* (1984), and *Your Native Land, Your Life* (1987).

AIDS

Altman, Dennis. *AIDS in the Mind of America*. New York: Anchor Books, 1987. Altman explores the social, psychological, and political impact of the AIDS epidemic. He indicts homophobia and the health care establishment as exacerbating the crisis.

Cahalan, Kathleen A. *AIDS: Issues in Religion, Ethics and Care*. Illinois: Park Ridge Center, 1987. This annotated bibliography covers materials published from 1980–1987.

Gong, Victor, and Norman Rudnick, eds. *AIDS: Facts and Issues*. New Brunswick, N.J.: Rutgers University Press, 1987. This book is a good single source of AIDS information covering medical, psychological, legal, ethical, and spiritual issues.

Nungesser, Lon G. *Epidemic of Courage: Facing AIDS in America*. New York: St. Martin's Press, 1986. People with AIDS, family members, friends, and caregivers tell their own stories of the AIDS epidemic.

O'Connor, Tom. *Living with AIDS*. San Francisco: Corwin Publishers, 1987. This practical and hopeful book is written by a person with AIDS for others who are living with HIV. O'Connor explores many approaches to enhancing health, longevity, and quality of life.

Quackenbush, Marcia, and Mary Nelson with Kay Clark, eds. *The AIDS Challenge: Prevention Education for Young People*. Santa Cruz: Network Publications, 1988. This comprehensive compilation of material suggests educational strategies for a wide range of ages, settings (including religious institutions), and special populations.

Additional Sources

Brod, Harry, ed. *A Mensch among Men: Explorations in Jewish Masculinity*. Trumansburg, N.Y.: Crossing Press, 1988. This anthology, reflecting a Jewish male pro-feminist perspective, offers a range of personal stories and scholarly essays, including articles related to homosexuality.

Browne, Susan E., Debra Connors, and Nanci Stern, eds. *With the Power of Each Breath: A Disabled Women's Anthology*. Pittsburgh: Cleis Press, 1985. This book includes the writings of fifty-four women, several of whom are lesbian, Jewish, or both.

Bulkin, Elly, Minnie Bruce Pratt, and Barbara Smith. *Yours in Struggle: Three Feminist Perspectives on Anti-Semitism and Racism*. Ithaca, N.Y.: Firebrand Books, 1984. Three women—Jewish, white Christian, and black—offer their insights into these distinct yet related forms of oppression.

Curry, Hayden, and Denis Clifford. *A Legal Guide for Lesbian and Gay Couples* 5th edition. Ed. Robin Leonard. Nolo Press, 1988. This updated guide is helpful to lesbians and gay men in or out of relationships. It addresses concerns about contracts, housing, insurance, parenting and custody, medical treatment, and wills, as well as other issues.

Demystifying Homosexuality: A Teaching Guide about Lesbians and Gay Men. New York: Irvington Publishers, 1984. This discussion guide for teachers, counselors, and parents includes a resource list, bibliography, and statements from professional and religious organizations.

Morse, Carl, and Joan Larkin, eds. *Gay and Lesbian Poetry in Our Time: An Anthology*. New York: St. Martin's Press, 1988. This new anthology includes the work of ninety-four poets, well-known and lesser-known, who cover the spectrum of age, race, ethnicity, and class. These poems were written between 1950 and 1988.

Shernoff, Michael, and William A. Scott. *The Sourcebook on Lesbian and Gay Health Care*, 2d edition. Washington, D.C.: National Lesbian and Gay Health

Foundation, 1988. This book includes excellent bibliographies and resource lists in addition to articles on sexuality, mental health, AIDS, substance abuse, family issues, and other topics.

Jewish Periodicals

The following section lists landmark articles and special journal issues on homosexuality that have appeared in Jewish periodicals during the past twenty years. They are placed in chronological order, in order to reflect trends as they have unfolded. A more exhaustive list is available from Rabbi Yoel Kahn, as previously noted, and is covered by the final entry in this bibliography.

Freehof, Solomon B. "Homosexuality." *Current Reform Responsa* (1969): 236–38. This short responsum (Jewish legal opinion) supports the traditional condemnation of homosexual acts. According to the author, the absence of lengthy discussion of homosexuality in Jewish sources "speaks well for the normalcy and purity of the Jewish people."

"Judaism and Homosexuality." *CCAR Journal* 20, no. 3 (Summer 1973). This symposium in the journal of the Reform movement was inspired by the application of Beth Chayim Chadashim, a gay and lesbian outreach congregation in Los Angeles, for admission to the Union of American Hebrew Congregations. The journal's eight articles range from Sanford Ragin's eloquent defense of the place of openly lesbian and gay Jews in the community ("An Echo of the Pleas of our Fathers") to hostile attacks ("A Congregation of the Emotionally Ill?"). Solomon Freehof, in his second responsum on the subject, reiterates his earlier objections and declares his opposition to gay and lesbian synagogues.

Lamm, Norman. "Judaism and the Modern Attitude towards Homosexuality." *Encyclopedia Judaica Yearbook* (1974), pp. 197–204. Lamm reviews historical Jewish sources and urges that homosexuality remain "Jewishly unacceptable." This article has been widely reprinted and circulated.

"Must Homosexuals Be Jewish Outcasts?" *Sh'ma* 5:98 (October 3, 1975), pp. 303–5. In the first published article by a gay Jew in a mainstream Jewish periodical, the author calls for tolerance and acceptance.

Mehler, Barry. "Gay Jews: One Man's Journey from Closet to Community." *Moment* 2, no. 5 (February/March 1977): 22–24. This article is a moving personal account of coming out and finding a home in the gay community.

Matt, Hershel J. "Sin, Crime, Sickness or Alternative Life Style?: A Jewish Approach to Homosexuality." *Judaism* 27 (1978): 13–24. For many years this essay was considered the authoritative liberal Jewish statement on homosexuality. Matt argues that since homosexuals are not free to choose their sexual orientation, they should not be considered sinners according to traditional Jewish law but accepted as they are. He calls for a marriage ceremony or similar affirmation for gay and lesbian Jews.

Spero, M. H. "Homosexuality: Clinical and Ethical Challenges." *Tradition* 17, no. 4 (Spring 1979): 17–53. An Orthodox Jewish therapist discusses clinical issues in treating homosexuals. Spero encourages "non-neurotic religious guilt" as a tool for change. Any suggestion that homosexuality is normal or acceptable is "deliberately misleading on a religious matter."

Schwartz, Robert D., and David Novak. "On Homosexuality." *Sh'ma* 11:201 (November 14, 1980), pp. 2–6. This exchange between a gay Jew and a Conservative rabbi highlights the limits of the debate involving those who consider themselves bound by halakhah. Robert Schwartz firmly states his refusal to go back into the closet in order to be welcomed in the synagogue and Jewish community.

"Homosexuals and Homosexuality: Religious Leaders and Laymen Compare Notes." *Judaism* 32 (Fall 1983). This symposium is marred by the distortion and homophobia of the lead article, which even the nongay-affirmative contributors dismiss. The contributors are rabbis and mental health professionals.

Marder, Janet R. "Getting to Know the Gay and Lesbian Shul." *Reconstructionist* 51, no. 2 (October/November 1985): 20–25. Marder describes her own growth as rabbi of Beth Chayim Chadashim. This journal issue, which includes three other gay-supportive articles, is one of the best short introductions to the topic.

"Homosexuality." *Keeping Posted* 32, no. 2 (October 1986). *Keeping Posted* is the Reform movement's magazine for high school and adult education. This excellent edition includes a description of gay congregations, medical and psychological facts, and two young Jews' personal narratives about coming out. An unfortunate inclusion is an interview with a psychiatrist who considers homosexuality to be an arrested state of development.

Matt, Hershel J. "Homosexual Rabbis?" *Conservative Judaism* 39, no. 3 (1987): 29–33. Having concluded that sexual orientation is an unalterable feature of personality, Matt calls for the complete rejection of traditional Jewish teaching and supports the ordination of gays and lesbians as rabbis.

Kirschner, Robert. "Judaism and Homosexuality: A Reappraisal." *Judaism* 37, no. 4 (Fall 1988): 450–58. Kirschner argues that since so little is understood about the origins of sexual orientation, halakhic creativity should be used to suspend the application of traditional Jewish law. Instead, the benefit of the doubt should be granted, with homosexuals therefore being fully accepted and integrated in Jewish communal life.

Kahn, Yoel. "Judaism and Homosexuality." *Journal of Homosexuality* 18, nos. 1–2 (Winter 1989). Kahn's essay surveys all writing on Judaism and homosexuality between 1968 and 1987. Asserting that the biblical and rabbinic world had no concept of homosexual orientation, Kahn argues that the traditional condemnation of homosexual behavior is inappropriate today and should no longer be invoked. He asserts that different sexual orientations are part of the diversity of creation and reflect humanity's creation in the image of God.

NOTES ON
THE CONTRIBUTORS

··

Adina Abramowitz lives in Media, Pennsylvania, where she is active in a newly formed synagogue, Mishkan Shalom. Both she and her lover serve on the synagogue's board of directors and as coordinators of its spiritual life committee. Adina directs a small business loan fund, and she is still looking for lesbian or gay graduates of the Hebrew Academy of Washington.

Martha A. Ackelsberg, professor of government at Smith College, was a founding member of *Ezrat Nashim* (the first Jewish feminist group to call for the equality of women within the Jewish community) and of *B'not Esh* (a Jewish feminist spirituality collective). She has long been active in Jewish feminist activities and has written and spoken widely on topics related to feminism, changing Jewish tradition, and changing families.

Rebecca T. Alpert was born and raised in Brooklyn, New York. She was ordained as rabbi at the Reconstructionist Rabbinical College, where she served for ten years as dean of students. She has published widely in the areas of Jewish history, medical ethics, and feminism. She is a member of *B'not Esh.* Rebecca lives with her partner and two children in Philadelphia.

Evelyn Torton Beck, scholar/teacher/activist, is professor and director of the Women's Studies Program and professor of Jewish studies at the University of Maryland—College Park. She is editor of *Nice Jewish Girls: A Lesbian Anthology* (1982); among her other books are *Kafka and the Yiddish Theater* (1971) and *The Prism of Sex* (1979). She lectures and writes widely in Jewish women's studies, lesbian studies, and feminist transformations of knowledge. She is currently at work on two books on feminist perspectives on Kafka and Jewish women and anti-Semitism, as well as a collection of her speeches and essays.

Denise L. Eger is rabbi of Congregation Beth Chayim Chadashim in Los Angeles. She is a graduate of Hebrew Union College, Jewish Institute of Religion. She has written several articles for *Compass* magazine, including an article on gay issues in the Reform movement.

Sue Levi Elwell is a rabbi who lives and works in Los Angeles. She is the author of *Jewish Women: A Mini-Course for Jewish Schools* and the editor of *The Jewish Women's Studies Guide*. She is a graduate of Hebrew Union College—Jewish Institute of Religion, and holds a Ph.D. in adult education from Indiana University. Sue is currently a member of the *P'nai Or Siddur* project and has been involved with numerous other Jewish organizations and publications.

Agnes G. Herman was born in New York City in 1922. She received her B.A. from the University of Michigan and her masters in social work from Columbia University. She married Rabbi Erwin Herman in 1945; they adopted their two children in the early 1950s. Agnes worked for social service agencies throughout the country until retiring in 1979. Since that time, she has been active as a writer, speaker, and volunteer. She was instrumental in launching the Union of American Hebrew Congregations (UAHC) program on the Changing Jewish Family and the Synagogue and now serves on its Committee on AIDS. She has collaborated with her husband on a book entitled *The Yanov Torah*.

Jody Hirsh is a Ph.D. candidate in Modern Hebrew Literature at UCLA and has lectured and published extensively in the fields of Jewish literature, Judaica, and Jewish education. He has taught at UCLA, University of California (Berkeley), and the University of San Francisco. He was a long-time board member and first West Coast coordinator of the Conference on Alternatives in Jewish Education (CAJE). In addition, he served as associate director of the San Francisco Bureau of Jewish Education. Jody is one of the very few Hebrew-speaking players of the viola da gamba.

Linda J. Holtzman, a native of Philadelphia, is a 1979 graduate of the Reconstructionist Rabbinical College. She served as rabbi of Congregation Beth Israel in Coatesville, Pennsylvania, and as part-time rabbi of Beth Ahavah, the gay and lesbian synagogue of Philadelphia. Currently she is director of practical rabbinics at the Reconstructionist Rabbinical College. She lives with her partner Betsy, their sons Jordan and Zachary, their dogs Lilith, Ulysses, and Circe, and their cat Miranda.

Paul Horowitz became Bar Mitzvah at an Orthodox synagogue, was a member of a Conservative movement youth organization (United Synagogue Youth), and spent summers at the secular socialist Camp Kinder-Ring of the Workmen's Circle. An activist in the antiwar, feminist, and gay liberation movements, his writing has appeared in *Out/Look*, the lesbian and gay quarterly, and NACLA's *Report on the Americas*. He is a member of New Jewish Agenda and Democratic Socialists of America.

Yoel H. Kahn was ordained at Hebrew Union College—Jewish Institute of Religion, in 1985. He is rabbi of Congregation Sha'ar Zahav in San Francisco.

Scott Klein was raised in Queens, New York, in a secular Jewish family. He first experienced being part of a Jewish minority when he attended Hamilton College, and he has since participated in Reform synagogues in San Francisco and New York. Active in lesbian and gay politics in both these cities, he served as president of Lambda Independent Democrats, Brooklyn's lesbian and gay Democratic club, and ran as a delegate pledged to Jesse Jackson in the 1988 Democratic primary.

La Escondida teaches Jewish history and religion at a small liberal arts college. A liturgist and musician, she also serves as rabbi of an egalitarian, *havurah*-style congregation.

Aliza Maggid is a founding member of Am Tikva, which began in Boston in 1977. She served as development director of the World Congress of Gay and Lesbian Jewish Organizations for three years. She has led workshops on organizational issues and leadership development and authored a booklet on leadership renewal used to train Congress board members. Aliza's accounts of World Congress conferences have been published in Boston's *Gay Community News* and in the anthology, *Nice Jewish Girls*. She adds, "My mom taught me to love people beyond labels and categories and always modeled this in her support for my people, gays and lesbians."

Janet R. Marder is a graduate of the University of California at Santa Cruz and was ordained in 1979 by Hebrew Union College—Jewish Institute of Religion, the seminary of the Reform movement. She served as the first ordained rabbi of Congregation Beth Chayim Chadashim in Los Angeles from 1983 to 1988. Currently, she is the associate director of the Union of American Hebrew Congregations, Pacific Southwest Region. She is married and the mother of two.

Judith Plaskow, associate professor of religious studies at Manhattan College, has been learning, teaching, speaking, and writing about feminist theology for almost twenty years. She is co-founder and co-editor of the *Journal of Femi-*

nist Studies in Religion, author of *Sex, Sin and Grace* and co-editor (with Carol P. Christ) of *Womanspirit Rising* and *Weaving the Visions*. Her essay in this volume is adapted from her Jewish feminist theology, soon to be published by Harper and Row, *Standing Again at Sinai: Rethinking Judaism from a Feminist Perspective*.

Tom Rawson is a computer consultant living in the Boston area. He is active in local and national progressive Jewish politics, and has co-led Unlearning Homophobia workshops for New Jewish Agenda.

Eric E. Rofes is an author, social service administrator, and community organizer currently serving as executive director of the Shanti Project, an AIDS organization in San Francisco. He recently worked as Executive Director of the Gay and Lesbian Community Services Center in Los Angeles, where he also served on the County AIDS Commission and as co-chair of the No on Larouche Committee in 1986. He has written for many publications, including *Gay Community News* and *The Guardian*, and has published six books including *The Kids' Book of Divorce* (Random House, 1981), *Socrates, Plato and Guys Like Me—Confessions of a Gay Teacher* (Alyson, 1984) and *Gay Life* (Doubleday, 1986). Eric has served on the boards of directors of the National Lesbian and Gay Health Foundation and the Pride Institute, an inpatient recovery center for lesbians and gay men.

Faith Rogow, a Ph.D. in women's and Jewish history, lives with her lover, Del, on the banks of the Susquehanna River in Binghamton, New York. She has been an educator in the Jewish community for over fifteen years, and has published several articles on Jewish women. She is also a composer of Jewish feminist music, a member of *B'not Esh*, and an activist in her local women's community. Her secret fantasy is to be a foot taller and the first Jewish woman point guard in the NBA.

Burt E. Schuman has had a variety of careers including teaching, community organizing, speechwriting, cable TV production, and directing an intergroup relations organization where he facilitated many workshops on heterosexism. Currently, he directs a Jewish agency in New York City.

Jeffrey Shandler, the grandson of East European Jewish immigrants, was born in Valley Forge, Pennsylvania, in 1956. He now lives in Brooklyn with his boyfriend, Stuart Schear. Jeffrey works and studies at the YIVO Institute for Jewish Research in New York. In addition to ethnographies on gay Jews, his academic work includes articles on the traditional education of women in Ashkenaz, the semiotics of American Yiddish primers, and Jewish self-portraiture on American television. His translation of Mani-Leyb's *Yingl Tsingl Khvat* has been published by Moyer Bell.

Lesley M. Silverstone, R.J.E., is a graduate of the Rhea Hirsch School of Education of the Hebrew Union College—Jewish Institute of Religion. She is presently the educational director and program director of Temple Menorah in Redondo Beach, California. She has written a student workbook on Israel and several educational articles, and she is presently working on a new textbook for primary grades for the Union of American Hebrew Congregations.

Rachel Wahba is a psychotherapist in private practice in San Francisco, where she also serves as a clinical supervisor at Operation Concern, a gay and lesbian mental health agency.

Felice Yeskel is a social change activist. She works as an organizational development consultant and human relations trainer with a variety of groups, including small businesses, religious and educational institutions, social service agencies, and community groups. She is at the dissertation phase of her doctoral program in organizational development and has a master's degree in psychology. She works for Diversity Works, Inc., social change educators and consultants, helping groups to deal with cultural difference.

Alan D. Zamochnick is an activist on disability and gay rights issues. A Philadelphia native, he holds degrees from Gallaudet and New York universities. He is currently the AIDS Project coordinator for a federal civil rights agency, is active in national and local disability and gay organizations, and is president of Beth Ahavah, Philadelphia's gay and lesbian synagogue.

Christie Balka is an activist who has written and spoken on the Middle East, feminism, and lesbian and gay issues. She served as national co-chair of New Jewish Agenda, and as associate director of the Shalom Center. Currently she works for a small public foundation based in Philadelphia, where she lives with her partner and two children. She is active in her local Jewish community and serves on her synagogue board.

Andy Rose is a social worker and community activist currently living in San Francisco. He is a graduate of Brandeis University and holds two masters degrees, an MSW from the University of Southern California and an M.A. in Jewish communal service from Hebrew Union College in Los Angeles. He has worked in many Jewish institutions, with people from ages 4 to 106.

Andy was a founding member and national co-chair of New Jewish Agenda. For the past four years he has focused his work and his political energies on AIDS issues, and he currently coordinates the Jewish community's AIDS Project in San Francisco. He also serves on the UAHC AIDS Committee and is a board member of the AIDS National Interfaith Network.

CREDITS

....